Detroit
Reprints
in
Music

Frederick Freedman, General Editor
Case Western Reserve University

Music
for
the
Bicentennial

Intended to honor the
American Revolution Bicentennial
1776-1976

A
MUSICAL
BIOGRAPHY

BY
JOHN ROWE PARKER

WITH
NEW INTRODUCTION
BY
FREDERICK FREEDMAN

Detroit Reprints in Music
INFORMATION COORDINATORS
1975

Copyright © 1975 by Information Coordinators, Inc.
Library of Congress Catalog Card Number 74-75895
International Standard Book Number 911772-73-1

Printed and bound in the United States of America
Designed by Vincent Kibildis
Published by
Information Coordinators, Inc.
1435-37 Randolph Street
Detroit, Michigan 48226

Introduction

John Rowe Parker's *A Musical Biography* **first appeared**
in 1824. Its historical significance rests upon the fact that this is the
first biographical music dictionary to be published in the United States,
written by a man who had some influence in developing America's
musical life during the first decades of the nineteenth century.

Biographical information about John Rowe Parker is somewhat
hard to come by as his name fails to appear in most American music
dictionaries; but such information as is generally available discloses
that both he and his brother, Matthew S. Parker, were quite active
in many aspects of Boston's musical life during a large portion of the
nineteenth century.

Matthew S. Parker (1780-1865) was a Founder and the first
Secretary (1815-1818) of Boston's Handel and Haydn Society
(generally considered to be the oldest active musical organization in
the United States), continued as a Trustee of that organization for
half a century and served as its Treasurer for more than two decades
(1841-1865). He also sang for many years in the choir of Trinity
Church, Boston, served as Treasurer of the Phil-Harmonic Society
(1809-1820), all the while earning his living as a cashier in Boston's
Suffolk Bank.[1]

His brother, John Rowe Parker, was known as a music merchant,
journal editor, lexicographer, music publisher, singer, and telegraph
operator. He is probably best remembered today, however, as the
editor of America's first *important* and highly influential music
periodical, *The Euterpeiad, or Musical Intelligencer*, the Boston
weekly (then bi-weekly and finally monthly) journal which came out
of his "Franklin Music Warehouse" at No. 6 Milk Street during the
period 1820-1823, printed and published by Thomas Badger, Jr.
Details about this widely circulated journal and its significance are
discussed extensively by Haskins,[2] Johnson,[3] and Wunderlich,[4] and
the journal itself with its musical supplements will soon be available

---

[1] Perkins, Charles C., & John S. Dwight. *History of the Handel and Haydn
Society of Boston, Massachusetts.* Boston: Alfred Mudge & Son, 1889-1893.

[2] Haskins, John C. "John Rowe Parker and the Euterpeiad," *Music Library
Association Notes* VIII/3 (June 1951), 447-56.

[3] Johnson, Harold Earle. "Early New England Periodicals Devoted to Music,"
The Musical Quarterly XXVI/2 (April 1940), 153-61; Johnson, Harold Earle.
Musical Interludes in Boston, 1795-1830 (NY: Columbia University Press,
1943), 250-55 ff.

[4] Wunderlich, Charles E. *A History and Bibliography of Early American
Musical Periodicals, 1782-1852.* Ph.D. Dissertation: University of Michigan,
1962. 783 p.

in reprint,[5] so there is little need to offer details here. Anyone interested in an early nineteenth century musical controversy, however, should read Crawford[6] to see how Parker criticized and vied with the New England tune book compiler, Andrew Law, in an exchange that vollied through five issues of this journal. Suffice it to say that *The Euterpeiad*, while short-lived, remained America's most significant journal during the first half of the nineteenth century, and it was superceded in quality only by John S. Dwight's *Journal of Music* which commenced publication some thirty years later in 1852.

Prior to setting up *The Euterpeiad*, however, Parker became proprietor of the Franklin Music Warehouse in the fall of 1816, close to and in strong competition with Gottlieb Graupner, perhaps the most esteemed musician and music publisher in Boston at that time. In 1820, Parker issued *A Catalog of Music and Musical Instruments;* and it is suggested that he must have done a thriving business, particularly since he sold publications of all Baltimore, Boston, New York and Philadelphia publishers, as well as musical instruments, and tickets to Boston concerts. He sang in the Trinity Church Choir, and was elected an Honorary Member of the Handel and Haydn Society on March 21, 1818, an organization he served for decades. Clearly, he had become a pillar of Boston's musical society.

His thriving music business, however, came to an end in the mid-1820's—the Philadelphia publisher, George E. Blake, indicated that Parker was his Boston music seller during the period 1818-1826—for reasons that still appear to be obscure[7] (perhaps the failure of *The Euterpeiad* had an impact upon his Franklin Music Warehouse as well?). In all events, it is generally known that he commenced operating a telegraphic office on the Central Wharf of Boston, and that he wrote no fewer than seven works on semaphoric matters between 1829 and 1842.[8] That he did not give up his musical editorial interests entirely is disclosed by the fact that his name is found on the Editorial Board of yet another music journal, *The Boston Musical Gazette*, as late as 1838.

---

[5] *The Euterpeiad* has been announced for publication in 1975, to be reprinted by Da Capo Press with a new introduction by Charles E. Wunderlich.

[6] Crawford, Richard A. *Andrew Law, American Psalmodist* (Evanston: Northwestern University Press, 1968), 245–46.

[7] An exceptional collection of John Rowe Parker correspondence (400-500 letters) is housed in The Charles Patterson Van Pelt Library, The University of Pennsylvania. Obviously, a thorough study of this correspondence would add significantly to our present sparse knowledge of Parker. Indeed, it seems that a doctoral dissertation on Parker is long overdue.

[8] They include the following titles: *Harbour Telegraph Signals* (Boston: 1829); *A Treatise Upon the Telegraphic Science* (Boston: 1835); *A New Semaphoric Signal Book, in three parts . . . To which is annexed the Boston Harbor Signal Book* (Boston: Light & Stearns, 1836); *History of Telegraphs* (Boston: Light & Stearns, 1836); *A Treatise Upon the Semaphoric System of Telegraphs* (Boston: 1838); *The New Semaphoric Signal Book . . .*, 2nd ed (Boston: Kidder & Wright, 1841); *A Treatise Upon Telegraphs Embracing Observations Upon the Semaphoric System . . .* (Boston: Kidder & Wright, 1842).

Although *A Musical Biography* was probably issued in a sizable print run, only five copies of the 1824 issue and nineteen copies of the 1825 reissue(?) are extant.[9] Examination of copies from both issues disclose no apparent difference except for a change of date on the title-page; indeed, a number of typographical errors seem to have been retained. Since the work was copyright December 18, 1824, by Moore and Prowse, in the District Court of Boston (the copyright notice appears in the front matter), one wonders whether the work was actually issued in a *single* press run that bridged into the new year.[10] Thomas Badger, Jr., Parker's usual printer, apparently was no longer in business.[11] This would explain why Stone and Fovell, the publishers who seemingly published no other book on music, issued this work.

Considering his personal interest in and honorary connection with the organization, it is not entirely surprising to see this work dedicated "To the President and Members of the Boston Handel and Haydn Society." From the standpoint of textual material, comparisons disclose that Parker drew upon his defunct journal, *The Euterpeiad*, although a careful analysis would be necessary to determine the extent of his "self-borrowing." Suffice it to say that had he not *The Euterpeiad* to draw upon, *A Musical Biography* might not have appeared in the format that has come down to us.

In the introduction he indicates his intent to compile *"Biographical Sketches of Eminent Musical Personages,"* and while these include three of the ". . . brightest luminaries of the musical world," namely Handel, Haydn, and Mozart, there is no entry for Beethoven. But Parker did not forget Beethoven completely, as he indicates (p. 114): ". . . from recent specimens of his unbounded fancy [implying, of course, that Beethoven's music was readily available in Boston] it is to be expected that he will extend the art of music, in a way never contemplated even by Haydn or Mozart." It could very well be that Parker was not fully prepared to assess Beethoven's position since Beethoven was very much alive in 1824, when this work went to press.

While this volume includes a number of biographical entries of European composers and performers, its most original and important entries are for musicians who were active in the New World. These include composers such as George K. Jackson (1742–1822) and Raynor Taylor (1747–1825), and performers such as Thomas Smith Webb,

[9] Shoemaker, Richard H., comp. *A Checklist of American Imprints, 1824* (Metuchen, NJ: The Scarecrow Press, 1969), 192; *op. cit., 1825,* 190.

[10] Perhaps one of the printers took the "liberty" to change the date, or Parker might have asked that the *new year* be used before the print run was completed. Richard J. Wolfe, *Secular Music in America 1801–1825, A Bibliography,* 3 vols. (NY: The New York Public Library, 1964), II, 664, suggests that the 1825 date reflects a reissue from standing type—certainly a more conventional conclusion. Wolfe, incidentally, only cites the location of four copies of the 1824 imprint and three copies of the 1825 imprint. Wolfe's copyright information, *ibid.,* should be corrected: "Moore and Prorose" should read "Moore and Prowse."

[11] Wolfe, *op. cit.,* III, 1137.

Miss Broadhurst, Nancy Oldmixon (née George), Sophia Ostinelli (daughter of James Hewitt), Alexi Eustaphieve, and Mrs. Eliza Salmon (née Munday). Both Miss Broadhurst and Lady Oldmixon distinguished themselves in London at Covent Garden, Drury Lane, and The Haymarket, but came to the United States in 1793, when Thomas Wignell and Alexander Reinagle opened their New Theater in Philadelphia. Miss Broadhurst sang in numerous cities along the eastern seaboard, from Boston to Charleston, S.C., and died suddenly in the latter city from ". . . the prevailing disease [yellow fever?]." Mrs. Oldmixon sustained her brilliant English stage reputation, but later retired from the stage to establish a girl's academy in Germantown (then a suburb of Philadelphia). Curiously, Parker seems to have had a special interest in women performers (perhaps a surprise to today's women's liberationists?). Although the free-flowing personalized accounts of these musicians do not provide all the detail that one finds scattered among the sundry studies by Sonneck, Wolfe, and numerous dictionaries, they are, nevertheless, among the most comprehensive entries to be found in any lexicon. Indeed, occasional later reference tools acknowledge Parker's work.

The latter portion of this volume contains eight articles on topics which were of considerable concern to the church musician, so it could very well be that this section might have been intended as a "mini-handbook" for his colleagues in the Haydn and Handel Society.

While this work lacks the strong lexicographic organization that one finds among its European counterparts (*e.g.*, Walther, Gerber, Choron, Sainsbury), it is clear, nevertheless, that European music dictionaries did not provide for the needs of the New World. Parker's *A Musical Biography*, which filled an important gap among American musical publications, consequently constitutes a landmark work in American music lexicography even if it is not comprehensive. It must be considered, however, in the context of Parker planning a second volume—which never became a reality—for he indicated on page 207: "End of Biographical Sketches of Volume One." Perhaps a thorough search of his papers will reveal more of the second volume than we now know.

FREDERICK FREEDMAN

Case Western Reserve University
December 1974

Design used to identify
publications issued by the
Franklin Music Warehouse

A

Musical Biography:

OR

SKETCHES

OF THE

Lives and Writings

OF

EMINENT MUSICAL CHARACTERS.

———

INTERSPERSED WITH AN EPITOME OF INTERESTING MUSICAL
MATTER.

Collated and Compiled

By JOHN R. PARKER.

————————•✳•————————

Boston :

PUBLISHED BY STONE & FOVELL......CONGRESS SQUARE

::::::::::::::

1825

Stone & Fovell, Printers.

CONTENTS.

DEDICATION.

———

To the President and Members of the

Boston Handel and Haydn Society.

With a view to transmit to posterity a record of musical talents, the following Sketches of Eminent Personages, are dedicated to the Members of an Institution, from whose exertions the practice of an art has increased, and a more extensive knowledge of the science of Music diffused.

Your Society having obtained a rank and character that promises long continuance, has proved itself highly useful to the community, by the dissemination of an improved style, in the performance of the sacred compositions of those authors, whose names it perpetuates.

While the scientific musician and the skilful practitioner, may speculate upon the wonderful effects of melody and harmony, the christian and philanthropist will feel their hearts glow with piety and devotion.

If the following sheets should in any degree tend to further your views, the endeavor of an individual to add his portion, it is hoped, will be appreciated.

The Compiler.

INTRODUCTION.

To place a value on the effect of a particular science, some writers are more subject to the anomaly of underrating its peculiar claims to cultivation and patronage than to any other error. This may apply to disquisitions on the properties of music; as treated by professed theorists, harmony and melody assume a moral and intellectual importance. Addison asserts, "*That music raises noble sentiments, and fills the mind with great conceptions,*" while Fenelon on the contrary, affirms, " *That harmony aims but to please the ear, and is qualified only to entertain the idle and effeminate;*" now, we say, that truth lies between the two extremes. If music aspires not to the value of ethics, political economy, or natural philosophy, neither does it yield to the beauty of poetical imagery, or the dignity of the nobler species of architecture. If mellifluous numbers and lively description can soothe the sense and enchant the fancy, musical compositions are qualified to charm the ear, awaken our finest feelings, and elevate the soul.

The Compiler having for several years past, conducted the editorial department of a publication, devoted to the diffusion of musical information in this city, possessed peculiar advantages in collating many interesting details, relative to those who have been distinguished for their scientific acquirements, or their practical skill in this art. His intention to compile " *Biographical Sketches of Eminent Musical Personages*," has long since occupied a considerable portion of time, and in the endeavor to collate such useful information as is eagerly sought for by the public generally, as well as the musical part of the community in particular, care has been taken to render these Sketches equally interesting to the Professor and Amateur. On a recurrence to the accumulated materials in his possession, so diversified a mass, rendered no small degree of perseverance and labor necessary to examine, collate, and arrange the characters most worthy of appearing in this collection. To make a selection, was, at least, a task of no ordinary magnitude : To preserve the judgment unperplexed, to reject by system, and adopt by rule ; in some instances to resist the influence of an unduly estimated name, to subdue in others the prejudices existing against absolute excellence ; to decide by the descent, not the reputation of an author, to give connection and order to prominent incident, and judiciously omit whatever would surcharge rather than adorn these Sketches, required, perhaps, not only much patience and labor, but a considerable degree of discrimination.

There are few sciences in which some conspicuous characters have not become eminent in their profession. There are always some standards at which we may aim, in our attempts at excellence, and which we may copy with safety. So also in the science of harmony, there are some who have acquired a skill and a reputation which has raised them far above their competitors. Eminent indeed have been other characters who have irradiated the science of harmony by the emanations of genius, or the productions of a fertile fancy. But in this group, as in others, there are some, who, like the prominent features of a perspective, arrest the attention from the minor objects.

Handel, *Haydn* and *Mozart* are the brightest luminaries of the musical world, and while harmony shall be cherished as a science, or be loved as an amusement, they will always stand conspicuous among those who have delighted mankind. For this reason, we have detailed *their* history with a minuteness that we could scarcely allow to others.

It will be necessary to premise, that in a work of this kind little originality can be expected. It is not the business of the Compiler to form fictitious incidents to amuse the public, but merely to present in a convenient form, the facts which tradition has preserved.

A

BIOGRAPHICAL SKETCH

OF THE LIFE OF

GEORGE FREDERIC HANDEL.

———

GEORGE FREDERIC HANDEL was born at Halle, a city in the circle of Upper-Saxony, the 24th February 1684, by a second wife of his father, who was an eminent surgeon and physician of the same place, and above sixty when his son was born. From his very childhood HANDEL had discovered such a strong propensity to Music, that his father, who always intended him for the study of the Civil Law, had reason to be alarmed. Perceiving that this inclination still increased, he took every method to oppose it. He strictly forbid him to meddle with any musical instrument ; nothing of that kind was suffered to remain in the house, nor was he ever permitted to go to any other, where such kind of furniture was in use. All this caution and art instead of restraining, did but augment his passion. He had found means to get a little clavichord privately conveyed to a room at the top of the house. To this room he constantly stole when the family was asleep. He had made some progress before Music had been prohibited, and by his assiduous practice at the hours of rest, had made such farther advances, as, though not attended to at that time, were no slight prognostics of his future greatness.

2

In such a situation it was not easy to keep him from getting at harpsichords, and his father was too much engaged
to watch him so closely there as he had done at home. His
father often mentioned to his friends, this uncontrollable
humour of his son, which he told them he had taken great
pains to subdue, but hitherto with little or no success. He
said it was easy to foresee, that if it was not subdued very
soon, it would preclude all improvements in the science for
which he intended him, and wholly disconcert the plan that
had been formed and agreed on for his education.

It happened one morning, that while he was playing on
the organ after the service was over, the Duke de Weisenfels was in the church. Something there was in the manner of playing, which drew his attention so strongly, that
his Highness, as soon as he returned, asked his valet de
chambre who it was that he had heard at the organ, when
the service was over. The valet replied, that it was his
brother. The Duke demanded to see him.

After he had seen him, and made all the inquiries which
it was natural for a man of taste and discernment to make
on such an occasion, he told his physician, that every father must judge for himself in what manner to dispose of
his children ; but that, for his own part, he could not but
consider it as a sort of crime against the public and posterity, to rob the world of such a rising Genius.

The Prince could not agree with him in his notions of
Music as a profession, which he said were much too low
and disparaging, as great excellence in any kind entitled
men to great honour. And as to profit, he observed how
much more likely he would be to succeed, if suffered to
pursue the path that Nature and Providence seemed to
have marked out for him ; than if he was forced into
another track to which he had no such bias ; nay, to which
he had a direct aversion. He concluded with saying, that
he was far from recommending the study of Music in ex-

clusion of the Languages, or of the Civil Law, provided it was possible to reconcile them together : what he wished was, that all of them might have fair play ; that no violence might be used, but the boy be left at liberty to follow the natural bent of his faculties, whatever that might be.

The first thing which his father did at his return to Halle, was to place him under one ZACKAW, who was organist to the cathedral church.

ZACKAW was proud of a pupil, who already began to attract the attention of all persons who lived near Halle, or resorted thither from distant quarters. And he was glad of an assistant, who, by his uncommon talents, was capable of supplying his place, whenever he had an inclination to be absent, as he often was, from his love of company, and a cheerful glass. It may seem strange to talk of an assistant at seven years of age, for he could not be more, if indeed he was quite so much, when first he was committed to the care of this person. But it will appear much stranger, that by the time he was nine he began to compose the church service for voices and instruments, and from that time actually did compose a service every week for three years successively. However it must not be forgot, that he had made some progress at home, before his father began to be alarmed, and, in consequence thereof, had forbid him to touch any musical instrument : that, after this severe prohibition, he had made further advances at stolen intervals by his practice on the clavichord ; and after that, he made the most of his moderate stay at the court of Weisenfels, where he found many instruments, and more admirers.

From the few facts just related it is easy to guess, that from the time of HANDEL's having a master in form, the Civil Law could have had no great share of his attention. The bent of his mind to Music was now so evident, and so

prevailing, that the Prince's advice was punctually followed. No further endeavours were used to alter or correct it. It was in the year 1698 that he went to Berlin.
The Opera there was in a flourishing condition, under the
direction of the King of Prussia, (grandfather of the present) who, by the encouragement which he gave to singers
and composers, drew thither 'some of the most eminent
from Italy, and other parts. Among these were BUONONCINI
and ATTILIO, the same who afterwards came to England
while HANDEL was here, and of whom the former was at
the head of a formidable opposition against him. This
person was in high request for his compositions, probably
the best which that court had known. But from his natural temper, he was easily elated with success, and apt to
be intoxicated with admiration and applause. Though
HANDEL was talked of as a most extraordinary player on
the harpsichord for one so young, yet on account of his
years he had always considered him as a mere child. But
as people still persisted in their encomiums, it was his fancy to try the truth of them. For this end he composed a
Cantata in the chromatic style, difficult in every respect,
and such as even a master, he thought would be puzzled
to play, or accompany without some previous practice.
When he found that he, whom he had regarded as a mere
child, treated this formidable composition as a mere trifle,
not only executing it at sight, but with a degree of accuracy, truth, and expression hardly to be expected even from
repeated practice ;—then indeed he began to see him in
another light, and to talk of him in another tone.

ATTILIO'S fondness for HANDEL commenced at his first
coming to Berlin, and continued to the time of his leaving
it. He would often take him on his knee, and make him
play on his harpsichord for an hour together, equally pleased and surprised with the extraordinary proficiency of so
young a person ; for at this time he could not exceed thir-

teen, as may easily be seen by comparing dates, The
kindness of ATTILIO was not thrown away ; as he was always welcome, he never lost any opportunity of being with
him or of learning from him all that a person of his age
and experience was capable of shewing him. It would be
injustice to BUONONCINI not to mention his civilities to
HANDEL, but they were accompanied with that kind of
distance and reserve, which always lessen the value of an
obligation, by the very endeavour to enhance it. The age
of the person to be obliged seems to remove all suspicion
of rivalship or jealousy. One so young could hardly be
the object of either ; and yet from what afterwards happened, such a notion may appear to some persons not altogether destitute of probability. Those who are fond of
explaining former passages by subsequent events, would
be apt to say that the seeds of enmity were sown at Berlin ; and that though they did not appear till the scene
was changed, they waited only for time and occasion to
produce them.

Thus much is certain that the little stranger had not
been long at court before his abilities became known to
the King, who frequently sent for him, and made him large
presents. Indeed his Majesty, convinced of his singular
endowments, and unwilling to lose the opportunity of pat-
ronizing so rare a genius, had conceived a design of culti-
vating it at his own expense. His intention was to send
him to Italy, where he might be formed under the best
masters, and have opportunities of hearing and seeing all
that was excellent in the kind. As soon as it was intima-
ted to HANDEL's friends (for he was yet too young to determine for himself) they deliberated what answer it would
be proper to return, in case this scheme should be proposed
in form. It was the opinion of many that his fortune was
already made, and that his relations would certainly em-
brace such an offer with the utmost alacrity. Others, who

better undesstood the temper and spirit of the court at Berlin, thought this a matter of nice speculation, and cautious debate. For they well knew, that if he once engaged in the King's service, he must remain in it, whether he liked it, or not ; that if he continued to please, it would be a reason for not parting with him ; and that if he happened to displease, his ruin would be the certain consequence. To accept an offer of this nature, was the same thing as to enter into a formal engagement, but how to refuse it was still the difficulty. At length it was resolved that some excuse must be found. It was not long before the King caused his intention to be signified, and the answer was that the Doctor would always retain the profoundest sense of the honour done to him by the notice which his Majesty had been graciously pleased to take of his son ; but as he himself was now grown old, and could not expect to have him long with him, he humbly hoped the King would forgive his desire to decline the offer which had been made him by order of his Majesty. From hence he went to Hamburgh.

Four or five years had elapsed from the time of his coming to Hamburgh, to that of his leaving it. Though he had continued to send his mother remittances from time to time, yet, clear of his own expenses, he had made up a purse of two hundred ducats. On the strength of this fund he resolved to set out for Florence.

At the age of eighteen he made the Opera of RODRIGO, for which he was presented with one hundred sequins, and a service of plate. This may serve for a sufficient testimony of its favorable reception. VITTORIA, who was much admired both as an Actress, and a Singer, bore a principal part in this Opera. She was a fine woman, and had for some time been much in the good graces of his Serene Highness. But, from the natural restlessness of certain hearts, so little sensible was she of her exalted situation, that she conceived a design of transferring her af-

fections to another person. HANDEL's youth and comeli-
ness, joined with his fame and abilities in Music, had made
impressions on her heart. Though she had the art to conceal them for the present, she had not perhaps the power,
certainly not the intention, to efface them.

The nature of his design in travelling made it improper for him to stay long in any one place. He had stayed
near a year at Florence, and it was his resolution to visit
every part of Italy, which was any way famous for its musical performances. Venice was his next resort. He
was first discovered there at a Masquerade, while he was
playing on a harpsichord in his visor. SCARLATTI happened to be there, and affirmed that it could be no one but
the famous Saxon, or the devil. Being thus detected, he was
strongly importuned to compose an Opera. But there was
so little prospect of either honor or advantage from such an
undertaking, that he was very unwilling to engage in it.
At last, however, he consented, and in three weeks he finished his AGRIPPINA, which was performed twenty-seven
nights successively ; and in a theatre which had been shut
up for a long time, notwithstanding there were two other
Opera-houses open at the same time ; at one of which
GASPARINI presided, as LOTTI did at the other. The audience was so enchanted with this performance, that a stranger who should have have seen the manner in which they
were affected, would have imagined they had all been dis-
tracted.

The theatre, at almost every pause, resounded with shouts
and acclamations of *viva il caro Sassone !* and other expressions of approbation too extravagant to be mentioned. They
were thunder-struck with the grandeur and sublimity of
his style : for never had they known till then all the powers of harmony and modulation so closely arraved, and so
forcibly combined.

This Opera drew over all the best singers from the other houses. Among the foremost of these was the famous VITTORIA, who a little before HANDEL's removal to Venice had obtained permission of the grand Duke to sing in one of the houses there. At AGRIPPINA her inclinations gave new lustre to her talent. HANDEL seemed almost as great and majestic as APOLLO, and it was far from the lady's intention to be so cruel and obstinate as DAPHNE.

Having mentioned the most material occurrences at Venice, we are now to relate his reception at Rome. The fame of his musical achievements at Florence and at Venice had reached that metropolis long before him. His arrival therefore was immediately known, and occasioned civil enquiries and polite messages from persons of the first distinction there. Among his greatest admirers was the Cardinal OTTOBONI, a person of a refined taste, and princely magnificence. Besides a fine collection of pictures and statues, he had a large library of Music, and an excellent band of performers, which he kept in constant pay. The illustrious CORELLI played the first violin, and had apartments in the Cardinal's palace. It was a customary thing with his eminence to have performances of Operas, Oratorios, and such other grand compositions, as could from time to time be procured. HANDEL was desired to furnish his quota ; and there was always such a greatness and superiority in the pieces composed by him, as rendered those of the best masters comparatively little and insignificant. There was also something in his manner so very different from what the Italians had been used to, that those who were seldom or never at loss in performing any other music, were frequently puzzled how to execute his. CORELLI himself complained of the difficulty he found in playing his Overtures. Indeed there was in the whole cast of these compositions, but especially in the opening of them, such a degree of fire and force, as never could consort with the mild graces, and placid elegancies of a genius so totally dissimilar. Several fruitless attempts HANDEL had one day made to instruct him in the manner of executing these spirited passages. Piqued at the tameness with which he still played them, he snatches the instrument out of his hand ; and to convince him how little he understood them, played the passages himself. But CORELLI, who was a person of great modesty and meekness, wanted no conviction of this sort ; for he ingenuously declared that he did not understand them ; *i. e.* knew not how to execute them properly, and give them the strength and expression required.

When HANDEL* appeared impatient, *Ma caro Sassone* (said he) *questa musica e nel stylo Francese di ch' io non m' intendo.*

* This celebrated composer, though of a very robust and uncouth external appearance, yet had such a remarkable irritability of nerves, that he could not bear to hear the tuning of instruments, and therefore this was always done before Handel arrived—A musical wag who knew how to extract some mirth from his irascibility of temper, stole into the orchestra on a night when the Prince of Wales was to be present at the performance of a new Oratorio, and untuned all the instruments, some half a note, others a whole note lower than the organ. As soon as the Prince arrived, Handel gave the signal of beginning conspirito, but such was the horrible discord, that the enraged musician started up from his seat, and having overturned a double bass which stood in his way, he seized a kettle-drum, which he threw with such violence at the head of the leader of the band, that he lost his full bottomed wig by the effort, without waiting to replace it, he advanced bareheaded to the front of the orchestra, breathing vengeance, but so much choaked with passion that utterance denied him. In this ridiculous attitude he stood staring and stamping for some minutes amidst a convulsion of laughter, nor could he be prevailed on to resume his seat till the prince went personally to appease his wrath, which he with great difficulty accomplished.

3

From Rome he removed to Naples, where, as at most other places, he had a palazzo at command, and was provided with table, coach, and all other accommodations. While he was at this capital, he made Acis and Galatea, the words Italian, and the Music different from ours.

HANDEL having now been long enough in Italy effectually to answer the purpose of his going thither, began to think of returning to his native country. Not that he intended this to be the end of his travels; for his curiosity was not yet allayed, nor likely to be so while there was any musical court which he had not seen. Hanover was the first he stopped at.

Here he met with a nobleman who had taken great notice of him in Italy, and who did him great service (as will appear soon) when he came to England for the second time. This person was Baron KILMANSECK. He introduced him at court, and so well recommended him to his Electoral Highness, that he immediately offered him a pension of fifteen hundred crowns per annum as an inducement to stay. Though such an offer from a prince of his character was not to be neglected, HANDEL loved liberty too well to accept it hastily, and without reserve. He told the Baron how much he owed to his kind and effectual recommendation, as well as to his Highness's goodness and generosity. But he also expressed his apprehensions that the favor intended him would hardly be consistent either with the promise he had actually made to visit the court of the Elector Palatine, or with the resolution he had long taken to pass over into England, for the sake of seeing that of London. Upon this objection, the Baron consulted his Highness's pleasure, and HANDEL was then acquainted, that neither his promise nor his resolution should be superseded by his acceptance of the pension proposed. He had leave to be absent for a twelve-month or more, if he chose it; and to go withersoever he pleased. On these easy conditions he thankfully accepted it.

When he had paid his respects to his relations and friends (among whom his old master ZACKAW was by no means forgot) he set out for Dusseldorp. The Elector Palatine was much pleased with the punctual performance of his promise, but as much disappointed to find that he was engaged elsewhere. At parting he made him a present of a fine set of wrought plate for a desert, and in such a manner as added greatly to its value.

From Dusseldorp he made the best of his way through Holland, and embarked for England.

The report of his uncommon abilities had been conveyed to England before his arrival, and through various channels. Some persons here had seen him in Italy, and others during his residence at Hanover. He was soon introduced at court, and honored with marks of the Queen's favor. Many of the nobility were impatient for an Opera of his composing. To gratify this eagerness, Rinaldo, the first he made in England, was finished in a fortnight's time.

After having remained a full twelve-month in England, it was time for him to think of returning to Hanover. When he took leave of the Queen at her court, and expressed his sense of the favors conferred on him, her Majesty was pleased to add to them by large presents, and to intimate her desire of seeing him again. Not a little flattered with such marks of approbation from so illustrious a personage, he promised to return, the moment he could obtain permission from the Prince, in whose service he was retained.

Towards the end of the year 1712, he obtained leave of the Elector to make a second visit to England, on condition that he engaged to return within a reasonable time.

The great character of the Operas which HANDEL had made in Italy and Germany, and the remembrance of Rinaldo joined with the poor proceedings at the Hay-market, made the nobility very desirous that he might again be employed in composing for that theatre. To their applications her Majesty was pleased to add the weight of her own authority ; and, as a testimony of her regard to his merit, settled upon him a pension for life, of 200*l per annum.*

The remaining two years he spent at Cannons, a place which was then in all its glory, but remarkable for having much more of art than nature, and much more cost than art. Of the music he made for the chapel there, some account will be given in another place. Whether HANDEL was *provided* as a mere implement of grandeur, or *chosen* from motives of a superior kind, it is not for us to determine. This, one may venture to assert, that the having such a composer, was an instance of *real* magnificence, such as no private person, or subject ; nay, such as no prince or potentate on the earth could at that time pretend to.

During the last year of his residence, at Cannons, a project was formed by the nobility for erecting an academy at the Hay-market. The intention of this musical society, was to secure to themselves a constant supply of Operas to be composed by HANDEL, and performed under his direction. For this end a subscription was set on foot: and as his late Majesty was pleased to let his name appear at the head of it, the society was dignified with the title of the Royal Academy. The sum subscribed being very large,* it was intended to continue for fourteen years certain. But as yet it was in its embryo-state, being not fully formed till a year or two after.

HANDEL therefore, after he quitted his employment at Cannons, was advised to go over to Dresden in quest of singers. Here he engaged SENESINO and DURISTANTI, whom he brought over with him to England.

At this time BUONONCINI and ATTILIO composed for the Opera, and had a strong party in their favor. Great rea-

* The King subscribed 1000*l.* and the nobility 40,000*l.*

son they saw to be jealous of such a rival as HANDEL,
and all the interest they had was employed to decry his
Music, and hinder him from coming to the Hay-market :
but these attempts were defeated by the powerful association above mentioned, at whose desire he had just been
to Dresden for singers.

In the year 1720, he obtained leave to perform his Opera of Radamisto. If persons who are now living, and
who were present at that performance may be credited,
the applause it received was almost as extravagant as his
Agrippina had excited : the crowds and tumults of the
house at Venice were hardly equal to those at London.
In so splendid and fashionable an assembly of ladies (to
the excellence of their taste we must impute it) there was
no shadow of form, or ceremony, scarce indeed any appearance of order, or regularity, politeness or decency.
Many, who had forced their way into the house with an
impetuosity but ill suited to their rank and sex, actually
fainted through the excessive heat and closeness of it.
Several gentlemen were turned back, who had offered
forty shillings for a seat in the gallery, after having despaired of getting any in the pit or boxes.

Such then was the state of things in the year 1720, at
the time Radamisto was performed. The succeeding
winter brought this musical disorder to its crisis. In order to terminate all matters in controversy, it was agreed
to put them on this fair issue. The several parties concerned were to be jointly employed in making an Opera,
in which each of them was to take a distinct act. And
he, who by the general suffrage, should be allowed to
have given the best proofs of his abilities, was to be put into possession of the house. The proposal was accepted,
whether from choice or necessity, I cannot say. The
event was answerable to the expectations of HANDEL's
friends. His act was the last, and the superiority of it so

very manifest, that there was not the least pretence for any further doubts or disputes. I should have mentioned, that as each made an overture as well as an act, the affair seemed to be decided even by the overture with which HANDEL's began. The name of the Opera was Muzio Scævola.

The academy being now firmly established, and HAN-DEL appointed composer to it, all things went on prosperously for a course of between nine and ten years. And this may justly be called the period of musical glory, whether we consider the performances or the performers, most certainly not to be surpassed, if equalled, in any age or country. The names and dates of the Operas exhibited within this memorable interval, may be found in their regular series by turning to the catalogue. And some brief and general account of their character is given in the observations at the end of it.

The perfect authority which HANDEL maintained over the singers and the band, or rather the total subjection in which he held them, was of more consequence than can well be imagined. It was the chief means of preserving that order and decorum, that union and tranquility, which seldom are found to subsist for any long continuance in musical societies. Indeed, all societies, like the animal body, seem to carry in their very frame and fabric, the seeds of their own dissolution. This happens sooner or later, only as those are forwarded or retarded by different causes.

SENESINO, who, from his first appearance, had taken deep root, and had long been growing in the affections of those, whose right to dominion the most civilized nations have ever acknowledged, began to feel his strength and importance. He felt them so much, that what he had hitherto regarded as legal government, now appeared to him in the light of downright tyranny. HANDEL, perceiving that he was grown less tractable and obsequious, resolved to subdue these Italian humors, not by lenitives, but sharp corrosives. To manage him he disdained ; to control him with a high hand, he in vain attempted. The one was perfectly refractory ; the other was equally outrageous. In short, matters had proceeded so far, that there were no hopes of an accommodation. The merits of the quarrel I know nothing of. Whatever they were, the nobility would not consent to his design of parting with SENESINO, and HANDEL was determined to have no further concerns with him. FAUSTINA and CUZZONI, as if seized with the contagion of discord, started questions of superiority, and urged their respective claims to it with an eagerness and acrimony, which occasioned a total disunion betwixt them.

And thus the Academy, after it had continued in the most flourishing state for upwards of nine years, was at once dissolved.

He remained inflexible in his resolution to punish SENESINO for refusing him that submission, which he had been used to receive, and which he thought he had a right to demand : but a little pliability would have saved him abundance of trouble. The vacancy made by the removal of such a singer was not easily supplied. The umbrage which he had given to many of the nobility, by his implacable resentments against a person whose talents they so much admired, was likely to create him a dangerous opposition. For, though he continued at the Hay-market, yet, in the heat of these animosities, a great part of his audience would melt away. New singers must be sought, and could not be had any nearer than Italy. The business of choosing, and engaging them, could not be despatched by a deputy. And the party offended might improve the opportunity of his absence to his disadvantage.

In spite of all these discouragements, to Italy he went, as soon as he had settled an agreement with HEIDEGGER.

to carry on Operas in conjunction with him. The agreement was for the short term of three years, and so settled as to subsist only from year to year.

After a short stay in Italy, he returned with STRADA, BERNACHI, FABRI, BERTOLDI, and others.

In the summer of the year 1733, he made a tour to Oxford, where there was a public act, at which he performed his Oratorio of ATHALIAH, composed for that solemnity. By this journey the damages he had suffered in his fortune were somewhat repaired, and his reputation more firmly established.

The observation that misfortunes rarely come single, was verified in HANDEL. His fortune was not more impaired, than his health and his understanding. His right arm was become useless to him from a stroke of the palsy ; and how greatly his senses were disordered at intervals, for a long time, appeared from an hundred instances, which are better forgotten than recorded. The most violent deviations from reason, are usually seen, when the strongest faculties happen to be thrown out of course.

In this melancholic state, it was in vain for him to think of any fresh projects for retrieving his affairs. His first concern was how to repair his constitution. But though he had the best advice, and though the necessity of following it was urged to him in the most friendly manner, it was with the utmost difficulty that he was prevailed on to do what was proper, when it was any way disagreeable. For this reason it was thought best for him to have recourse to the vapor-baths of Aix la Chapelle, over which he sat near three times as long as hath ever been the practice. Whoever knows any thing of the nature of those baths, will, from this instance, form some idea of his surprising constitution. His sweats were profuse beyond what can well be imagined. His cure, from the manner as well as from the quickness, with which it was wrought,

passed with the nuns for a miracle. When, but a few hours
from the time he quitted the bath, they heard him at the
organ in the principal church as well as convent, playing
in a manner so much beyond any they had ever been used
to, such a conclusion in such persons was natural enough.

Though his business was so soon despatched, and his
cure judged to be thoroughly effected, he thought it
prudent to continue at Aix about six weeks, which is the
shortest period usually allotted for bad cases.

Soon after his return to London in 1736, his Alexander's Feast was performed at Convent Garden, and was
well received.

About the year 1729, or 1730, Esther and Deborah
had been performed at the Hay-market with good success ;
with much better indeed than he met with at Convent Garden, when he tried them there but a few years after. He
seems not sufficiently to have considered the risques which
he ran in this new undertaking. The distance of this theatre from those parts of the town where the nobility chiefly
reside ; the relics of the opposition not yet extinct, though
somewhat abated ; a style little suited as yet to the apprehensions of the generality ; these, and probably some other causes, may have concurred to render his attempt in-
auspicious in its commencement. Too much accustomed
to disappointments to be easily dispirited, he continued
these new entertainments, so excellently adapted to the
season of the year in which they are exhibited, till the beginning of the year 1741. But at this time his affairs again
carried so ill an aspect, that he found it necessary to try the
event of another peregrination. He hoped to find that favour and encouragement in a distant capital, which London seemed to refuse him. For even his Messiah* had met

---

* When Handel's "Messiah" was first performed, the audience
were exceedingly struck and affected by the musick generally.

4

with a cold reception.   Either the sense of musical excellence was become so weak, or the power of prejudice so strong, that all the efforts of his unparalleled genius and industry proved ineffectual.

Dublin has always been famous for the gaiety and splendor of its court, the opulence and spirit of its principal inhabitants, the valour of its military, and the genius of its learned men.   Where such things were held in esteem he rightly reckoned, that he could not better pave the way to his success, than by setting out with a striking instance and

but when the chorus " For the Lord God Omnipotent reigneth" they were so transported, that they all, together with the King, (who happened to be present) started up and remained standing till the chorus ended, and hence it became the fashion in England for the audience to stand while that part of the music is performing.

The following anecdote is from a friend of Handel, and one who was upon the most intimate terms with him. He invited a friend to dine with him, the ingenious, but needy Author, who compiled the words of the Messiah, an admirable selection. The room in which they sat was a back parlour to which a closet with a window was annexed. Here was a harpsichord, Handel placed a pint of Port before his friend but retired frequently to the closet, exclaiming, " I have de tought" (thought.) It occurred so often that his friend was induced to peep through the key hole. He saw Handel lifting up to his lips a glass of wine, evidently hoarded for its rich flavour, and then carefully concealing the bottle. The Author's remuneration for the words of the Messiah, was, if we recollect rightly, *one Guinea*. Handel was a German, and epicurism is there national. The Foundling Hospital received from this Jupiter of the musical God's an Organ, and a benefaction of £10,299, and the profit arising to various charities from the performance of his Messiah, since its publication to the present, is probably little less than £100,000. Its services to the cause of piety in the way of impression cannot be inferior. The Messiah is one continual Scheckinah—one unceasing " blaze of glory."

public act of generosity and benevolence. The first step that he made, was to perform his Messiah for the benefit of the city prison. Such a design drew together not only all the lovers of Music, but all the friends of humanity. There was a peculiar propriety in this design from the subject of the Oratorio itself ; and there was a peculiar grace in it from the situation of HANDEL's affairs. They were brought into a better posture by his journey to Dublin, where he staid between eight and nine months. The reception that he met with, at the same time that it shewed the strong sense which the Irish had of his extraordinary merit, conveyed a kind of tacit reproach on all those on the other side of the water, who had enlisted in the opposition against him. Mr. POPE in the fourth book of the Dunciad has related this passsage of his history. A poor phantom, which is made to represent the genius of the modern Italian Opera, expresses her apprehensions, and gives her instructions to Dulness, already alarmed for her own safety. The lines are well known, but, for their strong characteristic imagery, deserve to be quoted in this place. They are as follows,

> But soon, ah soon, rebellion will commence,
> If Music meanly borrows aid from sense :
> Strong in new arms, lo ! giant Handel stands,
> Like bold Briarius with his hundred hands ;
> To stir, to rouse, to shake the soul he comes,
> And Jove's own thunders follow Mars's drums.
> Arrest him, empress ; or you sleep no more—
> She heard,—and drove him to the Hibernian shore.

At his return to London in 1741-2, the minds of most men were much more disposed in his favour. He immediately recommenced his Oratorios at Convent Garden. Sampson was the first he performed. And now (to use the excessive phrase of TACITUS) *blandiebatur cœptis fortuna* ; Fortune seemed rather to court and caress, than to countenance and support him. This return was the æra

of his prosperity. Indeed, in the year 1743, he had some
return of his paralytic disorder ; and the year after fell under the heavy displeasure of a certain fashionable lady. She
exerted all her influence to spirit up a new opposition
against him. But the world could not long be made to believe that her card assemblies were such proper entertainments for Lent, as his Oratorios. It is needless to enlarge
upon particulars which are easily remembered, or to give a
minute account of things generally known. It is sufficient
just to touch on the most remarkable. What is very much
so, his Messiah which had before been received with so
much indifference, became from this time the favourite Oratorio. As in the year 1741, it was applied to the relief
of persons exposed to all the miseries of perpetual confinement ; it was afterwards consecrated to the service of
the most innocent, most helpless, and most distressed part
of the human species. The Foundling Hospital originally
rested on the slender foundation of private benefactions.
At a time when this institution was yet in its infancy ;
when all men seemed to be convinced of its utility ; when
nothing was at all problematical but the possibility of sup-
porting it ;—HANDEL formed the noble resolution to lend
his assistance, and perform his Messiah annually for its
benefit. The sums raised by each performance were very
considerable, and certainly of great consequence in such a
crisis of affairs. But what was of much greater, was the
magic of his name, and the universal character of his sacred Drama. By these vast numbers of the nobility and
gentry were drawn to the hospital ; and many, who, at
the first, had been contented with barely approving the design, were afterwards warmly engaged in promoting it. In
consequence of this resort, the attention of the nation was
also drawn more forcibly to what was indeed the natural
object of it. So that it may truly be affirmed, that one of
the noblest and most extensive charities that ever was

planned by the wisdom, or projected by the piety of men, in some degree owes its continuance, as well as prosperity, to the patronage of HANDEL.

The very successful application of this wonderful production of his genius to so beneficent a purpose, reflected equal honour on the artist and the art.

He continued his Oratorios with uninterrupted success, and unrivalled glory, till within eight days of his death : the last was performed on the 6th of April, and he expired on Saturday the 14th of April 1759. He was buried the 20th by Dr. PEARCE, Bishop of Rochester, in Westminster-abbey, where, by his own order, and at his own expense a monument is to be erected to his memory.

In the year 1751, a gutta serena deprived him of his sight. This misfortune sunk him for a time into the deepest despondency. He could not rest until he had undergone some operations as fruitless as they were painful. Finding it no longer possible for him to manage alone, he sent to Mr. SMITH to desire that he would play for him, and assist him in conducting the Oratorios.

His faculties remained in their full vigour almost to the hour of his dissolution, as appeared from songs and choruses, and other compositions, which from the date of them may almost be considered as his parting words, his last accents! This must appear the more surprising, when it is remembered to how great a degree his mind was disordered at times towards the latter part of his life.

His health had been declining apace for several months before his death. He was very sensible of its approach, and refused to be flattered by any hopes of recovery. One circumstance was very ominous, I mean the total loss of appetite, which was come upon him, and which must prove more pernicious to a person always habituated, as he had been, to an uncommon portion of food and nourishment. Those who have blamed him for an excessive in-

dulgence in this lowest of gratifications,* ought to have considered, that the peculiarities of his constitution were
as great as those of his character. Luxury and in-
temperance are relative ideas, and depend on other circumstances besides those of quantity and quality. It
would be as unreasonable to confine HANDEL to the fare
and allowance of common men, as to expect that a London merchant should live like a Swiss mechanic. Not
that I would absolve him from all blame on this article.
He certainly paid more attention to it, than is becoming in
any man : but it is some excuse, that nature had given him
so vigorous a constitution, so exquisite a palate, and so craving an appetite ; and that fortune enabled him to obey
these calls, to satisfy these demands of nature. They

---

* At a time when Handel's circumstances were less prosperous
than they had been, he invited Goupy to dine with him. The
meal was plain and frugal, as he had warned his guest it must
be ; and for this Handel again apologized, adding that he would
give him as hearty a welcome as when he could treat with claret
and French dishes. Goupy returned a cordial reply ; and they
dined. Soon after dinner Handel left the room ; and his absence was so long, that Goupy at last, for want of other employ,
strolled into the adjoining back room, and walking up to a window which looked diagonally on that of a small third room, he
saw his host sitting at a table covered with such delicacies as he
had lamented his inability to afford his friend. Goupy, to whom
possibly such viands had little less relish than to his host, was so
enraged that he quitted the house abruptly, and published the
engraving or etching, for my memory does not retain the fact
accurately, in which Handel, figures as a hog in the midst of
dainties. It is impossible to defend, or even to excuse Handel ;
but we may extract from the fact some comfort for mediocrity
of talent, by calling attention to the almost invariable truth,
that, as if in mercy to the weakness of human nature, which
cannot endure any pretension to entire superiority, the balance
is generally pretty accurately adjusted between great excellence and great deficiency.

were really such.   For besides the several circumstances
just alleged, there is yet another in his favour ; I mean his
incessant and intense application to the studies of his profession.   This rendered constant and large supplies of nourishment the more necessary to recruit his exhausted spirits.
Had he hurt his health or his fortune by indulgencies of this
kind, they would have been vicious : as he did not, they
were at most indecorous.   As they have been so much the
subject of conversation and pleasantry, to have taken no
notice of them, might have looked like affectation.   But it
would be folly to enter into the particulars of this part of
his history, and contrary to the design of the foregoing
sheets, which is only " to give the reader those parts of his
character, as a man, that any way tend to open and explain
his character as an artist."

REMARKS ON HANDEL'S MUSIC.

The taste in Music both of the Germans and the Italians,
is suited to the different characters of the two nations.
That of the first is rough and martial ; and their Music
consists of strong effects, produced, without much delicacy,
by the rattle of a number of instruments.   The Italians,
from their strong and lively feelings, have endeavoured in
their Music to express all the agitations of the soul, from
the most delicate sensations of love, to the most violent
effects of hatred and despair ; and this in a great degree
by the modulation of a single part.

HANDEL formed his taste upon that of his countrymen,
but by the greatness and sublimity of his genius, he has
worked up such effects as are astonishing.   Some of the
best Italian masters, by the delicacy of their modulation,
have so deeply entered into all the different sensations of
the human heart, that they may almost be said to have the

passions of mankind at their command ; at least of that part of mankind, whose lively feelings are somewhat raised to a pitch with their own.

When we consider two kinds of Music so very different in character, as that of HANDEL, and that of the best Italians, and both carried to so great a degree of perfection, we cannot be surprised at seeing warm advocates for each. HANDEL's Music must be allowed to have had some advantages over theirs, independent of its real merit. The fulness, strength, and spirit of his Music, is wonderfully well suited to the common sensations of mankind, which must be roused a little † roughly, and are not of a cast to be easily worked upon by delicacies. Thus he takes in all the unprejudiced part of mankind. For in his sublime strokes, of which he has many, he acts as powerfully upon the most knowing, as upon the ignorant. Another advantage which he has over the Italians, is owing to themselves. The quantity of bad Music from Italy, prejudices many against the good.

I would conclude, that both those who indiscriminately condemn HANDEL's compositions, and those who in like manner condemn the Italian music, are equally to blame as prejudiced or ignorant deciders. And I would recommend it to all true lovers of Music, to examine with candor, and I may even add, with some degree of reverence, the compositions of men, whose great abilities in their profession do honor to human nature. I think it is highly probable, that whatever delicacies appear in HANDEL's Music, are owing to his journey into Italy ; and likewise that the Italians are much indebted to him for their management of the instrumental parts that accompany the voice ; in which

† It is only Handel's *general* character that is here opposed to that of the Italians. For though the cast of his mind was *more* towards the great and sublime than any *other* style, yet he sometimes excels the Italians themselves even in the passionate and pathetic.

indeed some few of them have succeeded admirably well. And as some proof of HANDEL's influence in Italy, it is, I believe, an undoubted fact, that French-horns were never used there as an accompaniment to the voice, till HANDEL introduced them.

But however well some of the Italians may have succeeded in the management of the instrumental parts in their Song-music, there is one point in which HANDEL stands alone, and in which he may possibly never be equalled ; I mean in the instrumental parts of his Chorusses, and full church Music. In these he has given innumerable instances of an unbounded genius. In short, there is such a sublimity in many of the effects he has worked up by the combination of instruments and voices, that they seem to be rather the effect of inspiration, than of knowledge in Music.

But in order to make a right judgment of his abilities in Music, attention must constantly be had to its two different species, viz. the instrumental and vocal.

The excellence of the former consists in the strength and fulness of its harmony : that of the latter in the delicacy and propriety of its melody.

HANDEL was not so excellent in air, where there is no strong character to mark, or passion to express. He had not the art, for which the Italians have ever been remarkable, the art of trifling with grace and delicacy. His turn was for greater things, in expressing which it is hard to say, whether he excelled most in his air, or in his harmony. This may be proved even from his Oratorios, where he has failed the most and the oftenest. But in his old operas there are numberless instances of his abilities in the vocal way, such as it would be difficult to parallel out of the greatest masters, whose excellence lay in that particular species.

5

And here I may observe, there are indeed some few
sounds, which nature herself employs to express the strong
emotions of the human heart, which the voice may imitate.
But it is common for the masters not only to forget the nature and extent of this imitative power in Music, but also to
mistake the subject on which to employ it. A too close
attachment to some particular words in a sentence, hath
often misled them from the general meaning of it. HAN-
DEL himself, from his imperfect acquaintance with the English language, has sometimes fallen into these mistakes.
A composer ought never to pay this attention to single
words, excepting they have an uncommon energy, and contain some passion or sentiment. To do HANDEL justice, he is
generally great and masterly, where the language and poetry are well adapted to his purpose. The English tongue
abounds with monosyllables and consonants. Though these
cannot always be avoided, yet the writers of musical dra-
mas should always pick out such as are the least harsh and
disagreeable to the ear. The same regard must be had to
the sentiments, as to the language. The more simple and
natural they are, the more easily will Music express them.
There was a time (says Mr. Addison) when it was laid
down as a maxim, that nothing was capable of being well
set to Music, that was not nonsense. This satyr is equally
just and beautiful. But though the sense of such productions canot be too strong, the poetry of them may be too
fine. If it abounds with noble images, and high wrought
descriptions, and contains little of character, sentiment, or
passion, the best composer will have no opportunity of ex-
erting his talents. Where there is nothing capable of being expressed, all he can do is to entertain his audience
with mere ornamental passages of his own invention. But
graces and flourishes must rise from the subject of the composition in which they are employed, just as flowers and

festoons from the design of the building. It is from their relation to the whole, that these minuter parts derive their value.

It was not to be dissembled that the manly cast of HANDEL's mind often led him into a kind of melody ill suited to the voice ; that he was apt to depart from the style which the species of composition demanded, and run into passages purely instrumental. Yet so admirable is the contrivance, and so beautiful the modulation in some of his pieces, where this deviation is most conspicuous, that the best judge of Music, who examines them as a critic, will hardly have the heart to execute his office ; and, while the laws of it compel him to arraign the fault, will almost be sorry to see it corrected.

To conclude, there is in his works, such a fulness, force, and energy, that the harmony of HANDEL may always be compared to the antique figure of HERCULES, which seems to be nothing but muscles and sinews ; and his melody may often be likened to the Venus of Medicis, which is all grace and delicacy.

Whatever shall be thought of this attempt to do justice to his memory, too much reason there is for believing that the interests of religion and humanity are not so strongly guarded, or so firmly secured, as easily to spare those succors, or forego those assistances which are ministered to them from the elegant arts.

They refine and exalt our ideas of pleasure, which when rightly understood, and properly pursued, is the very end of our existence. They improve and settle our ideas of taste ; which, when founded on solid and consistent principles, explains the causes, and heightens the effects, of whatever is beautiful or excellent, whether in the works of creation, or in the productions of human skill.

They adorn and embellish the face of nature ; the talents of men they sharpen and invigorate ; the manners

they civilize and polish ; in a word, they soften the cares
of life, and render its heaviest calamities much more supportable by adding to the number of its innocent enjoy-
ments.

———

FRANCIS JOSEPH HAYDN.

———

FRANCIS JOSEPH HAYDN was born on the last day of
March, 1732, at Rohrau, a small town, fifteen leagues distant from Vienna.   His father was a cartwright ; and his
mother, before her marriage, had been cook in the family of
Count HARRACH, the Lord of the village.   The father of
HAYDN united to his trade of a cartwright, the office
of parish sexton.   He had a fine tenor voice, was fond
of his organ, and of Music in general.   On one of those
journies, which the artisans of Germany often undertake,
being at Frankfort-on-the-Mayne, he learned to play a little on the harp :   and in holidays, after church, he used to
take his instrument, and his wife sung.   The birth of Joseph did not alter the habits of this peaceful family.   The
little domestic concert returned every week, and the child,
standing before his parents, with two pieces of wood in his
hands, one of which served him as a violin, and the other as
a bow, constantly accompanied his mother's voice.   A
cousin of the cartwright, whose name was FRANK, a school-
master at Haimburg, came to Rohrau, on Sunday, and assisted at the trio.   He remarked, that the child, then
scarcely six years old, beat the time with astonishing ex-
actitude and precision.   This FRANK was well acquainted

with Music, and proposed to his relations to take little Joseph to his house, and to teach him. They accepted the offer with joy, hoping to succed more easily in getting Joseph into holy orders, if he should understand music.

From his most tender age, Music had given him unusual pleasure. At any time, he would rather listen to any instrument whatever, than run about with his little companions. When at play with them in the square, near St. Stephen's as soon as he heard the organ, he quickly left them, and went into the church. Arrived at the age of composition, the habit of application was already acquired : besides, the composer of Music has advantages over other artists ; his productions are finished as soon as imagined.

Less precocious than Mozart, who, at thirteen years produced an applauded Opera, Haydn, at the same age, composed a mass, which honest Reuter very properly ridiculed. This sentence surprised the young man, but full of good sense at that early period, he was aware of its justice : he was sensible that it was necessary to learn counterpoint, and the rules of melody. But from whom was he to learn them ? Reuter did not teach counterpoint to the children of the choir, and never gave more than two lessons in it to Haydn. Mozart had an excellent master in his father, who was an esteemed performer on the violin. It was otherwise with poor Joseph, a friendless chorister in Vienna, who could only obtain lessons by paying for them, and who had not half a penny. His father, notwithstanding his two trades, was so poor, that when Joseph had been robbed of his clothes, on his communicating the misfortune to his family, his father making an effort, sent him six florins to refit his wardrobe.

Haydn bought, at a second hand shop, some theoretical books, among others the Treatise by Fux, and he set about studying it with a perseverance, which the horrible obscurity of the rules could not overcome. Labouring alone, without a master, he made an infinite number of little discoveries, which were afterwards of use to him. Without either money, or fire, shivering with cold in his garret, and oppressed with sleep as he pursued his studies to a late hour of the night, by the side of a harpsichord out of repair, and falling to pieces in all parts, he was still happy. The days and years flew on rapid wing, and he has often said, that he never enjoyed such felicity at any other period of his life. HAYDN's ruling passion was rather the love of music than the love of glory : and even in his desire of glory, not a shadow of ambition was to be found. In composing Music, he sought rather his own gratification, than to furnish himself with the means of acquiring celebrity.

HAYDN was in his nineteenth year, when he composed the Tempest. MOZART wrote his first Opera at Milan, at the age of thirteen, in competition with HASSE, who, after having heard the rehearsal, said publicly, " this boy will throw us all into the shade." HAYDN was not so successful ; his talent was not for the theatre : and though he has produced Operas which no master would be ashamed to avow, he has, nevertheless, remained far behind the *Clemenza di Tito* and *Don Juan.*

It was at twenty that he produced his first quartett in B♭ $\frac{6}{4}$ time, which all the musical amateurs immediately learned by heart. I do not know for what reason HAYDN, about this time, left the house of his friend KELLER ; but it is certain, that his reputation, though rising under the most brilliant auspices, had not yet raised him above poverty. He went to reside with a M. MARTINEZ, who offered him board and lodging, on condition that he would give lessons on the piano-forte, and in singing, to his two daughters. It was then, that the same house, situated near the church of St. Michael, contained in two rooms, one over the other, in the third and fourth stories, the first poet of the age, and the first symphonist of the world.

METASTASIO, also, lodged with MARTINEZ, but, as poet to the Emperor Charles VI., he lived in easy circumstances, while poor HAYDN passed the winter days in bed for want of fuel. The society of the Roman poet was, nevertheless a great advantage to him. A gentle and deep sensibility had given METASTASIO a correct taste in all the arts. He was passionately fond of Music, and understood it well ; and this singularly harmonious soul appreciated the talents of the young German. METASTASIO, dining every day with HAYDN, gave him some general rules respecting the fine arts ; and in the course of his instructions, taught him Italian.

This struggle against want, the early companion of almost all artists who have arrived at distinction, lasted with respect to HAYDN, for six long years. If some rich nobleman had brought him out at that time, and sent him to travel, for two years, in Italy, with a pension of one hundred louis, nothing, perhaps, would have been wanting to his talent ; but, less fortunate than METASTASIO, he had not his *Gravina*. At length, he obtained a situation in a family ; and in 1758, left the house of MARTINEZ, to enter the service of the count MORTZIN.

HAYDN, was received into the Esterhazy family, placed at the head of a grand orchestra, and attached to the service of a patron immensely rich, found himself in that happy union of circumstances, too rare for our pleasures, which gives opportunity to genius to display all its powers. From this moment his life was uniform, and fully employed. He rose early in the morning, dressed himself very neatly, and placed himself at a small table by the side of his piano forte, where the hour of dinner usually found him still seated. In the evening, he went to the rehearsals, or to the Opera, which was performed, in the Prince's palace, four times every week. Sometimes, but not often, he devoted a morning to hunting. The little time which he had to spare, on common days, was divided between his friends and mademoiselle Bosselli. Such was the course of his life, for more than thirty years. This accounts for the astonishing number of his works. They may be arranged in three classes : instrumental music, church music, and operas.

The general character of the instrumental music of our author is that of romantic imagination. In vain would you seek in it the correctness of Racine ; it is rather the style of Ariosto, or of Shakespeare. For this reason I cannot account for the reputation of HAYDN in France,

His genius ranges in every direction with the rapidity of the eagle. The astonishing, and the alluring, succeed each other alternately, and are painted with the most brilliant tints. It is this variety of coloring, it is the absence of every thing tedious, which has probably obtained for him so rapid and extensive a success. Scarcely had he composed his symphonies, before they were performed in America, and the Indies.

The magic of his style seems to me to consist in a predominating character of liberty and joy. This joy of HAYDN is a perfectly natural, pure, and continual exultation ; it reigns in the *allegros* ; it is perceptible even in the grave parts, and pervades the *andantes* in a sensible degree.

In those compositions, where it is evident from the rythm, the tone, and the general character, that the author intends to inspire melancholy, this obstinate joy, being unable to shew itself openly, is transformed into energy and strength. Observe, this sombre gravity is not pain, it is joy constrained to disguise itself ; which might be called the concentrated joy of a savage ; but never sadness, dejection, or melancholy. HAYDN has never been really melancholy more than two or three times ; in a verse of his *Stabat Mater*, and in two of the *adagios* of the *Seven Words*.

This is the reason why he has never excelled in Dramatic music. Without melancholy, there can be no impassioned music, and, for this cause, the French people, lively, vain, and light, expressing with quickness all their sentiments, sometimes oppressed with ennui, but never melancholic, will never have any music.

HAYDN did not set himself to write a symphony, except he felt himself in a good disposition for it. It has been said, that fine thoughts come from the heart ; and the truth of this remark is the more observable, in proportion as the subject, on which an author is employed, is removed from the precision of the mathematical sciences.

HAYDN, like Buffon, thought it necessary to have his hair put in the same nice order, as if he were going out, and dressed himself with a degree of magnificence. Frederic II, had sent him a diamond ring ; and HAYDN confessed that, often, when he sat down to his piano, if he had forgotten to put on his ring he could not summon a single idea. The paper on which he composed, must be the finest and whitest possible, and he wrote with so much neatness and care that the best copyist could not have surpassed him, in the regularity and clearness of his characters. It is true, that his notes had such little heads, and slender tails, that he used, very properly to call them his *flies legs*.

After these mechanical precautions, HAYDN commenced his work, by noting down his principal idea, his *theme*, and choosing the keys through which he wished to make it pass. His exquisite feeling gave him a perfect knowledge of the greater, or less degree of effect, which one chord produces, in succeeding another ; and he afterwards imagined a little romance, which might furnish him with musical sentiments and colors.

Notwithstanding a cast of physiognomy rather morose, and a short way of expressing himself, which seemed to indicate an ill-tempered man, the character of HAYDN was

6

gay, open, and humorous. This vivacity, it is true, was
easily repressed by the presence of strangers, or persons of
superior rank. In Germany, nothing is suffered to level
the distinctions of society ; it is the land of ceremony. At
Paris, the *cordons bleus* went to see D'Alembert in his garret ; in Austria, Haydn never associated with any but the
musicians, his colleagues ; society, as well as himself, were
doubtless losers by this circumstance. His gaiety, and
the copiousness of his ideas, well fitted him for the display
of the comic in instrumental music, a genus almost new,
and in which he would have made great progress ; but to
succeed in which, as in every thing which relates to comedy, it is indispensible that the author be in the habit of the
most elegant society. Haydn was not introduced to the
great world till the decline of life, during his visits to London.

After the death of his female friend, he accepted the
proposals of a London professor, named Salomon, who had
undertaken to give concerts in that city. Salomon thought
that a man of genius, drawn from his retirement, purpose-
ly for the amateurs of London, would bring his concerts into fashion. He gave twenty concerts in the year, and offered Haydn 100 sequins (50*l.*) for each concert. Haydn,
having accepted these terms, set out for London in 1790,
at the age of fifty-nine. He spent more than a year there.
The new music which he composed for these concerts was
greatly admired* The simplicity of his manners, added to

* Haydn has produced some of his most striking effects by the
sudden change of key. Every practitioner in the art must have
noticed the various complexions, so to speak, by which they are
characterized. By *Key*, we mean any system of notes which
regards a certain tone as its base or centre, to which all the ad-
jacent harmonies gravitate, or tend. In the 15th century, Music was generally written in the key of F, and its relative D minor. This order of sounds was first adopted, probably on ac-

certain indications of genius, could not fail to succeed with a generous and reflecting nation. The English would often observe him, as he walked in the street, eye him in silence from head to foot, and go away saying, " That is certainly a great man."

count of its being the most agreeable to the ear. And as some of the grandest sounds of the natural world,—the rushing of the storm, the murmurs of the brook, and the roar of the sea, are to be referred to this harmony, it may be denominated the *Key of Nature.* As science improved, other notes were taken as the centres of systems, by which other keys were formed, and we have now not less than 24 keys, both major, and minor.

We shall endeavor to characterize some of them.

F its relative.	This key is rich, mild, sober and contemplative.
D Minor.	Possesses the same qualities, but of a heavier and darker cast : more doleful, solemn and grand.
C	Bold, vigorous, and commanding : suited to the expression of war and enterprize.
A Minor.	Plaintive, but not feeble.
G	Gay and sprightly. Being the medium key, it is adapted to the greatest range of subjects.
E Minor.	Persuasive, soft and tender.
D	Ample, grand, and noble. Having more fire than C, it is suited to the loftiest purposes. In choral music, it is the highest key, the treble having its cadence note on the 4th line.
B. Minor.	Bewailing, but in too high a tone to excite commiseration.
A.	Golden, warm, and sunny.
F sharp Minor.	Mournfully grand.
E in sharps	Bright and pellucid : adapted to brilliant subjects. In this key Haydn has written his most elegant thoughts. Handel mistook its properties when he used it in the chorus, " *The many rend the skies with loud applause.*" Though higher than D, it is less loud, as it stretches the voice beyond its natural power.
B in sharps.	Keen and piercing. Seldom used.

During his residence in London, our author enjoyed two great gratifications. One was, in hearing HANDEL's music ; the other, in going to the ancient concert. This last is a society established for the purpose of preserving music, which, in the fashionable world, is called ancient. They give concerts, at which are performed the master-pieces of Pergolese, Leo, Durante, Marcello, Scarlatti,— in a word, of that constellation of distinguised men, who appeared almost at the same time, about the year 1730.

HAYDN undertook a second journey to London, in 1794. Gallini, the manager of the King's theatre, in the Hay-market, had engaged him to compose an opera, which he intended to get up with the greatest magnificence. The subject was the descent of Orpheus to hell. HAYDN began to work, but Gallini found a difficulty in obtaining permission to open his theatre. The composer, who was hankering after home, had not patience to wait till permission could be ob-

B flat	The least interesting of any. It has not sufficient fire to render it majestic, or grand, and is
G Minor.	too dull for song. Meek and pensive. Replete with melancholy.
E flat Major.	Full and mellow ; sombre, soft and beautiful. It is a key in which all musicians delight.— Though less decided in its character than some of the others, the regularity of its beauty renders it a universal favorite.
C. Minor.	Complaining, having something of the whining cant of B. minor.
A flat Major.	The most lovely of of the tribe. Unassuming, gentle, soft, delicate and tender, having none of the pertness of A in sharps. Every author has been sensible of the charm of this key, and has reserved it for the expression of his most refined sentiments.
F Minor.	Religious, penitential, and gloomy.
D flat Major.	Awfully dark. In this remote key, Haydn and Beethoven have written their sublimest thoughts. They never enter it but for tragic purposes.

It is sufficient to have hinted at these effects. To account for them, is difficult ; but every musician is sensible of their existence.

tained. He left London, with eleven parts of his Orpheus, which, as I am informed, are his best productions in theatrical music, and returned to Austria, never more to leave it.

He often saw, in London, the celebrated Mrs. Billington, whom he enthusiastically admired. He found her one day, sitting to Reynolds, the only English painter, who has succeeded in portraits.—He had just taken that of Mrs. Billington, in the character of St. Cecilia, listening to the celestial music, as she is usually drawn. Mrs. Billington shewed the picture to HAYDN. "It is like," said he, "but there is a strange mistake."—"what is that?" asked Reynolds, hastily :—"you have painted her listening to the angels ; you ought to have represented the angels listening to her." Mrs. Billington sprung up, and threw her arms round his neck. It was for her that he composed his *Ariadne abbandonata*, which rivals that of Benda.

One of the English princes commissioned Reynolds to take HAYDN's portrait. Flattered by the honor, he went to the painter's house, and sat to him, but soon grew tired Reynolds, careful of his reputation, would not paint a man of acknowledged genius, with a stupid countenance, and deferred the sitting to another day. The same weariness and want of expression occurring at the next attempt, Reynolds went to the prince, and informed him of the circumstance. The prince contrived a stratagem ; he sent to the painter's house a pretty German girl, in the service of the queen his mother. HAYDN took his seat for the third time, and as soon as the conversation began to flag, a curtain fell, and the fair German, elegantly attired in white, and crowned with roses, addressed him in his native tongue : " O, great man, how happy am I to have an opportunity of seeing thee, and of being in thy presence !" HAYDN, delighted, overwhelms the lovely enchantress with questions ; his countenance recovered its animation, and Reynolds seized it with rapidity.

George III. who liked no music but Handel's was not
insensible to that of HAYDN.   He and the queen gave a
flattering reception to the German professor ; and the
University of Oxford sent him a doctor's diploma, a dignity
which had been conferred on only four persons since the
year 1400, and which Handel himself had not obtained.

HAYDN left London, delighted with Handel's music, and
carrying with him a few hundred guineas, which seemed to
him a treasure.   On his return through Germany, he gave
a few concerts ; and for the first time his little fortune received an augmentation.   His appointments in the Esterhazy family, were of small amount ; but the condescension
with which he was treated by the members of that august
house, was of more value to a man whose works are the
production of his feelings, than any pecuniary advantages.
He had always a cover at the prince's table ; and when his
highness gave a uniform to his orchestra, HAYDN received
the dress usually worn by persons coming to Eisenstadt to
pay their court to the prince.   It is by a course of attentions such as these, that the great families of Austria gain
the affections of all by whom they are surrounded ; it is by
this moderation that they render tolerable and even agreeable, privileges and manners which put them almost on an
equality with crowned heads.   German pride is ridiculous
only in the printed accounts of their public ceremonies ;
the air of kindness which accompanies the reality, gives a
pleasing colour to every thing.

HAYDN took with him, from London, 15,000 florins.
Some years afterwards, the sale of the score of the *Creation*, and the *Four Seasons*, brought him an additional sum
of 2,000 sequins. with which he purchased the small house
and garden in the fauxbourg Gumpendorff, on the road to
Schonbrunn, where he resides.   Such is the state of his
fortune.

Long before HAYDN rose to the Creation, he had composed (in 1774) an Oratorio entitled *Tobias*, an indifferent performance, two or three passages of which only, announces the great master. You know that while in London, HAYDN was struck with Handel's music : he learned from the works of the English musician the art of being majestic. One day at Prince Schwartzenberg's when HANDEL's *Messiah* was performed, upon expressing my admiration of one of the sublime chorusses of that work, HAYDN said to to me thoughtfully, " *This man is the father of us all.*"

I am convinced that if he had not studied Handel, he would never have written the Creation : his genius was fired by that of this master. It was remarked by every one here, that after his return from London, there was more grandeur in his ideas ; in short he approached, as far as is permitted to human genius, the unattainable object of his songs. Handel is simple ; his accompaniments are written in three parts only ; but to use a Neapolitan phrase of Gluck's, there is not a note that does not *draw blood.*

HAYDN was sixty-three years old when he undertook this great work and was employed two whole years upon it. When urged to bring it to a conclusion, he calmly replied, "I spend much time over it, because I intend it to last a long time."

In the beginning of the year 1798, the oratorio was completed ; and in the following Lent, it was performed, for the first time, in the rooms of the Schwartzenberg palace, at the expense of the *Dilettanti* society, who had requested it from the author.

Who can describe the applause, the delight, the enthusiasm of this society. I was present ; and I can assure you, I never witnessed such a scene. The flower of the literary and musical society of Vienna were assembled in the room, which was well adapted to the purpose, and HAYDN himself directed the orchestra. The most profound sience, the most scrupulous attention, a sentiment I might almost say of religious respect, were the dispositions which prevailed when the first stroke of the bow was given. The general expectation was not disappointed. A long train of beauties, to that moment unknown, unfolded themselves before us ; our minds, overcome with pleasure and admiration experienced, during two successive hours, what they had rarely felt,—a happy existence, produced by desires ever lively, ever renewed, and never disappointed.

HAYDN wrote his Creation to German words, which is not capable of Italian melody. How could he, even if he had wished it, have written melodies like those of Sacchini ? Born in Germany, knowing his own feelings, and those of his countrymen, he apparently wished to please them in the first place. We may criticise a man when we see him mistake the road to his object ; but is it reasonable to quarrel with him on the choice of the object ?

A great Italian master has produced the only criticism worthy of HAYDN and of himself. He has re-cast from one end to the other, all the music of the Creation, which will not see the light till after his death. This master thinks that HAYDN, in symphony is a man of genius, but in every thing else, only estimable. For my own part, I am of opinion, that when the two *Creations* shall both have been published, the German one will always be preferred at Vienna, and the Italian at Naples.

Two years after the Creation, Haydn, animated by success, and encouraged by his friend Von Swieten, composed a new oratorio, *The Four Seasons.* The descriptive baron had taken the text of them from Thompson. There is less sentiment in this work than in the Creation, but the subject admitted of gaiety, the joy of the vintage, profane love ; and the Four Seasons would be the finest things extant, in the department of descriptive music, if the Creation did not exist.

The music of it is more learned and less sublime, than that of the Creation. It, nevertheless, surpasses its elder sister in one point ; that is, the quartetts.

The text of the Four Seasons is despicable. As to the music, represent to yourself a gallery of pictures, differing in style, subject and colouring. This Gallery is divided into four apartments, in the middle of each of which, appears a large principal picture.

The subjects of these four pictures are, for the first, the snow, the north winds, the frost, and its horrors.

In the Summer, a storm ; in the Autumn, hunting ; and in Winter the village evening.

It immediately occurs, that an inhabitant of a more fortunate climate, would not have introduced snow, and the horrors of winter, into a picture of the spring. According to my taste, it is but a dismal commencement of the work. According to the amateurs, these rude sounds have a wonderful tendency to increase the subsequent pleasure.

With you, my friend, I shall not go through the Four Seasons, step by step.

In representing the summer's sun, HAYDN was under the necessity of endeavouring to keep clear of the first sunrise in the Creation ; and this art, which we would fain consider as descriptive, is so vague, so anti descriptive, that notwithstanding the incredible pains which the first symphonist of the world has taken, he has fallen into some degree of repetition.

The critics objected to the Four Seasons, that it contained even fewer airs than the Creation, and said that it was a piece of instrumental music, with a vocal accompaniment.

The author was growing old. He is also accused, ridiculously enough in my opinion, of having introduced gaiety into a serious subject. And why is it serious ? Because it is called an *oratorio*. The title may be ill chosen ; but is it not rather a fortunate thing that a symphony, which

7

produces no very profound emotions, should be occasionally lively ? The *chilly* accuse him, with more justice of
having put two winters into one year.

The words of the Four Seasons, common-place enough
in themselves, were flatly translated into several languages.
The music was arranged in quartetts, and quintetts, and
was introduced still more than that of the Creation, into
amateur concerts. The little melody contained in it, being
principally in the orchestra, the air remains almost entire,
even when the vocal part is taken away.

I think I see in HAYDN, the Tintoret of music. Like the
Venetian painter, he unites to the energy of Michel Angelo,
fire, originality, and fertility of invention. All this is in-
vested with a lovelines of colouring, which renders pleasing even the minutest details. I am, nevertheless, of opinion,
that the Tintoret of Eisentadt, was more profound in his art
than the Venetian one ; more particularly, he knew how
to work slowly.

The mania of comparisons seizes me. I trust you with
my collection, on condition that you will not laugh at it too
much. I fancy, then that

Pergolese, and Cimarosa	are the Raphaels of music
Paesiello — is —	Guido
Durante — — — — —	Lionardo da Vinci
Hasse — — — — —	Rubens
Handel — — — — —	Michel Angelo
Galluppi — — — —	Bassano
Jomelli — — — — —	Lewis Caracci
Gluck — — — — —	Caravaggio
Piccini — — — — —	Titian
Sacchini — — — — —	Correggio
Vinci — — — — —	Fra Bartolommeo
Anfossi — — — — —	Albano.

Zingarelli	-	-	-	-	Guerchino
Mayer	-	-	-	-	-	Carlo Maratti
Mozart	-	-	-	-	-	Dominichino.

The least imperfect resemblance, is that of Paesiello and Guido. As for Mozart, Dominichino should have a still stronger cast of melancholy, to resemble him entirely.

The musical career of HAYDN terminates with the Four Seasons. The labour of this work exhausted his declining strength. "I have done," said he to me, a short time after finishing this oratorio, "my head is no longer what it was. Formerly ideas came to me unsought ; I am now obliged to seek for them, and for this I feel I am not formed."

He wrote, after this, a few quartetts, but could never finish that numbered 84, though he was employed upon it, almost without interruption, for three years. In the latter part of his time he employed himself in putting bases to ancient Scotch airs, for each of which he received two guineas from a London bookseller. He arranged near three hundred of these, but in 1805, by order of his physician he discontinued this occupation also. Life was retiring from him ; he was seized with vertigoes as soon as he sat down to the piano forte. From this time, he never left his garden at Gumpendorff. He sent to his friends, when he was desirous of reminding them of him, a visiting card of his own composition. The words of it are,

"My strength is gone, I am old and feeble."

The music which accompanies them, stopping in the middle of the period, without arriving at the cadence, well expresses the languishing state of the author,

All my strength is gone.   Old and weak am I.

Hin ist alle mien Kraft.   All und schwach bin ich.

At present, this great man, or rather what remains of him here, is occupied by two ideas only : the fear of falling ill, and the fear of wanting money. He is continually sipping a few drops of Tokay, and receives with the greatest pleasure presents of game, which serve to diminish the expense of his little table.

The visits of his friends rouse him a little, and he sometimes follows an idea pretty well. For instance. In 1805, the Paris papers announced that he was dead ; and, as he was an honorary member of the Institute, that illustrious body, which has nothing of the German sluggishness about it, caused a mass to be celebrated in honour of him. The idea of this, much amused HAYDN, He remarked, " If these gentlemen had given me notice, I would have gone myself to beat the time to the fine mass of Mozart's which they have had performed for me." But, notwithstanding his pleasantry, in his heart, he was very grateful to them.

A short time afterwards, Mozart's widow and son gave a concert at the petty theatre De la Wieden, to celebrate HAYDN's birth-day. A cantata was performed, which the young Mozart had composed in honor of the immortal rival of his father. The native goodness of German hearts should be known, to form an idea of the effect of this concert. I would engage, that during the three hours it lasted, not a single pleasantry, of any kind, passed in the room.

That day reminded the public of Vienna of the loss they had already sustained, as well as of that which they were about to experience.

It was agreed to perform the Creation, with the Italian words of Carpani, and one hundred and sixty musicians assembled at the palace of prince Lobkowitz.

They were aided by three fine voices, Madame Frischer, of Berlin, Messrs. Weitmuller and Radichi. There were more than fifteen hundred persons in the room.

The poor old man, notwithstanding his weakness, was desirous of seeing, once more, that public for which he had
so long laboured. He was carried into the room in an easy chair. The princess Esterhazy, and his friend, Madame de Kurzbeck, went to meet him. The flourishes of
the orchestra, and still more the agitation of the spectators,
announced his arrival. He was placed in the middle of
three rows of seats, destined for his friends, and for all
that was illustrious in Vienna. Salieri, who directed the
orchestra, came to receive HAYDN's orders before they began. They embraced ; Salieri left him, flew to his
place, and the orchestra commenced amidst the general
emotion. It may easily be judged, whether this religious
music would appear sublime to an audience, whose hearts
were affected by the sight of a great man about to depart
out of life. Surrounded by the great, by his friends, and
by the artists of his profession, and by charming women,
of whom every eye was fixed upon him, HAYDN bid a glorious adieu to the world, and to life.

The chevalier Capellini, a physician of the first rank,
observed that HAYDN's legs were not sufficiently covered.
Scarcely had he given an intimation to those who stood
around, than the most beautiful shawls left their charming
wearers, to assist in warming the beloved old man.

HAYDN, whom so much glory, and affection, had caused
to shed tears more than once, felt himself faint at the end
of the first part. His chair was brought. At the moment
of leaving the room, he ordered the chairman to stop ;
thanked the public, first, by an inclination of his head;
then, turning to the orchestra, with a feeling truly German, he raised his hands to heaven, and with his eyes
filled with tears, pronounced his benediction on the ancient
companions of his labors.

On my return to the Austrian capital, I have to inform you,
my dear friend, that the larva of HAYDN has also quitted us.

That great man no longer exists, except in our memory. I have often told you, that he was become extremely weak before he entered his seventy-eighth year. It was the last of his life. No sooner did he approach his piano-forte, than the vertigo returned, and his hands quitted the keys to take up the rosary, that last consolation.

The war broke out between Austria and France. This intelligence roused HAYDN, and exhausted the remnant of his strength.

He was continually inquiring for news ; he went every moment to his piano, and sang, with the small thread of voice which he yet retained,

" God preserve the emperor."

The French armies advanced with gigantic strides. At length, on the night of the 10th of May, having reached Schonbrunn, half a leagues's distance from HAYDN's little garden, they fired, the next morning, fifteen hundred cannon-shot, within two yards of his house, upon Vienna, the town which he so much loved. The old man's imagination represented it as given up to fire and sword. Four bombs fell close to his house. His two servants ran to him full of terror. The old man, rousing himself, got up from his easy chair, and with a dignified air, demanded : "Why is this terror ? Know that no disaster can come where HAYDN is." A convulsive shivering prevented him from proceeding, and he was carried to his bed. On the 26th of May, his strength diminished sensibly. Nevertheless, having caused himself to be carried to his piano, he sung thrice, as loud as he was able,

"God preserve the emperor !"

It was the song of the swan. While at the piano, he fell into a kind of stupor, and, at last, expired on the morning of the 31st, aged seventy-eight years and two months.

Madame de Kurzbeck, at the moment of the occupation, of Vienna, had entreated him to allow of his being removed to her house in the interior of the city : he thanked her, but declined leaving his beloved retreat.

HAYDN was buried at Gumpendorff, as a private individual. It is said, however, that prince Esterhazy intends to erect a monument to him.

A few weeks after his death, Mozart's *requiem* was performed in honor of him, in the Scotch church. I ventured into the city, to attend this ceremony. I saw there some generals and administrators of the French army, who appeared affected with the loss which the arts had just sustained. I recognized the accents of my native land, and spoke to several of them ; and, among others, to an amiable man, who wore that day the uniform of the Institute of France, which I thought very elegant.

A similar respect was paid to the memory of HAYDN at Breslau, and at the Conservatoire of Paris, where a hymn of Cherubini's composition was performed. The words are insipid, as usual ; but the music is worthy of the great man whom it celebrates.

During all his life, HAYDN was very religious. Without assuming the preacher, it may be said, that his talent was increased by his sincere faith in the truths of religion. At the commencement of all his scores, the following words are described,

In nomine Domini,

or,   *Soli Deo gloria.*

and at the conclusion of all of them is written,

Laus Deo.

When, in composing, he felt the ardour of his imagination decline, or was stopped by some insurmountable difficulty, he rose from the piano-forte, and began to run over his rosary. He said, that he never found this method fail. "When I was employed upon the Creation," said he, "I felt myself so penetrated with religious feeling, that, before I sat down to the piano forte, I prayed to God, with earnestness, that he would enable me to praise him worthily."

HAYDN's heir is a blacksmith, to whom he has left thirty-eight thousand florins in paper, deducting twelve thousand, which he bequeathed to his two faithful servants. His manuscripts were sold by auction, and purchased by prince Esterhazy.

Prince Lichtenstein was desirous of having our composer's old parrot of which many wonderful stories were told. When he was younger, it was said, he sung, and spoke several languages, and people would have it, that he had been instructed by his master. The astonishment of the blacksmith, when he saw the parrot sold for one thousand four hundred florins, diverted all who were present at the sale. I do not know who purchased his watch. It was given to him by admiral Nelson, who called upon him, when he passed through Vienna, and asked him to make him a present of one of his pens, begging him to accept, in return, the watch he had worn in so many engagements.

HAYDN wrote for his epitaph,

Veni, scripsi, vixi.

He has left no posterity. Cherubini, Pleyel, Neukomm, and Weigl, may be considered as his disciples.

HAYDN had the same weakness as the celebrated Austrian minister, prince Kaunitz ; he could not bear to be painted as an old man. In 1800, he was seriously angry with a painter who had represented him as he then was : that is to say, in his seventy-eighth year. " If I was HAYDN, when I was forty," said he to him, " why would you transmit to posterity a HAYDN of seventy-eight ? Neither you nor I gain by the alteration."

Such were the life and death of this celebrated man.

JOHN C. W. T. MOZART.

John Chrysostom Wolfgang Theophilus Mozart, was born at Salzburg, on the 27th of January, 1756. A few years afterwards, his father discontinued giving lessons in the town, and determined to devote all the time which the duties of his office left at his disposal, to the superintendance of the musical education of his two children.

Mozart was scarcely three years old when his father began to give lessons on the harpsichord to his sister, who was then seven. His astonishing disposition for music immediately manifested itself. His delight was to seek for thirds on the piano, and nothing could equal his joy when he had found this harmonious chord. The minute details into which I am about to enter, will, I presume, be interesting to the reader.

When he was four years old, his father began to teach him, almost in sport, some minuets, and other pieces of music, an occupation which was as agreeable to the master, as to the pupil. Mozart would learn a minuet in half an hour, and a piece of greater extent in less than twice that time. Immediately after, he played them with the greatest clearness, and perfectly in time. In less than a year, he made such rapid progress, that, at five years old, he already invented little pieces of music which he played to his father, and which the latter, in order to encourage the rising talent of his son, was at the trouble of writing down.

During some months, a fondness for the usual studies of childhood gained such an ascendancy over Wolfgang, that he sacrificed every thing, even music, to it. While he was learning arithmetic, the tables, the chairs, and even the walls, were covered with figures which he had

8

chalked upon them. The vivacity of his mind, led him to attach himself easily to every new object that was presented to him. Music, however, soon became again the favorite object of his pursuit. He made such rapid advances in it, that his father, notwithstanding he was always with him, and in the way of observing his progress, could not help regarding him as a prodigy.

As soon, therefore, as Wolfgang had attained his sixth year, the MOZART family, consisting of the father, the mother, the daughter, and Wolfgang, took a journey to Munich. The two children performed before the elector, and received infinite commendations. This first expedition succeeded in every respect. The young artists, delighted with the reception they had met with, redoubled their application on their return to Salzburg, and acquired a degree of execution on the piano, which no longer required the consideration of their youth, to render it highly remarkable.— During the autumn of the year 1762, the whole family repaired to Vienna, and the children performed before the court.

From his most tender age, MOZART, animated with the true feeling of his art, was never vain of the compliments paid him by the great. He only performed insignificant trifles when he had to do with people who were unacquainted with music. He played, on the contrary, with all the fire, and attention, of which he was capable, when he was in the presence of connoisseurs ; and his father was often obliged to have recourse to artifice, and to make the great men, before whom he was to exhibit, pass for such with him   When MOZART, at the age of six years, sat down to play in the presence of the emperor Francis, he addressed himself to his majesty, and asked : " Is not M. Wagenseil here ? We must send for him : he understands the thing." The emperor sent for Wagenseil, and gave up his place to him, by the side of the piano. " Sir," said MOZART to the composer, "I am going to play one of your concertos ; you must turn over the leaves for me."

On his return from Vienna to Salzburg with his parents, he brought with him a small violin, which had been given him during his residence at the capital, and amused himself with it. A short time afterwards, Wenzl, a skilful violin player, who had then just begun to compose, came to Mozart, the father, to request his observations on six trios, which he had written during the journey of the former to Vienna. Schachtner, the archbishop's trumpeter, to whom Mozart was particularly attached, happened to be at the house, and we give the following anecdote in his words :

"The father," said Schachtner, "played the bass, Wenzl the first violin, and I was to play the second. Mozart requested permission to take this last part ; but his father reproved him for this childish demand, observing, that as he had never received any regular lessons on the violin, he could not possibly play it properly. The son replied, that it did not appear to him necessary to receive lessons in order to play the second violin. His father, half angry at this reply, told him to go away, and not interrupt us. Wolfgang was so hurt at this, that he began to cry bitterly. As he was going away with his little violin, I begged that he might be permitted to play with me, and the father, with a good deal of difficulty, consented. Well, said he to Wolfgang, you may play with M. Schachtner, on condition that you play very softly, and do not let yourself be heard : otherwise, I shall send you out directly. We began the trio, little Mozart playing with me, but it was long before I perceived, with the greatest astonishment, that I was perfectly useless. Without saying any thing, I laid down my violin, and looked at the father, who shed tears of affection at the sight.—The child played all the six trios in the same manner. The commendations we gave him made him pretend that he could play the first violin. To humor him, we let him try, and could not forbear laughing on hearing him execute this part, very imperfectly, it is true, but still so as never to be set fast."

Every day afforded fresh proofs of MOZART's exquisite organization for music. He could distinguish, and point out, the slightest differences of sound, and every false or even rough note, not softened by some chord, was a torture to him. It was from this cause that during the early part of his childhood, and even till he had attained his tenth year, he had an insurmountable horror for the the trumpet, when it was not used merely as an accompaniment. The sight of this instrument produced upon him much the same impression as that of a loaded pistol does upon other children, when pointed at them in sport. His father thought he could cure him of this fear, by causing the trumpet to be blown in his presence, notwithstanding his son's entreaties to be spared that torment ; but, at the first blast, he turned pale, fell upon the floor, and would probably have been in convulsions, if they had not immediately ceased.

In the month of July, 1763, when he was in his seventh year, his family set out on their first expedition beyond the boundaries of Germany ; and it is from this period that the celebrity of the name of MOZART in Europe is to be dated.

The tour commenced with Munich, where the young artist played a concerto on the violin, in presence of the elector, after an extempore prelude. At Augsburg, Manheim, Francfort, Coblentz, and Brussels, the two children gave public concerts, or played before the princes of the district, and received every where the greatest commendations.

In the month of November they arrived at Paris, where they remained five months. They performed at Versailles, and Wolfgang played the organ of the king's chapel before the court. They gave in Paris two grand public concerts, and universally met with the most distinguished reception. They were even so far honored as to have their portraits taken ; the father was engraved between his two children, from a design of Carmontelle's. It was at Paris that MOZART composed and published his two first works, one of which he dedicated to the princess Victoire, second daughter of Louis XV., and the other to the countess de Tesse.

In April, 1764, the MOZARTS went to England, where they remained till about the middle of the following year. The children performed before the king, and as at Ver sailles, the son played the organ of the royal chapel. His performance on the organ was thought more of, at London, than his exhibitions on the harpsichord. During his stay there, he and his sister gave a grand concert, all the symphonies of which were his own composition.

During his residence in England, that is, when he was eight years old, Wolfgang composed six sonatas which were engraved at London, and dedicated to the queen.

In the month of July, 1765, the MOZART family returned to Calais, from whence they continued their journey through Flanders, where the young artist often played the organs of the monasteries, and cathedral churches. At the Hague, the two children had an illness which endangered their lives, and from which they were four months in recovering. Wolfgang composed six sonatas for the pianoforte during his convalescence, which he dedicated to the princess of Nassau-Weilbour. In the beginning of the year 1766, they passed a month at Amsterdam, from whence they repaired to the Hague, to be present at the installation of the prince of Orange. MOZART composed for this solemnity a *quodlibet* for all the instruments, and also different airs and variations for the princess.

After having performed several times before the Stadtholder, they returned to Paris, where they staid two months, and then returned to Germany, by Lyons and Switzerland.

At Munich, the elector gave Mozart a musical *theme*, and required him to develope it, and write it down immediately, which he did in the prince's presence, without recurring either to the harpsichord or the violin. After writing it, he played it : which excited the greatest astonishment in the elector and his whole court. After an absence of more than three years, they returned to Salzburg, towards the end of November, 1766, where they remained till the autumn of the following year, and this tranquility seemed further to augment the talents of Wolfgang. In 1768, the children performed at Vienna in presence of the emperor, Joseph II. who commissioned Mozart to compose the music of an opera buffa—The *Finta Semplice*. It was approved of by Hasse, the maitre de chapelle, and by Metastasio, but was never brought upon the stage.

He returned to pass the year 1769 at Salzburg. In the month of December, his father took him into Italy, just after he had been appointed director of the archbishop of Salzburg's concert. We may imagine the reception given in that country to this celebrated child, who had excited such admiration in the other parts of Europe.

The house of count Firmian, the governor general, was the theatre of his glory at Milan. After having received the poem of the opera to be performed during the carnival of 1771, and of which he undertook to write the music. Wolfgang quitted that city in the month of March, 1770. At Bologna, he found an enthusiastic admirer in the celebrated Father Martini, the same person of whom Jomelli came to take lessons. Father Martini, and the Bologna amateurs, were transported at seeing a child of thirteen, whose small stature made him appear still younger, develope all the subjects of fugues proposed by Martini, and execute them on the piano-forte, without hesitating, and with the greatest precision. At Florence, he excited similar astonishment by the correctness with which he played, at sight, the most difficult fugues and themes, proposed to him by the marquis de Ligneville, a distinguished amateur.

In the passion-week, the MOZARTS repaired to Rome, where, as may be supposed, they did not fail to hear the celebrated Miserere,* performed in the Sixtine chapel, on the evening of Ash-Wednesday.

* The difficulty of what he thus accomplished is much greater than may at first be imagined. But for the sake of explanation I shall enter into a few details respecting the Sixtine chapel, and the Miserere.

The Miserere, which is performed there twice in passion-week, and which produces such an effect upon strangers, was composed, about two hundred years since, by Gregorio Allegri, a descendant of Antonio Allegri, better known by the name of Correggio. At the moment of its commencement, the pope and cardinals prostrate themselves. The light of the tapers illumine the representation of the last judgment, painted by Michel Angelo, on the wall with which the altar is connected. As the service proceeds, the tapers are extinguished, one after the other, and the impression produced by the figures of the damned, painted with terrific power, by Michel Angelo, is increased in awfulness, when they are dimly seen by the pale light of the last tapers. When the service is on the point of concluding, the leader, who beats the time, renders it imperceptibly slower ; the singers diminish the volume of their voices, and the sinner, confounded, before the majesty of his God, and prostrated before his throne, seems to await in silence, his final doom.

The sublime effect of this composition depends, as it appears, on the manner in which it is sung, and the place in which it is performed. There is a kind of traditional knowledge, by which the pope's singers are taught certain ways of managing their voices, so as to produce the greatest effect, and which it is impossible to express by notes. Their singing possesses all the qualities which render music affecting. The same melody is repeated to all the verses of the psalm, but the music, though similar in the masses, is not so in the details. It is accordingly easy to be understood, without being tiresome. The peculiarity of the Sixtine chapel, consists in accelerating or retard

From Rome, the Mozarts went to Naples, where Wolfgang played on the piano-forte at the Conservatorio alla pieta. When he was in the middle of his sonata, the audience took it into their heads, that there was a charm in in the ring which he wore. It became necessary to ex-

ing the time in certain expressions, in swelling or diminishing the voice according to the sense of the words, and in singing some of the verses with more animation than others.

The following anecdote will shew still more clearly the difficulty of the exploit performed by Mozart in singing the Miserere.

It is related that the emperor Leopold I. who not only was fond of music, but was himself a good composer, requested of the pope, through his ambassador, a copy of the Miserere of Allegri, for the use of the imperial chapel at Vienna. The request was complied with, and the director of the Sixtine chapel caused a copy to be written out, which was immediately transmitted to the emperor, who had in his service the first singers of the day.

Notwithstanding their talents, the Miserere of Allegri produced, at Vienna, no more effect than the dullest common chant, and the emperor and his court were persuaded that the pope's maitre de chapelle, desirous of keeping the Miserere to himself, had eluded his master's orders, and sent an inferior composition. A courier was immediately despatched to complain to the pope of this want of respect, and the director was dismissed without being allowed to say a word in his own justification. The poor man, however, prevailed on one of the cardinals to intercede for him, and to represent to his holiness that the manner of performing the Miserere, could not be expressed in notes ; but required much time, and repeated lessons from the singers of the chapel, who possessed the traditional knowledge of it. The pope, who knew nothing of music, could scarcely comprehend how the same notes should not be just as good at Vienna, as at Rome. He, however, allowed the poor maitre de chapelle to write his defence to the emperor, and, in time, he was received again into favor.

It was this well-known anecdote, which occasioned the people of Rome to be so astonished when they heard the child sing their Miserere, correctly, after two lessons. Nothing is

plain to him the cause of the disturbance which arose, and
and he was at last obliged to take off this supposed magic
circle. We may imagine the effect produced upon such
an auditory, when they found that after the ring was taken off, the music was not less beautiful. Wolfgang gave
a second grand concert, at the house of Prince Kaunitz,
the emperor's ambassador, and afterwards returned to
Rome. The pope desired to see him, and conferred on
him the cross and brevet of a knight of the Golden Militia
(*auratœe Militiœ Eques.*) At Bologna, he was nominated,
unanimously, member and master of the Philharmonic
Academy. He was shut up alone, agreeably to usage, and
in less than half an hour he composed an antiphony for
four voices.

Mozart's father hastened his return to Milan, that he
might attend to the opera which he had undertaken. The
time was advancing, and they did not reach that city till
the close of October, 1770. Had it not been for this
engagement, MOZART might have obtained what is considered in Italy the first musical honor,—the composition of
a serious opera for the theatre of Rome.

On the 26th of December, the first representation of the
Mithridates took place at Milan. This opera, composed by
MOZART, at the age of fourteen, was performed twenty
nights in succession ; a circumstance which sufficiently in-

more difficult than to excite surprise in Rome, in any thing re_
lating to the fine arts. The most brilliant reputation dwindles
into insigificance in that celebrated city, where the finest productions of every art are the subjects of daily, and familiar contemplation.

I know not whether it arose from the reputation which it
procured him, but it appears that the solemn and affecting
chant of the Miserere, made a deep impression in the mind of
Mozart, who shewed, ever afterwards, a marked preference for
Handel and the tender Boccherini.

9

dicates its success. The manager immediately entered into a written agreement with him for the composition of the
first opera for the year 1773. Mozart left Milan, which
resounded with his fame, to pass the last days of the carnival at Venice, in company with his father. At Verona,
which he only passed through, he was presented with a diploma, constituting him a member of the Philharmonic Society of that city. Wherever he went in Italy, he met
with the most distinguished reception, and was generally
known by the name of the Philharmonic Knight : *Il Cava-
liere Filarmonico.*

When Mozart returned with his father to Salzburg, in
March, 1771, he found a letter from count Firmian of Milan, who commanded him in the name of the empress Maria Theresa, to compose a dramatic cantata on occasion of
the marriage of the archduke Ferdinand. The empress had
chosen the celebrated Hasse, as the oldest professor, to
write the opera, and she was desirous that the youngest
composer should undertake the cantata, the subject of
which was *Ascanius in Alba.* He undertook the work, and
in the month of August, set out for Milan, where, during the
solemnities of the marriage, the opera and the serenade
were performed alternately.

In 1772, he composed for the election of the new archbishop of Salzburg, the cantata entitled *Il sogno di Scipione ;*
and at Milan, where he passed the winter of the year following, he wrote *Lucio Silla,* a serious opera, which had
twenty six successive representations. In the spring of
1773, Mozart returned to Salzburg, and during some ex-
cursions which he made in the course of this year to Vienna and Munich, he produced various compositions of merit,
as, *La Finta Giardiniera,* an opera buffa, two grand masses for the elector of Bavaria's chapel, &c. In 1775, the
archduke Maximilian spent some time at Salzburg, and it was

on this occasion that Mozart composed the cantata enti-
tl ed *Il Re Pastore*.

Arrived at the age of nineteen, Mozart might flatter himself that he had attained the summit of his art, since of this
he was repeatedly assured, wherever he went ;—from London to Naples. As far as regarded the advancement of his
fortune, he was at liberty to choose among all the capitals
of Europe. Experience had taught him that he might every where reckon on general admiration. His father thought
that Paris would suit him best, and accordingly in the
month of September, 1777, he set out for that capital, accompanied by his mother only.

It would have been, unquestionably, very advantageous
to him to have settled there, but the French music, of that
time, did not accord with his taste ; and the preference
shewn for vocal performances would have given him little
opportunity of employing himself in the instrumental department. He had also the misfortune to lose his mother in the
year after his arrival. From that time, Paris became in-
supportable to him. After having composed a symphony
for the *Concert Spirituel*, and a few other pieces, he hastened
to rejoin his father in the beginning of 1779.

In the month of November, of the year following, he repaired to Vienna, whither he had been summoned by his
sovereign, the archbishop of Salzburg. He was then in his
twenty fourth year. The habits of Vienna were very agreeable to him, and the beauty of its fair inhabitants, it appears
still more so. There he fixed himself, and nothing could
ever prevail upon him afterwards to leave it. The empire
of the passions having commenced in this being, so exquisitely sensible to his art, he soon became the favourite composer of his age, and gave the first example of a remarkable
child becoming a great man.

To give a particular analysis of each of Mozart's works
would be too long, and too difficult ; an amateur ought to

know them all.   Most of his operas were composed at Vienna, and had the greatest success, but none of them was a greater favourite than the *Zauber Flote*, which was performed one hundred times in less than a year.

Like Raphael, MOZART embraced his art in its whole extent.   Raphael appears to have been unacquainted with one thing only, the mode of painting figures on a ceiling, in contracted proportion, or what is termed *fore-shortening*. He always supposes the canvas of the piece to be attached to the roof, or supported by allegorical figures.

As for MOZART, I am not aware of any department in which he has not excelled : operas, symphonies, songs, air, for dancing—he is great in every thing.   Haydn's friend the baron Von Swieten, went so far as to say, that if MOZART had lived, he would have borne away the sceptre of instrumental music, even from that great master.   In the comic opera, MOZART is deficient in gaiety.   In this respect he is inferior to Galuppi, Guglielmi, and Sarti.

The most remarkable circumstance in his music, independently of the genius displayed in it, is the novel way in which he employs the orchestra, especially the wind instruments.   He draws surprising effects from the flute, an instrument of which Cimarosa hardly ever made any use. He enriches the accompaniment with all the beauties of the finest symphonies.

MOZART has been accused of taking interest only in his own music, and of being acquainted with none but his own works.   This is the reproach of mortified vanity.   Employed all his life in writing his own ideas, MOZART had not, it is true, time to read all those of other masters.   But he readily expressed his approbation of whatever he met with that possessed merit, even the simplest air, provided it was original ; though, less politic than the great artists of Italy, he had no consideration for mediocrity.

He most esteemed Porpora, Durante, Leo, and Alessandro Scarlatti, but he placed Handel above them all. He knew the principal works of that great master by heart. He was accustomed to say ; " Handel knows best of us all what is capable of producing a great effect When he chooses, he strikes like the thunder-bolt."

We possess nine operas composed by MOZART to Italian words : *La Finta Semplice,* comic opera, his first essay in the dramatic department : *Mitridate,* serious opera : *Lucio Silla,* serious opera : *La Giardiniera,* comic opera : *Idomeneo,* serious opera : *Le Nozze di Figaro,* and *Don Giovanni,* composed in 1787 : *Cosi fan tutte,* comic opera ; and *La Clemenza di Tito* an opera of Metastasio, which was performed, for the first time, in 1792.

He wrote only three German operas, *Die Entfuhrung aus dem Serail, Der Schauspieldirector,* and *Die Zauber, Flote,* in 1792.

He has left seventeen symphonies, and instrumental pieces of all kinds.

MOZART was also one of the first piano-forte players in Europe. He played with extraordinary rapidity ; the execution of his left hand, especially, was greatly admired.

As early as the year 1785, Haydn said to MOZART's father, who was then at Vienna : " I declare to you, before God, and on my honour, that I regard your son as the greatest composer I ever heard of."

Such was MOZART in music. To those acquainted with human nature, it will not appear surprising, that a man, whose talents in this department were the object of general admiration, should not appear to equal advantage in the other situations of life.

MOZART possessed no advantages of person, though his parents were noted for their beauty.

MOZART never reached his natural growth. During his whole life, his health was delicate. He was thin and pale :

and though the form of his face was unusual, there was nothing striking in his physiognomy, but its extreme variableness. The expression of his countenance changed every moment, but indicated nothing more than the pleasure or pain which he experienced at the instant. He was remarkable for a habit which is usually the attendant of stupidity. His body was perpetually in motion ; he was either playing with his hands, or beating the ground with his foot. There was nothing extraordinary in his other habits, except his extreme fondness for the game of billiards. He had a table in his house, on which he played every day by himself, when he had not any one to play with. His hands were so habituated to the piano, that he was rather clumsy in every thing beside. At table, he never carved, or if he attempted to do so, it was with much awkwardness, and difficulty. His wife usually undertook that office. The same man, who from his earliest age, had shewn the greatest expansion of mind in what related to his art, in other respects remained always a child. He never knew how properly to conduct himself. The management of domestic affairs, the proper use of money, the judicious selection of his pleasures, and temperance in the enjoyment of them, were never virtues to his taste. The gratification of the moment was always uppermost with him. His mind was so absorbed by a crowd of ideas, which rendered him incapable of all serious reflection, that, during his whole life, he stood in need of a guardian to take care of his temporal affairs. His father was well aware of his weakness in this respect, and it was on this account that he persuaded his wife to follow him to Paris, in 1777, his engagements not allowing him to leave Salzburg himself.

But this man, so absent, so devoted to trifling amusements, appeared a being of a superior order as soon as he sat down to a piano-forte. His mind then took wing, and his whole attention was directed to the sole object for which nature designed him, *the harmony of sounds.* The most numerous orchestra did not prevent him from observing the slightest false note, and he immediately pointed out, with surprising precision, by what instrument the fault had been committed, and the note which should have been made.

When Mozart went to Berlin, he arrived late on the evening. Scarcely had he alighted, than he asked the waiter of the inn, whether there was any opera that evening. "Yes, the *Entfuhrung aus dem Serail*"—"That is charming!" He immediately set out for the theatre, and placed himself at the entrance of the pit, that he might listen without being observed. But, sometimes, he was so pleased with the execution of certain passages, and at others, so dissatisfied with the manner, or the time, in which they were performed, or with the embellishments added by the actors, that continually expressing either his pleasure, or disapprobation, he insensibly got up to the bar of the orchestra. The manager had taken the liberty of making some alterations in one of the airs. When they came to it, Mozart, unable to restrain himself any longer, called out almost aloud, to the orchestra, in what way it ought to be played. Every body turned to look at the man in a great coat, who was making all this noise. Some persons recognised Mozart, and in an instant, the musicians and actors were informed that he was in the theatre. Some of them, and amongst the number a very good female singer, were so agitated at the intelligence, that they refused to come again upon the stage. The manager informed Mozart of the embarassment he was in. He immediately went behind the scenes, and succeeded, by the compliments which he paid to the actors, in prevailing upon them to go on with the piece.

Music was his constant employment, and his most gratified recreation. Never, even in his earliest childhood, was persuasion required to engage him to go to his piano.   On the contrary, it was necessary to take care that he did not injure his health by his application.   He was particularly fond of playing in the night.   If he sat down to the instruments at nine o'clock in the evening, he never left it before midnight, and even then it was necessary to force him away from it, for he would have continued to modulate and play voluntaries, the whole night.   In his general habits he was the gentlest of men, but the least noise during the perform-ance of music offended him violently.   He was far above above that affected or mis-placed modesty, which prevents many performers from playing till they have been repeat-edly entreated.   The nobility of Vienna often reproached him with playing, with equal interest, before any persons that took pleasure in hearing him.

An amateur, in a town through which MOZART passed in one of his journies, assembled a large party of his friends, to give them an opportunity to hear this celebrated musician. MOZART came, agreeably to his engagement, said very lit-tle, and sat down to the piano-forte.   Thinking that none but connoisseurs were present, he began a slow movement, the harmony of which was sweet, but extremely simple, intending by it to prepare his auditors for the sentiment which he designed to introduce afterwards.   The company thought all this very common-place. The style soon became more lively ;   they thought it pretty enough.   It became severe, and solemn, of a striking, elevated, and more diffi-cult harmony.   Some of the ladies began to think it quite tiresome, and to whisper a few criticisms to one another : soon, half the party were talking.   The master of the house was upon thorns, and MOZART himself, at last perceived how little his audience were affected by the music.   He did not abandon the principal idea with which he commenc-ed, but he developed it with all the fire of which he was ca-

pable ; still he was not attended to. Without leaving off
playing, he began to remonstrate rather sharply with his
audience, but as he fortunately expressed himself in Italian,
scarcely any body understood him. They became however more quiet. When his anger was a little abated, he
could not himself forbear laughing at his impetuosity. He
gave a more common turn to his ideas, and concluded with
playing a well known air, of which he gave ten or twelve
charming variations. The whole room was delighted, and
very few of the company were at all aware of what had
passed. Mozart, however, soon took leave, inviting the
master of the house, and a few connoisseurs, to spend the
evening with him at his inn. He detained them to supper,
and upon their intimating a wish to hear him play, he sat
down to the instrument, where, to their great astonishment
he forgot himself till after midnight.

An old harpsichord tuner came to put some strings to his
travelling piano forte. "Well, my good fellow," says
Mozart to him, "what do I owe you ? I leave to-mor-
row." The poor man regarding him as a sort of deity, replied stammering and confounded, "Imperial Majesty !
Mr. the maitre de chapelle of his imperial majesty ! I cannot. It is true that I have waited upon you several times,
You shall give me a crown." "A crown !" replied Mozart,
"a worthy fellow, like you, ought not to be put out of his
way for a crown ;" and he gave him some ducats. The
honest man as, he withdrew, continued to repeat with low
bows. "Ah ! Imperial Majesty !"

Of his operas, he esteemed most highly the _I domeneus_,
and _Don Juan_. He was not fond of talking of his own
works ; or if he mentioned them ; it was in few words.
Of _Don Juan_ he said one day, "This opera was not composed for the public of Vienna, it is better suited to
Prague ; but, to say the truth, I wrote it only for myself,
and my friends."

10

The time which he most willingly employed in composition, was the morning, from six or seven o'clock till ten, when he got up. After this, he did no more the rest of the day, unless he had to finish a piece that was wanted. He always worked very irregularly. When an idea struck him, he was not to be drawn from it. If he was taken from the piano forte, he continued to compose in the midst of his friends, and passed whole nights with his pen in his hand. At other times, he had such a disinclination to work, that he could not complete a piece till the moment of its performance. It once happened that he put off some music which he had engaged to furnish for a court concert, so long, that he had not time to write out the part which he was to perform himself. The emperor Joseph, who was peeping every where, happening to cast his eyes on the sheet which MOZART seemed to be playing from, was surprised to see nothing but empty lines, and said to him : where's your part ?" " Here," replied MOZART, putting his hand to his forehead.

The same circumstance nearly occurred with respect to the overture of *Don Juan*. It is generally esteemed the best of his overtures ; yet it was only composed the night previous to the first representation, after the general rehearsal had taken place. About eleven o'clock in the evening, when he retired to his apartment, he desired his wife to make him some punch, and to stay with him, in order to keep him awake. She accordingly began to tell him fairy tales, and odd stories, which made him laugh till the tears came. The punch, however, made him so drowsy, that he could only go on while his wife was talking, and dropped asleep as soon as she ceased. The efforts which he made to keep himself awake, the continual alternation of sleep and watching, so fatigued him, that his wife persuaded him to take some rest, promising to awake him in an hours time. He slept so profoundly, that she suffered him to repose for two hours. At five o'clock in the morning she awoke him. He had appointed the music-copiers, to come at seven, and by the time they arrived, the overture was finished. They had scarcely time to write out the copies necessary for the orchestra, and the musicians were obliged to play it without a rehearsal. Some persons pretend that they can discover in this overture the passages where MOZART dropped asleep, and those where he suddenly awoke again.

Don Juan had no great success at Vienna at first. A short time after the first representation, it was talked of in a large party, at which most of the connoisseurs of the capital and amongst others Haydn, were present, MOZART was not there. Every body agreed that it was a very meritorious performance, brilliant in imagination, and rich in genius ; but every one had also some fault to find with it. All had spoken except the modest Haydn. His opinion was asked, "I am not," said he, with his accustomed caution, " a proper judge of the dispute : all that I know is, that MOZART is the greatest composer now existing." The subject was then changed.

MOZART, on his part, had also a great regard for HAYDN. He has dedicated to him a set of quartetts, which may be classed with the best productions of the kind. A professor of Vienna, who was not without merit, though far inferior to Hadyn, took a malicious pleasure in searching the compositions of the latter, for all the little inaccuracies which might have crept into them. He often came to shew MOZART symphonies, or quartetts, of Haydn's, which he had put into score, and in which he had, by this means, discovered some inadvertencies of style. MOZART always endeavoured to change the subject of conversation : at last, unable any longer to restrain himself, " Sir," said he to him, sharply, " if you I and were both melted down together, we should not furnish materials for one Haydn."

A painter, who was desirous of flattering Cimarosa, said to him once, that he considered him superior to MOZART, " I, sir," replied he smartly ; " what would you say to a person who should assure you that you were superior to Raphael ?"

MOZART judged his own works with impartiality, and often with a severity, which he would not easily have allowed in another person. The emperor Joseph II., was fond of MOZART, and had appointed him his maitre de chapelle ; but this prince pretended to be a dilettante. His travels in Italy had given him a partiality for the music of that country, and the Italians who were at his court did not fail to keep up this preference, which, I must confess, appears to me to be well founded.

These men spoke of MOZART's first essays with more jealousy than fairness. and the emperor, who scarcely ever judged for himself, was easily carried away by their decisions. One day, after hearing the rehearsal of a comic opera (die Entfuhrung aus dem Serail,) which he had himself demanded of MOZART, he said to the composer : "My dear MOZART, that is too fine for my ears ; there are to many notes there."—"I ask your majesty's pardon," replied MOZART, drily ; "there are just as many notes as there should be" The emperor said nothing, and appeared rather embarrassed by the reply ; but when the opera was performed, he bestowed on it the greatest encomiums.

MOZART was himself less satisfied with this piece afterwards, and made many corrections and retrenchments in it. He said, in playing on the piano-forte one of the airs which had been most applauded ; " This is very well for the parlour, but it is too verbose for the theatre. At the time I composed this opera, I took delight in what I was doing, and thought nothing too long."

MOZART was not at all selfish ; on the contrary, liberality formed the principal feature of his character. He often gave without discrimination, and still more frequently expended his money without discretion.

During one of his visits to Berlin, the king, Frederic William, offered him an appointment of 3,000 crowns a year, if he would remain at his court, and take upon him the direction of his orchestra. Mozart made no other reply than "Shall I leave my good emperor?" Yet at that time, Mozart had no fixed establishment at Vienna. One of his friends blaming him afterwards for not having accepted the king of Prussia's proposals, he replied : I am fond of Vienna, the emperor treats me kindly, and I care little aoout money."

Some vexatious intrigues, which were excited against him at court, occasioned him, nevertheless, to request his dismissal ; but a word from the emperor, who was partial to the composer, and especially to his music, immediately changed his resolution. He had not art enough to take advantage of this favorable moment, to demand a fixed salary ; but the emperor himself, at length thought of regulating his establishment. Unfortunately, he consulted on the subject a man who was not a friend to Mozart. He proposed to give him 800 florins (about 100l.) and this sum was never increased. He received it as a private composer to the emperor, but he never did any thing in this capacity. He was once required, in consequence of one of the general government-orders, frequent at Vienna, to deliver in a statement of the amount of his salary. He wrote, in a sealed note, as follows : "Too much for what I have done: to little for what I could have done."

The music-sellers, the managers of the theatres, and others, daily took advantage of his well known disinterestedness. He never received any thing for the greater part of his compositions for the piano. He wrote them to oblige persons of his acquaintance, who expressed a wish to possess something in his own writing for their private use. In these cases he was obliged to conform to the degree of proficiency which those persons had attained ; and this explains why many of his compositions for the harpsichord appear unworthy of him. Artaria, a music-seller, at Vienna, and others of his brethren, found means to procure copies of these pieces, and published them without the permission of the author ; or, at any rate, without making him any pecuniary acknowledgment.

One day, the manager of the theatre, whose affairs were in a bad state, and who was almost reduced to despair, came to Mozart, and made known his situation to him, adding, " You are the only man in the world who can relieve me from my embarrassment."—" I," replied Mozart, " how can that be ?"—" by composing for me an opera to suit the taste of the description of people who attend my theatre. To a certain point you may consult that of the connoisseurs, and your own glory ; but have a particular regard to that class of persons who are not judges of good music. I will take care that you shall have the poem shortly, and that the decorations shall be handsome ; in a word, that every thing shall be agreeable to the present mode." Mozart, touched by the poor fellow's entreaties, promised to undertake the business for him. " What remuneration do you require ?" asked the manager. " Why, it seems that you have nothing to give me," said Mozart, " but that you may extricate yourself from your embarrassments, and that, at the same time, I may not altogether lose my labor, we will arrange the matter thus : You shall have the score, and give me what you please for it, on condition that you will not allow any copies to be taken. If the opera succeeds, I will dispose of it in another quarter. The manager, enchanted with this generosity, was profuse in his promises. Mozart immediately set about the music, and composed it agreeable to the instructions given him. The opera was performed ; the house was always filled ; it was

talked of all over Germany, and was performed a short
time afterwards, on five or six different theatres, none of
which had obtained their copies from the distressed manager.

On other occasions, he met only with ingratitude from
those to whom he had rendered service, but nothing could
extinguish his compassion for the unfortunate. Whenever any distressed artists, who were stangers to Vienna, applied to him, in passing through the city, he offered them
the use of his house and table, introduced them to the acquaintance of those persons whom he thought most likely
to be of use to them, and seldom let them depart without
writing for them concertos, of which he did not even keep
a copy, in order that being the only persons to play them,
they might exhibit themselves to more advantage.

Mozart often gave concerts at his house on Sundays. A
Polish Count, who was introduced on one of these occasions, was delighted, as well as the rest of the company,
with a piece of music for five instruments, which was performed for the first time. He expressed to Mozart how
much he had been gratified by it, and requested that, when
he was at leisure, he would compose for him a trio for the
flute. Mozart promised to do so, on condition that it
should be at his own time. The Count, on his return home,
sent the composer one hundred gold demi-sovereigns,
(about 100*l*) with a very polite note, in which he thanked
him for the pleasure he had enjoyed. Mozart sent him
him the original score of the piece for five instruments,
which had appeared to please him. The count left Vienna. A year afterwards he called again upon Mozart, and
enquired about his trio. "Sir," replied the composer, " I
have never felt myself in a disposition to write any thing
that I should esteem worthy of your acceptance."—"Probably," replied the count, " you will not feel more disposed
to return me the 100 demi-sovereigns, which I paid you

beforehand for the piece." Mozart, indignant, immediately returned him his sovereigns ; but the Count said nothing about the original score of the piece for five instruments ; and it was soon afterwards published by Artaria,
as a quatuor for the harpsichord, with an accompaniment
for the violin, alto, and violincello.

It has been remarked, that Mozart very readily acquired new habits. The health of his wife, whom he always
passionately loved, was very delicate. During a long illness which she had, he always met those who came to see
her, with his finger on his lips, as an intimation to them not
to make a noise. His wife recovered, but, for a long time
afterwards, he always went to meet those who came to visit him with his finger on his lips, and speaking in a subdued
tone of voice.

In the course of this illness, he occasionally took a ride,
on horseback, early in the morning, but before he went, he
was always careful to lay a paper near his wife, in the
form of a physician's prescription. The following is a copy
of one of these : "Good morning, my love, I hope that you
have slept well, and that nothing has disturbed you :
be careful not take cold, or to hurt yourself in stooping : do not vex yourself with the servants ; avoid
every thing that would be unpleasant to you, till I return :
take good care of yourself : I shall return at nine o'clock.

Constance Weber was an excellent companion for Mozart, and often gave him useful advice. She bore him
two children, whom he tenderly loved. His income was
considerable, but his immoderate love of pleasure, and the
disorder of his affairs, prevented him from bequeathing any
thing to his family, except the celebrity of his name, and
the attention of the public. After the death of this great
composer, the inhabitants of Vienna testified to his children, their gratitude for the pleasure which their father
had so often afforded them.

During the last years of Mozart's life, his health, which had always been delicate, declined rapidly. Like all persons of imagination, he was timidly apprehensive of future evils, and the idea that he had not long to live, often distressed him. At these times, he worked with such rapidity and unremitting attention, that he sometimes forgot every thing that did not relate to his art. Frequently, in the height of his enthusiasm, his strength failed him, he fainted, and was obliged to be carried to his bed. Every one saw that he was ruining his health by this immoderate application. His wife, and his friends, did all they could to divert him. Out of complaisance, he accompanied them in the walks and visits to which they took him, but his thoughts were always absent. He was only occasionally roused from this silent and habitual melancholy, by the presentiment of his approaching end, an idea which always awakened in him fresh terror.

His insanity was similar to that of Tasso, and to that which rendered Rousseau so happy in the valley of Charmettes, by leading him, through the fear of approaching death, to the only true philosophy, the enjoyment of the present moment and the forgetting of sorrow. Perhaps, without that high state of nervous sensibility which borders on insanity, there is no superior genius in the arts which require tenderness of feeling.

His wife, uneasy at these singular habits, invited to the house those persons whom he was most fond of seeing, and who pretended to surprise him, at times, when after many hour's application, he ought naturally to have thought of resting. Their visits pleased him, but he did not lay aside his pen ; they talked, and endeavoured to engage him in the conversation, but he took no interest in it ; they addressed themselves particularly to him, he uttered a few inconsequential words, and went on with his writing

11

It was in this state of mind that he composed the *Zau-*
ber Flote, the Clemenza di Tito, the Requiem, and some
other pieces of less celebrity. It was while he was writing
the music of the first of these operas, that he was seized
with the fainting fits we have mentioned. He was very partial to the Zauber Flote, though he was not quite satisfied
with some parts of it, to which the public had taken a fancy, and which were incessantly applauded. This opera
was performed many times, but the weak state in which
MOZART then was, did not permit him to direct the orchestra, except during nine or ten of the first representations.
When he was no longer able to attend the theatre, he used
to place his watch by his side, and seemed to follow the
orchestra in his thoughts. " Now the first act is over," he
would say—" now they are singing such an air." &c.; then
the idea would strike him afresh, that he must soon bid
adieu to all this forever.

The effect of this fatal tendency of mind was accelera-
ted by a very singular circumstance. I beg leave to be
permitted to relate it in detail, because we are indebted to
it for the famous Requiem, which is justly considered one
of MOZART's best productions.*

* This great work is a solemn mass in D. minor for the burial
of the dead hung round with the funeral pomp and imagery
which the forebodings of the author inspired. At its opening,
the ear is accosted by the mournful notes of the *Corni di basset-*
to, mingling with the bassoons in a strain of bewailing harmony, which streams with impressive effect amidst the short sorrowful notes of the accompanying orchestra.

The *Dies irae* follows in a movement full of terrour and dis-
may. The *Tuba mirum*, is opened by a sonorous *tromboni*, to
awaken the sleeping dead. Every one acquainted with the powers of this instrument acknowledges the superiority of its tone s
for the expression of this sublime idea.

Rex tremendæ Majestatis, is a magnifiicent display of regal

One day, when he was plunged in a profound reverie, he heard a carriage stop at his door. A stranger was announced, who requested to speak to him. A person was introduced, handsomely dressed, of dignified, and impressive manners. " I have been commmissioned, Sir, by a man of considerable importance, to call upon you." " Who is he ?" interrupted Mozart.—" He does not wish to be known."—" Well, what does he want ?"—" He has just lost a person whom he tenderly loved, and whose memory will be eternally dear to him. He is desirous of annually commemorating this mournful event by a solemn service, for which he requests you to compose a requiem." Mozart was forcibly struck by this discourse, by the grave manner in which it was uttered, and by the air of mystery in which the whole was involved. He engaged to write the Requiem. The stranger continued, " Employ all your genius on this work ; it is destined for a connoisseur." " So much the better,"—" What time do you require ?"— " A month."—" Very well : in a month's time I shall return.—What price do you set on your work ?"—" A hundred ducats." The stranger counted them on the table, and disappeared.

Mozart remained lost in thought for some time ; he

grandeur, of which none but a Mozart would have dared to sketch the outline. It is followed by the beautiful movement *Recordare*, which supplicates in the softest inflexions. The persuasive tone of the Corni di bassetto is again introduced with unexampled effect.

It is too evident where the pen of our author was arrested ; and this wonderful performance is very absurdly finished by repeating some of the early parts of the work to words of a very contrary import. *The lux æterna*, is a subject worthy of the pen of Beethoven, and it is to be hoped he will yet finish this magnificent work, in a style worthy of its great progenitor.

then suddenly called for pen, ink, and paper, and, in spite of his wife's entreaties, began to write. This rage for composition continued several days ; he wrote day and night, with an ardour which seemed continually to increase; but his constitution, already in a state of great debility, was unable to support his enthusiasm : one morning, he fell senseless, and was obliged to suspend his work. Two or three days after, when his wife sought to divert his mind from the gloomy presages which occupied it, he said to her abruptly : " It is certain that I am writing this Requiem for myself ; it will serve for my funeral service." Nothing could remove this impression from his mind.

As he went on, he felt his strength diminish from day to day, and the score advanced slowly. The month which he had fixed, being expired, the stranger again made his appearance. " I have found it impossible," said Mozart, " to keep my word"—" Do not give yourself any uneasiness," replied the stranger ; " what further time do you require ?"—"Another month. The work has interested me more than I expected, and I have extended it much beyond what I at first designed." " In that case, it is but just to increase the premium ; here are fifty ducats more." —" Sir," said Mozart, with increasing astonishment, " who then are you ?"—"That is nothing to the purpose ; In a month's time I shall return."

Mozart immediately called one of his servants, and ordered him to follow this extraordinary personage, and find out who he was ; but the man failed for want of skill, and returned without being able to trace him.

Poor Mozart was then persuaded that he was no ordinary being ; that he had a connection with the other world, and was sent to announce to him his approaching end. He applied himself with the more ardour to his Requiem, which he regarded as the most durable monument of his genius.

While thus employed, he was seized with the most alarming fainting fits, but the work was at length completed before the expiration of the month. At the time appointed, the stranger returned, but MOZART was no more.

His career was as brilliant as it was short. He died before he had completed his thirty-sixth year ; but in this short space of time he has acquired a name which will never perish, so long as feeling hearts are to be found.

MOZART, philosophically contemplated, is still more astonishing, than when regarded as the author of sublime compositions. Never was the soul of a man of genius exhibited so naked, if we may be allowed the expression. The corporeal part had as little share as possible in that extraordinary union called MOZART. To this day the Italians designate him by the appellation of " quel mostro d'ingegno," that prodigy of genius.

HENRY PURCELL.

In tracing the progress of English music through the reigns of James and Charles I. the gloomy era of the Protectorate, and the days of revelry of Charles the second, we have found among secular compositions little to admire. In fact, almost the whole of the above period may, in a musical point of view, be considered as the reign of dullness and insipidity.

It is therefore with peculiar pleasure that we are now permitted, in the course of our labors, to speak of HENRY PURCELL, who, considered as a musician, is as justly the pride of an Englishman, as Shakspeare in dramatic productions, Milton in epic poetry, Locke in metaphysics, or Sir Isaac Newton in mathematics and philosophy.

Unluckily for PURCELL, he built his fame with such perishable materials, that the knowledge of his worth and works is daily diminishing, while the reputation of our Poets and philosophers increases daily by the study and utility of their productions. And so much of our great musician's celebrity is already consigned to tradition, that it will soon be as difficult to find his songs, or at least to hear them, as those of his predecessors Orpheus and Amphion, with which Cerberus was lulled to sleep, or the city of Thebes constructed.

HENRY PURCELL was born in 1658. His father Henry, and uncle Thomas Purcell, were both musicians, and gentlemen of the chapel Royal, at the Restoration. From whom HENRY received his first instructions in music cannot be ascertained, But his father dying in 1664, when he was only six years old, it is probable, that he was qualified for a chorister by captain Cook, who was master of the children from the Restoration, till his death in 1672. As PURCELL was appointed organist of Westminster Abbey at 18 years of age, he must have learned the elements of his art at an early period of his life. He certainly was taught to sing in the King's Chapel, and received lessons from Pelham Humphrey, Cook's successor, till his voice broke ; an accident, which usually happens to youth at sixteen or seventeen years of age.

After this, perhaps, he had a few lessons on composition from Dr. Blow, which were sufficient to cancel all the instructions he had received from other masters, and to occasion the boast inscribed on his tomb-stone, that he had been

" *Master to the famous* Mr. HENRY PURCELL."

Nothing is more common than this petty larceny among musicians. If the first master has drudged eight or ten years with a pupil of genius, and it is thought necessary,

in compliance with fashion or caprice, that he should receive a few lessons from a second, the persevering assiduity
of the first and principal instructor is usually forgotten,
while the second arrogates to himself the *whole* honor, both
of the talents and cultivation of his new scholar.

PURCELL is said to have profited so much from his first
lessons, and early application, as to have composed, while
a singing boy in the chapel, many of his anthems, which
have been constantly sung in our cathedrals ever since.
Eighteen was a very early age for the appointment of
organist of Westminster Abbey, one of the first cathedrals
in the kingdom for choral compositions and performance.

It was not likely he would stop here : the world is more
partial to promising youth, than to accomplished age. At
twenty-four, in 1682, he was promoted to one of the three
places of organist of the Chapel Royal, on the death of
Edward Low, the successor of Dr. Christopher Gibbons, in
the same station. After this, he produced so many admirable compositions for the church and chapel, of which he
was organist, and where he was certain of having them
better performed than elsewhere, that his fame soon extended to the remotest parts of the kingdom. From this time,
his anthems were procured with eagerness, and heard with
pious rapture wherever they could be performed ; nor was
he long suffered to devote his talents exclusively to the
service or the church. He was very early in life solicited
to compose for the stage and chamber, in both which undertakings he was so decidedly superior to all his predecessors, that his compositions seemed to speak a new and more
intelligible language. His songs contain whatever the ear
could then wish, or heart feel. In fact no other vocal music was listened to with pleasure, for nearly thirty years after PURCELL's death : when they gave way only to the favorite opera songs of Handel.

The unlimited powers of this musician's genius, embraced
every species of composition that was then known, with equal
felicity In writing for the church, whether he adhered to
the elaborate and learned style of his great predecessors, Tal-
list, Bird, and Gibbons, in which no instrument is employed
but the organ, and the several parts moving in fugue, imitation, or plain counterpoint; or, on the contrary, giving way to
feeling and imagination, adopted the new and more expressive style, of which he was himself one of the principal in-
ventors, accompanying the voice parts with instruments, to
enrich the harmony, and enforce the melody and meaning
of the words, he manifested equal abilities and resources.
In compositions for the *theatre*, though the colouring and
effects of an orchestra were then but little known, yet as
he employed them more than his predecessors, and gave to
the voice a melody more interesting and impassioned, than
during that century had been heard in this country, or even,
perhaps, in Italy, he soon became the delight and darling
of the nation. And in the several species of *chamber music*,
which he attempted, whether sonatas, for instruments,
or odes, cantatas, songs, ballads and catches for the voice,
he so far surpassed whatever our country had produced or
imported before, that all other musical compositions seemed
to have been instantly consigned to contempt and oblivion.

Many of his numerous compositions for the church, particularly those printed in the second and third volumes of
Dr. Boyce's Collection, are still retained in our cathedrals,
and in the King's chapel.

The superior genius of PURCELL, can be fairly estimated
by those only who make themselves acquainted with the
state of music previous to his time ; compared with which,
his productions for the church, if not more learned, will be
found infinitely more varied and expressive : and his *secular*
compositions appear to have descended from another more

happy region, with which neither his predecessors nor contemporaries had any communication.

To enter into a critical examination of PURCELL's numerous compositions, would exceed the limits, and be foreign to the purpose of this work. The public are greatly indebted to Mr. Corfe and Dr. Clarke, of Cambridge, both of whom have published very excellent selections from the secular works of this great musician, under the title of " *The Beauties of Purcell.*" Were it not for such occasional meritorious exertions, on the part of the professors, it is greatly to be feared that the stream of oblivion would in a few years, draw into their insatiable vortex the productions of PURCELL and even of Handel, their names, like those of many of their predecessors, might float awhile on the surface, when their works were buried in the abyss beneath.

Feeling an enthusiastic attachment to the fame of this truly English musician, and anxious to contribute our mite to draw the public attention to a fair examination of the characteristic and manly strains which abound in every part of his productions, we have ventured to extend our remarks upon this scientific musician.

We cannot take our leave of PURCELL's vocal music, without a grateful memorial of his Catches, Rounds, and Glees, of which the humor, originality, and melody, were so congenial with the national taste, as to render them almost the sole productions of that facetious character, in general use for nearly four score years ; and though the countenance, and premiums recently bestowed upon this species of composition, united with the modern refinements in melody and performance, have given birth to many Glees of a more elegant, graceful, and exalted kind, than any which PURCELL produced ; yet he seems hardly ever to have been equalled in the wit, pleasantry, and contrivance of his Catches.

12

We shall here conclude our history of HENRY PURCELL, which we fear, by many Italianized readers, may be considered already too circumstantial. Had his short life been protracted, we might perhaps have had a school of secular music of our own, which we cannot to this day boast of. In many instances he has surpassed even Handel, in the expression of English words and national feelings ; and we may fairly sum up his merits as a musician in a single sentence. His beauties in composition were entirely his own, while his occasional barbarisms may be considered as unavoidable compliances with the false taste of the age in which he lived.

THOMAS A. ARNE.

Of England's musical composers, no one, his merits aggregately viewed, certainly no one except Purcell, claims a higher distinction than the late DR. ARNE. To a a strong and clear conception, he added all the polish of his time and with a copious store of science, was the musician of sentiment and of nature. It were a praise sufficient to establish his general pre-eminence, that his genius marked out a course for itself ; but the flowers with which his path was profusely adorned, by his simple and easy, yet elegant imagination, combined with the force and originality of his ideas, place him in a station perfectly his own, and exhibit his professional character in a beautiful and brilliant light.

THOMAS AUGUSTINE ARNE, son of an eminent upholsterer in King Street, Covent Garden, received his education at Eton College. The provident wisdom of his father de-

signed him for the legal profession, but the native taste for
music that afterwards rendered him so conspicuous an ornament of his country, disclosed itself in his earliest youth,
and, by his school fellows, has been said to have interfered with the progress of his academical attainments. According to some of his biographers, a flute too often supplied the place of Virgil and Horace ; and, on leaving the
grammar school, he brought with him so strong a predilec-
tion for the *concord of sweet sounds*, that he was frequently
tempted to avail himself of the privileges of a liveried ser-
vant, by going in a borrowed garb to the part of the opera
house then usually allotted to the domestics of the nobility.
Sensible of the pain and displeasure that would be created
in his father's mind, should he know that his son's partiality
was devoted to the charms, and his time to the cultivation,
of music, he secretly procured, and conveyed to the attic
story, an old spinnet. On this instrument, after cautiously
muffling the strings, he guardedly and timidly practised during the hours when suspicion and the family were asleep.
While improving his execution on the spinnet, and applying himself to the acquisition of thorough bass, he contrived to procure the advantage of some instructions on the violin. Under Festing, he made so great so rapid a progress,
that not many months after the commencement of his application to that instrument, his father, calling at the house
of a friend, detected his son in the very act of leading a
chamber band. His astonishment yielded to a degree of anger that was not speedily appeased : but at length cool reflection, and the apparent desperation of the case determined him to indulge the pertinacious bent of nature, and
afford his son every possible opportunity of turning his
talents and inclination to a profitable account.

DR. ARNE was a singular instance of that predestinate

taste, which is to be accounted for only by peculiar organization, the existence of which among other less splendid instances has been since confirmed by Crotch Himmel and Mozart. His first stealthy acquisition in musical science, made chiefly during night, contrary to the direction of the principal pursuit of his life, and in opposition to the will of his Father, are proofs of that irresistible propensity by which genius governs its possessors. His was the pure and unbought love of the art, generated by the pleasurable perception of sweet sounds. There was in ARNE's compositions a natural ease and elegance, a flow of melody which stole upon the senses, and a fullness and variety in the harmony which satisfied without surprising the auditor by any new affected or extraneous modulation. He had neither the vigour of Purcell, nor the grandeur, simplicity, and magnificence of Handel, he apparently aimed at pleasing, and he has succeeded.

CHARLES BURNEY.

CHARLES BURNEY, Mus. Doct. F. R. S. whose celebrity is equally great in the literary and musical world, was a native of Shrewsbury, and was born in 1726. He received the rudiments of his education at the free grammar school of that town, and completed it at the public school of Chester, at the latter place, he commenced his musical studies under Mr. Baker, organist of the Cathedral, who was a pupil to Dr. Blow. He returned to Shrewsbury about the year 1741, and continued the study of music under the half-brother, Mr. James Burney, who was an eminent organist and teacher, of that town. In 1744, he met with

Dr. Arne, at Chester, who perceiving his talents to be respectable, prevailed upon his friends to send him to London. In 1749 he was elected organist of St. Dione's Back Church, Fenchurch-Street, with an annual salary of only thirty-pounds ; and the same year was engaged to take the organ part of the new concert established at the king's Arms, Cornhill, instead of that which had been held at the Swan Tavern, burnt down the year before. Being in an ill state of health, which in the opinion of his physicians indicated a consumption , he was prevailed upon to retire into the country. Accordingly he went to Lynn Regis, in Norfolk, where he was chosen organist, with a salary of one hundred pounds a year. Here he continued nine years, and formed the design of compiling his general History of Music. In 1760, his health being established, he gladly returned once more to the metropolis, with a large and young family, and entered upon his profession with an increase of profit and reputation. His eldest daughter, who was then about eight years old, obtained great success in the musical world by her astonishing performances on the harpsichord. Soon after his arrival in London he composed several much admired Concertos ; and in 1766 he brought out, at Drury Lane theatre, a translation of Rosseau's " *Devine du Village*, which he had executed during his residence at Lynn. It had, however, no great success. In 1769 he had the honorary degree of Doctor of Music conferred upon him by the University of Oxford, on which occasion he performed an exercise, in the Musical School of that University. This exercise, consisting of an Anthem of great length, with an Overture, airs, recitatives, and Choruses, was several times afterwards performed at the Oxford music meetings, and under the direction of the famous EMANUEL BACH, in St. Catharine's Church, Hamburgh. The year following he travelled through France

and Italy, as well with a view to improvement in his profession, as to collect materials for his intended " *History of*
Music,"–an object which he seldom kept out of mind, from
the time he first conceived the idea of such a work. In
1777 he published his Musical Tour, or present state of music in France and Italy. This work was very well received by the public ; and is so good a model for travellers to
keep their journals by, that Dr. Johnson professedly adopted it as his, when he visited the Hebrides. Speaking of
his own book, " I had," said the Doctor, " that clever dog,
BURNEY's Musical Tour in my eye."

In 1772 he travelled through the Netherlands, Germany,
and Holland ; and in the course of the next year he published an account of his journey, in two volumes octavo.
The same year he was elected fellow of the Royal Society.

In 1776 appeared his first volume, in quarto, of his " General History of Music." The remaining volumes of this
very elaborate and intelligent work were published at irregular periods ; and the four, of which it now consists,
were not completed till the year 1789. In 1779, at the
desire of Sir John Pringle, Dr. BURNEY drew up for the
Philosophical Transactions, " An account of little Crotch,
the infant musician, now professor of music in the University of Oxford. The grand musical festival of 1785, in
commemoration of Handel, held in Westminster Abbey,
was considered as deserving of a particular memoir. The
Historian of Music was fixed upon as the most proper person to draw it up. Accordingly the same year a splendid volume was published by Dr. BURNEY, in quarto, for the benefit of the musical fund. In this work the doctor displayed
eminent talents as a biographer, and the life of Handel is
one of the few good memoirs which exist in our language.
In 1796 he published the life of Metastasio in three vol-

umes, octavo, but this performance wants that arrangement
and judicious selection which characterizes his former
productions.

Doctor BURNEY has been twice married, and has had
eight children of whom several have manifested very superior abilities. His eldest daughter was celebrated for her
extraordinary musical powers. The second, Madame Dar-
blay, is universally known and admired as the author of
Evelina, Cecilia and *Camilla.* The eldest son James, sailed
round the world with Capt. Cook, and afterwards commanded the Bristol of 50 guns, in the East Indies, he has published
some very judicious tracts on the best means of defend-
ing our Island against an invading enemy. The second son,
Charles Burney, L. L. D. is master of a respectable Academy at Greenwich, and well known in the learned world
by his profound knowledge of the Greek language, and his
masterly criticisms in the Monthly Review. For many
years DR. BURNEY resided in the house, (No 36 St. Mar-
tins Street Leicester fields) formerly occupied by Sir Isaac
Newton ; during the last ten years he has inhabited an elegant suite of apartments in Chelsea College, where he enjoys a handsome independency. He still spends several
hours every day in his library, which is stored with a great
variety of valuable and curious books, many of them col-
lected during his travels.

SAMUEL ARNOLD.

Dr. SAMUEL ARNOLD, born in August, 1740, was at a very
early age received into the King's Chapel, and by consequence, received his musical education under Mr. Gates
master of the children of that establishment. Endowed

with a considerable portion of natural talent, and a persevering spirit, he, in his twenty third year, found himself
qualified to enter upon dramatic composition. Engaged at
Covent Garden Theatre as one of its regular composers,
he gave the first public evidence of his abilities, by his
composition and compilation of the music of the *Maid of
the Mill.* His success in this undertaking both stimulated
further exertion, and expanded his professional ambition.
Aspiring to the very highest rank of his art, he prosecuted
his studies with new ardour, cultivated with avidity the
principle arcana of counterpoint, and in 1767 produced his
oratorio of the *Cure of Saul,* written by Dr. Brown. The
piece was received with sufficient favour to encourage the
continuance of his efforts in the same high province, and
the following year, he brought forward his *Abimelech.*
The applause obtained by this second oratorial production,
established the reputation of its composer ; and in 1773,
he successfully submitted to the public judgment his *Prodigal Son,* the tenor and bass songs of which I am reminded,
were sung by Mr. Vernon and Mr. Merideth. Four years
after this, appeared his oratorio of the *Resurrection,* the
general merit of which was well calculated to sustain the
reputation he had acquired.

Of the four oratorios already named, the *Prodigal Son*
acquired the superior renown ; and when Lord North was
elected Chancellor of the University of Oxford, the composer was applied to, for the use of that piece, to celebrate
the installation. The oratorio performed, Mr. ARNOLD
availed himself of the opportunity of presenting to the
musical professor a probationary exercise for a Doctor's degree. Dr. William Hayes had heard the oratorio in London, and with a politeness that equalled his judgment, declined scrutinizing the submitted composition. " It is, Sir,"
said the professor, returning to the ingenious candidate

his score unopened " unnecessary to examine an exercise composed by the author of the Prodigal Son."

In 1783, Dr. ARNOLD succeeded Dr. Nares, brother of Judge Nares, as organist to his majesty, and composer to the chapel Royal ; and in the following year, was nominated one of the sub-directors of the grand commemoration of Handel, which took place in Westminster Abbey. The new interest given to the productions of the Prince of Modern Musicians, by this Royal celebration of German genius, suggested to Dr. ARNOLD the idea of furnishing the public with a complete edition of Handel's works ; and in thirty-six folio volumes he effected his design, with the exception of a few of those Italian operas of the great composer least in public request. The reperusal of Handel's compositions necessary to the prosecution of this undertaking gave birth to the idea of converting those portions of his productions least familiarly known, into materials for a new oratorio ; which the Doctor produced, under the title of Redemption. The judgment displayed in this laborious adaptation, was worthy of the compiler's long experience in orchestral compilation ; and his effort was received at Drury Lane Theatre with the most cordial approbation.

Dr. ARNOLD was an educated and industrious musician, rapid alike in his designs and execution, he imagined and he wrote by impulse or for pay, and there is little trace in any of his works for the stage, of more than a facility and ease which rarely raise him above the common level of amusing and lively composition, he divided his time and attention among too many objects to be eminently successful in any one department. He was at one and the same time deeply engaged in writing, publishing, conducting and teaching. His genius lacked the austerity and devotion as well as the enthusiasm necessary to the perfection and

13

completion of great undertakings, or the maturity of any capital performance. As a writer of operas, he stood below Storace, and very little above his immediate successor.

Dr. ARNOLD's general habits were not the most abstemious ; and a train of disorders brought upon his constitution, already enfeebled by the long confinement hastened his dissolution. After an illness of many months, too severe to admit the hope of his recovery, he expired at his house in Duke-street, Westminster, on the 22nd of October, 1802. His remains were interred near the north exterior of the choir of Westminster Abbey. The funeral was attended by the gentlemen of the three choirs of Westminster, St. Paul's, and the King's Chapel ; and among the mourners, were the late Sir William Parsons. Dr. Ayrton, and Dr. Busby.

JEAN BAPTISTE VIOTTI.

JEAN BAPTISTE VIOTTI was born in Piedmont about 1745, and was without doubt the first performer on the violin of the age.—After having travelled through the courts of the North he arrived at Paris, preceded by the fame of his performance, and which he even surpassed on his debut at the Concert Spirituel, which took place in March, 1782. He played a concerto of his own composition, and this as well as those he afterwards published contained an original character which appeared to fix the limits of this kind of performance, a fruitful imagination, a happy freedom, and all the fire of youth tempered by a pure and noble taste

They applauded these beautiful pieces, which from the first bars announced the genius of the composer, the display of an originality of thought, where the progression of sentiment carries the effect to the highest degree. And with regard to the execution, what energy and grace combined ! what finish in the adagio ! What brilliancy in the allegro ! Thus when he was heard for the first time in France, this great, sublime, and learned performance excited extraordinary enthusiasm.

The Queen of France, Maria Antoinette, wished VIOTTI to come to Versailles. The day was fixed for a concert.— The whole court arrived and the concert began. The first bars of the Solo commanded the greatest attention, when, on a sudden, a cry in the chamber was heard of " Room for Count D'Artois ;" in the midst of the tumult, Viotti put his Violin under his arm and departed, leaving the court to the great scandal of all the spectators.

It was but a short time after, that this virtuoso determined to play no more in public, but his friends still had the privilege of hearing him in private concerts.

In 1790, a deputy of the constituted assembly, an intimate friend of VIOTTI's, lodged in a fifth story. The latter consented to give a concert at his house ; princes and ladies of rank were invited to it.—" Often enough," said VIOTTI, " have we gone down to them, to-day they must come up to us."

VIOTTI possessed a quick spirit of repartee. One day the minister, Calonne, asked him which was the most correct violin ? that, replied he, which is the least incorrect.

M. Eymar has described the mind of VIOTTI in the following terms——

" Never did man attach such great value to the simplest gifts of nature, never did a child more supremely enjoy them

If he found a violet hidden under the grass, it transported him with joy ; or if he gathered fresh fruit, it rendered him the happiest of mortals ; he found in the one a perfume ever new, in the other a flavor ever delicious. His organs so delicate and sensible, seemed to have preserved their virgin inviolability ; while stretched on the grass he passed whole hours in admiring the colour or inhaling the odour of a rose. Every thing in the country, was to this extraordinary man a new object of amusement, interest and enjoyment. His faculties were roused at once by the slightest sensation : every thing struck his imagination ; every thing spoke to his soul, and his heart abounded with effusions of sentiment.

Towards the end of this year, 1792, Viotti left France and came to London, where he has since resided.

This great Violin player reckons among his pupils, M. Rode, Alday, Libon, La Barre, J. B. Cartier, Vacher, Mori, &c.

He has printed nineteen ancient, and six modern concertos, a volume of quartetts, several volumes of trios, amongst which are particularly distinguished the numbers 16, 17, 18, and 19, six books of duetts, four sonatas, and airs with variations for the violin. He has also composed two symphonies for a full band which he performed with Mr. Imbault before the queen of France in 1787.

To this memoir we may add, that Mr. Viotti is at this time in England, but he has long since quitted the public profession of this art.

His genius was continually acquiring strength, he was brilliantly successful whenever he appeared before the public ; he united a vigour, a new grace, an animated style, and in short, with this rare assemblage of qualities bestowed by nature and by art, he was heard with rapture and astonishment. He died in Paris March, 1824.

G. PAISIELLO.

G. Paisiello, son of Francois and of Grazazia Fogiale, was born at Tarentum on the 9th of May, 1741. His father was a veterinary Surgeon particularly distinguished in his art, and the reputation he had acquired, not only in the province of Lucca but in the whole kingdom, procured him the honor of being employed by the King of Naples, Charles the Third, during the war of Velletri. His father determined as soon as he had attained his fifth year, that he should study till he was thirteen with the Jesuits who had a College at Tarentum ; and as it was the custom of these fathers to have the service for the Virgin sung in all their feasts, they remarked when their young pupil sung the hour of Matins, that he had a fine contralto voice and an excellent ear. Upon this observation, a Chevalier D. Girolamo Carducci, of the same city, and who superintended the music for the Holy Week in the Church of the Capuchins, endeavoured to make him sing some pieces from memory. Young Paisiello acquitted himself in such a manner that it might have been imagined he had studied music for a length of time.

He set out for Naples with his father, and in June, 1754, he was received into the Conservatorio of St. Onofrio, where he had the happiness of finding the celebrated Durante, master. It was under him that he studied, at the end of five years he became first master among the pupils of the Conservatorio.

The revolution having broken out in 1789, the government assumed the republican form. The court abandoning

Naples and returning into Sicily, the government named
PAISIELLO, composer to the nation. But the Bourbon family being re-established, they made it a crime to have accepted this employment, and till the moment that he was
freed from the reproaches cast on him, his appointments
were suspended. At last, after two years had elapsed, he
was restored to his situation. He was afterwards demanded by the first consul of France, Napolean Bonaparte ; and
Ferdinand king of Naples gave him a despatch with an order to go to Paris, and place himself at the disposal of the
first consul. Alquier, the minister of France, resident at
Naples, pressed him on this occasion to declare his inten-
tions respecting the fees and the treatment he desired. M.
PAISIELLO replied that the honor of serving the first consul
sufficed him.

On arriving at Paris he was provided with a furnished
apartment, and one of the court carriages ; he was assigned a salary of twelve thousand francs, and a present of
eighteen thousand francs for the expenses of his stay besides those of his journey. He was offered at Paris several employments such as those of Director of the Imperial Academy, and of the Conservatorio ; he refused them
all and contented himself with that of Director of the
Chapel which he filled with excellent artists. He composed for this Chapel, sixteen sacred services, consisting of
masses, motetts, prayers, &c, and besides these he composed the opera of *Proserpine*, for the Academy of Music, and
a grand mass for two choirs, a Te Deum and prayers for
the coronation of the emperor.

Finding that the climate of Paris did not agree with his
wife he quitted this city after residing in it two years and
a half, and notwithstanding his distance from thence he
continued to send every year, to Napoleon, a sacred composition for the anniversary of his birth, the 15th of Au-

gust.   A year after his departure, the emperor proposed to
to him to return to Paris, but the bad state of his health
prevented him from accepting the invitation.

The Bourbon family being obliged to quit Naples, king
Joseph Napolean confirmed to him the place of Master of
the Chapel, of composer and director of the music of his
chamber and of his chapel, with an appointment of eighteen
hundred ducats.   He composed for this chapel twenty-four
services, consisting of masses, motetts, and prayers.

At the same time Napolean sent him the Cross of the
Legion of Honor, which Joseph himself presented to him,
with a pension of a thousand francs.   He has since com
posed the opera *Dei Pillagorici*, which might serve as a
model both to poets and to musicians, and which procured
him the decoration of the order of the two Sicilies from
the king ; he was also named a member of the Royal
Society of Naples, and President of the Musical direction
of the Royal Conservatorio.   Joseph having gone to Spain,
Murat, who succeeded him, confirmed PAISIELLO in all
his employment.

At the time of the emperor's marriage with her royal
highness the archduchess of Austria, PAISIELLO thought
it his duty to present his majesty with a sacred composition, and in token of his thanks, his majesty sent
him a present of four thousand francs, which was accompanied with a letter, addressed to him, from the grand
marshall of the palace, containing the acknowledgments of
his majesty.

Besides the offices already spoken of M. PAISIELLO is
chapel master, of the cathredral of Naples, for which he
has composed several services *alla Palestrina*, he is also
chapel master to the municipality.   He has composed for
different religious houses, now destroyed, a great number
of offices, such as three masses for two choirs, two masses

for five voices, three masses for four voices, two dixits for four voices, three Motetts for two choirs, six Motetts for four voices, a Miserere for five voices, alla Palestrina, with an accompaniment for a violincello and tenor, a Christus, besides three cantatas for a single voice, for Amateurs, four notturnos for two voices, six concertos for the piano-forte, composed expressly for the infanta Princess of Parma, afterwards queen of Spain, (wife of Charles IV.)

Paisiello is the first who introduced the tenor into the comic theatres of Naples ; an instrument which was not at all in use. He is also the first who brought into these theatres and the chnrches the use of concerted bassoons and clarionets.

It was he who took off the prohibition of applauding in the theatre of San Carlos, singers and composers. The king set the example by applauding an air sung by Carlo Raina, in the opera of L. Papirius.

Paisiello has been named a member of many learned societies, such as of the Napolean Academy, of Lucca, the Italian Academy, sitting at Livourne, and the society of the children of Apollo, at Paris. On the 30th of December, 1809, he was elected an associate of the institution of France.

To complete the account M. Paisiello thus rendered of himself, some remarks on the nature of his talents, and on those qualities which characterised him are merely necessary. To do this in few words, they are fertility of invention, an extraordinary and happy felicity of finding subjects full both of nature and originality, a talent unique in developing them by the resources of melody, and embellishing them by interesting details, an arrangement always full of of fancy and learning, a taste; grace and freshness of melody by which he has far surpassed all other composers, and has been a model to those who have laboured after him.

His composition always very simple, and divested of all affectation of learning ; is not only extremely correct, but exceedingly elegant, and his accompaniments always very clear, are at the same time brilliant and full of effect. With regard to expression, although simplicity seems to be its principal and ruling character, it is not less true that he knows perfectly how to introduce variety, to seize on the different methods of producing effect, and to pass from the comic, from the simple and unaffected to the pathetic, to the Majestic, and even to the terrible, without losing that grace and elegance, from which it appears impossible for him to depart.

Such are the qualities which have obtained M. Paisiello the suffrages of all, both those of the public and of amateurs, as well as those of the learned and masters.

No composer could at any time have been more universally admired, sought, applauded, and respected in all the nations of Europe, nor have better deserved the distinguished reception his works have every where met. No one has more enjoyed such universal success. Placed at the same time among the most delightful authors, and among the finest classics, he has received the homage of his age, and has assured to himself that of posterity.

CHARLES HAGUE.

CHARLES HAGUE, was born on the 4th May 1769 at Tadcaster, in Yorkshire. From early youth he manifested

14

great fondness for music. A violin was placed in his hand,
and his brother, who was many years older than himself,
became his preceptor. · In 1779 he left his native place for
Cambridge, where his brother had begun to reside. From
the last mentioned period he had the advantage of excellent instruction, both in the practice and in the theory of
his future profession. He became the pupil of Manini,
an eminent professor on the violin, and studied the rudiments of thorough bass, and the rudiments of composition,
under the elder Hellendal, a man of undoubted attainments in musical science.

Under these favourable circumstances, Charles Hague
rapidly acquired celebrity, by his exquisite performances
on the violin, which to the close of his life continued to be
his favourite instrument.   As he became known he acquired friends. Indeed it would have been surprising if a youth
of his interesting appearance and admirable talents, had
not secured many friends in the University. Among those
who were the most anxious for his success in life, and the
most zealous to promote it, there would be great injustice
in omitting to mention the late Rev. Dr. Jewett, at that
time Regius, Professor of Civil Law, a gentleman, who
while eminent for his acquirements as a scholar, possessed
a refined taste in music, and an accurate knowledge of its
principles.

About the year 1785 Manini died , and by the advice, as
it is believed, of his University friends, young Hague then
resided for a time in London, and became pupil of Solomon.   Already an excellent performer, he could avail himself to the uttermost of the instructions of that great master, and from Solomon, without doubt, he acquired no
small portion of that skill and power which enabled him to
give such delightful effect to the compositions of Haydn.
During this period, he had the good fortune to be assisted

in the study of vocal harmony by Dr. Cooke ; of glee writers in modern times second to few in point of elegance,
and, perhaps the most learned. On his return to Cambridge, the subject of this memoir had the satisfaction of
numbering among his pupils many members of the University, eminent both for rank and talent. In 1791 he married Harriet, daughter of J. Hussey, Esq. of Clopton, Mid-
dlesex. In 1794 he was admitted to the degree of Bachelor of Music, in the University of Cambridge. In 1799
the Professorship of Music became vacant in consequence
of the death of Dr. Randall ; when, encouraged by his numerous friends among the members of the Senate, he became a candidate for the appointment, and was successful.
Soon after his election to the professorship he succeeded to
the degree of Doctor of Music.

Dr. HAGUE, from that time, considered himself as completely settled in Cambridge, where he continued to reside to
the day which discovered what small reliance can be placed
on a constitution even of great apparent strength. During
the Spring of 1821, he frequently complained of being un-
well ; but no danger was apprehended. Towards the end
of May, he was making arrangements for some Concerts on
a grand scale, which were to be performed at the approaching commencement, when he became suddenly ill
He remained two or three weeks in a state which gradually destroyed all hopes of his recovery ; and on the 18th of
June 1821 he expired, deeply regretted by his family and
friends.

Of the children of Dr. HAGUE, one only, a daughter, sur-
vives, and if it were in any degree the object of the present
writer to premise the living, he could not leave unrecorded
the taste and talents of Sophia Hague.

Dr. HAGUE was well acquainted with the principles of
of playing on keyed instruments, although not a performer

himself besides the violin, he was a complete master of the tenor and violincello. On public occasions, on which his services were more particularly called forth, he was accustomed to lead the musical performances with a precision and a contrariety which shewed that he was clearly entitled to the situation in which he was placed. In quartetts, his style of playing was the most delightful that can be imagined. If, however, we were required to state one department in which he more particularly excelled, we should mention his violin accompaniment to the Pianoforte. In *that*, we are almost inclined to think he was unrivalled ; so prompt was the intelligence with which he seized the meaning of the Composer, so facinating the *eloquence* with which he developed his ideas.

Dr. HAGUE, was well accquainted with the *theory* of music. Whoever would understand the principles of composition will find it an advantage to consult many writers, for the purpose of illustration ; but it is indispensable that he study one standard author thoroughly. We may observe that students in music are not only students to whom this hint may be useful. The late Professor had an exclusive admiration, either of antient or of modern music, he knew the peculiar value of each. He was anxious to preserve a sensible distinction between the secular and the ecclesiastical style. Of the productions of his cotemporaries, Dr. HAGUE was always disposed to speak with liberality. He dwelt with rapture, upon that admirable Oratorio of Dr. Crotch, *Palestine.* For a short period during the early years of that extraordinary genius, he was the pupil of CHARLES HAGUE, who was also at that time very young, being but six years older than his pupil. In a journal of Dr. HAGUE's yet remaining, the circumstance is stated, with admiration of the rapid progress which his pupil had made ; and with a declaration that to have had such a pu-

pil, would always appear to him the greatest honour of his
life. In due time Dr. Crotch became Professor of music
at Oxford. Many were the friends who became attached
to Dr HAGUE, when living, and who lamented him now he
is no more.

—

DR. CROTCH.

—

Dr CROTCH, the subject of the present memoir, was
born at Norwich, July 5, 1775. His father, by trade a car-
penter, an ingenious mechanic, and of good reputation,
having a passion for music, of which, however, he had no
knowledge, undertook to build an organ, on which, as soon
it would speak, he learned to play two or three common
tunes, such as, *God save the King* ; *Let ambition fire thy
mind* ; and the *Easter Hymn* ; with which, and such chords
as were pleasing to his ear, he used to try the perfection of
his instrument.

About Christmas, 1776, when Master CROTCH was only
a year and a half old, he discovered a great inclination for
music, by leaving even his food to attend to it, when the organ was playing ; and about Midsummer, 1777, he would
touch the key note of his particular favorite tunes, in order
to persuade his father to play them. Soon after this, as he
was unable to name these tunes, he would play the first two
or three notes of them, when he thought the key note did
sufficiently explain what he wished to have played. But according to his mother's account it seems to have been in

consequence of his having heard the superior performance of Mrs. Lulman, a musical lady, who came to try his father's organ, and who not only played on it, but sung to to her own accompaniment, that he first attempted to play a tune himself: for, the same evening, after her departure, the child cried and was so peevish that his mother was wholly unable to appease him. At length, passing through the dining room, he screamed and struggled violently to go to the organ, in which, when he was indulged, he eagerly bent down the keys with his little fists, as other children usually do, after finding themselves able to produce a noise, which pleases them more than the artificial performance of real melody or harmony by others. The next day, however, being left, while his mother went out, in the dining-room with his brother, a youth about fourteen years old, he would not let him rest till he blew the bellows of the organ, while he sat on his knee and bent down the keys, at first promiscuously, but presently, with one hand, he played enough of *God save the King* to awaken the curiosity of his father, who being in a garret, which was his workshop, hastened down stairs to inform himself who was playing this tune upon the organ. When he found it was the child, he could hardly believe what he heard and saw. At this time, he was exactly two years and three weeks old, as appears by the register, in the parish of St. George, Colgate, Norwich. Although he showed such a decided inclination for music, he could no more be prevailed on to play by persuasion than a bird to sing.

When his mother returned, the father, with a look that at once implied joy, wonder and mystery, desired her to go up stairs with him, as he had something curious to show her. She obeyed, and was as much surprised as as the father, on hearing the child play the first part of *God save the King*. The next day he made himself master of the treble of the second part ; and the day after he attempted the base, which he performed nearly correct in every particular, except the note immediately before the close, which being an octave below the preceding sound, was out of the reach of his little hand. In the beginning of November, 1777, he played both the treble and base of *Let Ambition fire thy mind* ; an old tune now called, *Hope thou Nurse of Young Desire.*

Upon the parents' relating this extraordinary circumstance to their neighbors, they were laughed at, and advised not to mention it, as such a marvellons account would only expose them to ridicule. However, a few days afterwards, Mr. Crotch being ill, and unable to go out to work, Mr. Paul, a master weaver, by whom he was employed, passing accidentally by the door, and hearing the organ fancied that he had been deceived, and that Crotch had staid at home, in order to divert himself on his favorite instrument. Fully prepossessed with this idea, he entered the house, and suddenly opening the dining room door, saw the child playing on the organ, while his brother was blowing the bellows. Mr. Paul thought the performance so extraordinary, that he immediately brought two or three of the neighbors to hear it, who propagating the news, a crowd of nearly a hundred persons came the next day to hear the young performer ; and, on the following days, a still greater number flocked to the house from all quarters of the city ; till, at length, the child's parents were obliged to limit his exhibition to certain days and hours, in order to lessen his fatigue and exempt themselves from the inconvenience of constant attendance on the curious multitude. At four years old, his ear for music was so astonishing,that he could distinguish at a great distance from any instrument, and out of sight of the keys, any note that was struck, whether A. B. C. &c. In this, Dr. Burney

used repeatedly to try him, and never once found him mista-
ken, even in the half notes ; a circumstance the more extraordinary, as many practitioners, and good performers,
are unable to distinguish by ear, at the opera or elsewhere,
in what key any piece or air is executed.   At this early
age, when he was tired of playing on an instrument, and his
musical faculties appeared wholly blunted, he could be
provoked to attention, even though engaged in any new
amusement, by a wrong note being struck in any well
known tune ; and, if he stood by the instrument when
such a note was designedly struck, he would instantly put
down the right, in whatever key the air was playing.

The extraordinary musical talents, exhibited by Dr.
CROTCH in infancy was matured by study and practice, so
as afterwards he was enabled to attain the highest rank in
his profession, and as a professor of music.

Among the numerous musical compositions published by
Dr. CROTCH, we cannot help mentioning two which more
particularly advanced his reputation ; " Palestine, a sacred
Oratorio," and " Specimens of various kinds of Music," in
three vols. folio.   He is also author of a work on the Ele-
ements of Musical Compositions.

WILLIAM SHIELD.

Late as WILLIAM SHIELD appeared, it is difficult to
speak of him in terms which will adequately describe our
sense of his superior merit, he struck out for himself, a
style of writing, pure, chaste, and original.   His great

characteristic, however, is *simplicity*. No composer has ever woven so few notes into such sweet and impressive melodies, while the construction of the bass and harmony is alike natural, easy, and unaffected. We cannot open one of his operas without being instantly captivated with this quality of his music. In such delightful entertainments as *Marian* and *Rosina*, his airs breath all the freshness, purity and beauty of rural life, though the ornamented and difficult parts are carried far beyond the common style of bravura.

SHIELD appears to have been singularly fortunate in the great compass and agility of the female singers, for whom he wrote his airs of execution. In Marian, there is an oboe sang of amazing extent and much complication. In most of his works where he introduces bravuras, we find passages combining the difficulties of execution, in a manner, which, if not absolutely new, lays considerable claim, to novelty, and full of the same ingenious cast of expression that is discernable throughout all the parts of his style. Perhaps no writer is so remarkable for songs containing so much that is strictly national. After Purcell, we consider SHIELD to be the finest and most perfect example of really English writers. Ballads, in all the different modes of sentiment and description, abound in his operas. Sea and hunting song, the rural ditty, the convivial song and glee, the sweet sentimental ballad are so frequent, that indeed, with the occasional interposition of songs of execution, they may be said to make up the customary and continual alternations from air to air. It will strike the observer as singular, that late composers for the stage should have made so little use of the minor key. SHIELD has applied it in a most beautiful manner. In analyzing his compositions, we have been led, from time to time, to regret the incessant appetite for novelty in the public, which calls for such con-

15

tinual changes of food, and that can lure us " from this fair mountain," but too of ten " tobattern on the moor." Yet nevertheless the taste of our own age bears us out in the belief that as much ot Mr. SHIELD's music will descend to posterity, carrying with it the intrinsic marks of 'English genius, as any other writer since the days of Arne, as a whole we have found nothing superior to Rosina. His works are very numerous, though in many of his pieces he has availed himself, with felicity of popular airs and of selections from Handel and foreign composers.

LEWIS VAN BEETHOVEN.

This stern colossus of harmony, was born in the year 1772 at Bonn, in Germany, where his father served as a tenor singer in the chapel of the late elector of Cologne, he was a pupil of Haydn and Albrechtberger, one of the greatest German Theorists, though less perfect than Haydn; he exceeds him in power of imagination ; from recent specimens of his unbounded fancy, it is to be expected that he will extend the art of music, in a way never contemplated even by Haydn or Mozart.

The symphonies of Haydn may be compared to little operas, formed upon natural occurrences, all within the verge of probability ; those of BEETHOVEN, are romances of the wildest invention, exhibiting a supernatural agency, which powerfully affects the feelings and the imagination. His genius seems to anticipate a future age. In one comprehensive view, he surveys all that science has hitherto produced ; but regards it only as the basis of that super-structure which harmony is capable of raising

He measures the talents of resources of every preceding artist ; and, as it were, collects into a focus their scattered rays. He discovers that Haydn and Mozart alone have followed nature, yet he explores the hidden treasures of harmony, with a vigour superior to either. In sacred mu-sic, he is pre-eminently great ; the dark tone of his mind, is in unison with that solemn style which the services of the church require ; and the gigantic harmony which he wields, enables him to excite by sounds, a tenor hitherto unknown.

His austere, energetic, and deeply thoughtful counte-nance, pourtrays features, in which a smile must be as tran-sient as a sunny gleam through an awful stormy cloud ; his phisognomy is the index of his mind, and the mind of man is reflected in his productions in general, this is more particularly the case in works of art, and above all in mu-sic, because music is a medium, the least clogged by posi-tive material forms, and therefore the least liable to warp the emanations of our minds and feelings. The works of Handel, Gluck, Haydn, Paisiello, Mozart and Pleyel &c. display their respective characters and being ; but none more conspicuously than the compositions of Beethoven. It would lead us too far away, to enumerate all the charac-istic features in the style of this great composer. It is evi-dent, that in point of melody he falls short of Mozart, at least as to proportioned quantity. On the other hand, when BEETHOVEN chooses to be melodious, and such paroxisms are neither frequent, nor of long duration ; we think his subjects of a higher order, more original, more deeply affecting, more general, more fervid, we had almost said more superhuman, than the strains of any other composer. They work more powerfully upon our sympathies, we feel something like the sensation produced by an odour never smelt before. Such his melodies appear, his harmonies are equally peculiar.

That a genius like BEETHOVEN, should have ventured further than any other upon the rugged domain of dissonance, is not surprising ; but even in the treatment and combination of his parts, he stands single. Disregarding the inconvenience of the performer, he disdains the fetters of established forms of accompaniments, he crowds zig zag notes into subservient parts, not so much from whim, as the sake of particular effect. Hence the comparative difficulty of BEETHOVEN's music, the danger even for the experienced player to trust to the forebodings of the ear, the necessity of the eye being forever on the watch, and the impossibility of executing many of his works at sight, however great the reward of perseverance in mastering these obstacles.

The works of this great master, are less remarkable for purity and correctness, than for a certain brilliancy and masculine energy of style which are more easily to be felt than described. He is not so correct, so polished, and so regular as Haydn and Mozart.

BEETHOVEN is the most celebrated, among the living composers in Vienna, and in certain departments the foremost of the day. His powers of harmony are prodigious. Though not an old man, he is lost to society in consequence of his extreme deafness, which has rendered him almost unsocial. The neglect of his person which he exhibits, gives him a somewhat wild appearance. His features are strong and prominent, his eye is full of energy ; his hair which neither comb nor scissors seem to have visited for years, overshadows his broad brow in a quantity and confusion to which only the snakes around a Gorgon's head offer a parallel. His general behaviour does not ill accord with his compromising exterior. Except when he is among his chosen friends, kindliness and affability are not his characteristics. The total loss of hearing, has deprived him of all the pleasure which society can give, and perhaps soured his temper.—Even among his oldest friends, he must be humored like a spoiled child. He has always a small paper book, and what conversation takes place, is carried on in writing. The moment he is seated at the piano, he is evidently unconscious there is any thing in existence but himself and his instrument, and, considering how very deaf he is, it seems impossible he should hear all he plays. Accordingly, when he is playing very *piano*, he often does not bring out a single note. He hears it himself in the " *minds ear.*" While his eye, and the almost imperceptable motion of his fingers, show that he is following out the strain in his own soul through all its dying gradations, the instrument is actually as dumb as the musician is deaf. He seems to feel the bold, the commanding, and the impetuous, more than what is soothing or gentle. The muscles of the face swell, and its veins start out ; the wild eye rolls doubly wild ; the mouth quivers, and quivers, and BEETHOVEN looks like a wizard overpowered by the demons whom he himself has called up.

The strong pinions of his *"music of fire,"* bears him upward, in general, to high vantage ground above his competitors, but though standing alone, in these days, the mountain eminence which he has attained, is not always the region of classical flowers. Thorns and brambles and flinty asperities are scattered among the wild luxuriances of its more beautiful productions. We are admirers of BEETHOVEN's excellencies, not of his correctness, his extravagance or his imperfections. When BEETHOVEN nods like Homer, he errs against his own knowledge, we look upon him as amenable to the canons of sound criticism, and never dream of holding up his errors, as new lights and dis-

coveries in the art ; and or of opposing them to the uniform
doctrines of the best theorists, and the unvariable practice
of the great body of the most eminent composers. We
would just as soon think of taking a line of Byron or
Campbell, and turning it against the established sense of the
best English poets, as the settled rules of the best gramma-
rians and philologers.

The career of this Musical Composer, furnishes few very
striking incidents : his residence having been stationary at
Vienna for nearly thirty years, enjoying an annuity of four
thousand florins from some Austrian nobleman, on the express condition of his not leaving the Austrian dominions
without their consent*

The following account of a present of an elegant piano
forte, by Thomas Broadwood, London, to LEWIS VAN BEE-
THOVEN the celebrated German Music composer is translated from a German newspaper.

" Arts belong to no particular country, but find a home
among the enlightened in every part of the world, be it on
the Ganges, or the banks of the Oronoco ; where sympathies present themselves to the magic of excitement, a union is offered to all that is sublime in human nature. The
empire of genius is boundless and undisputed. Such is the

---

*"Being in Germany a short time since, I took an opportunity
of spending part of a day with our friend Beethoven at Modlin,
near Vienna. *He is very deaf, but seems otherwise to be in fne
feather :* running about the hills, and bringing down notes for
innumerable fine things every evening. He shewed us a prodi-
giously fine piano forte, which has just been sent him by Mr.
Broadwood, of London ; a noble specimen of the admiration
with which the genius of this great man is regarded in every
part of the world. The instrument is by far the finest we ourselves ever saw, and had attracted immense applause from all
the cognoscenti of Vienna."

reign of the great BEETHOVEN, at the sound of his lyre "*divine*," a spell of ecstacy falls upon every German heart ;
the soft strain of Italy bursts into grandeur, and the song
of melting ardour pours forth, even from the icy shores of
the Neva.

The noble Briton, less rapid, but perhaps more steady
in his admiration, offers a tribute worthy to the " *God of
Music.*" We have reference to that prodigy of art, received by BEETHOVEN at Modlin his summer residence, and
presented to him as a token of respect by Mr. Broadwood
of London. This precious instrument, a *Horizontal Grand
Piano Forte*, has never yet been equalled. It has six octaves from the lowest C, to the uppermost. The tone
is the most exquisite that can be conceived, any particular notes can be softened at pleasure, and nothing is omitted to make this masterpiece perfect. Besides the pedals
on the left, there are two on the right for the bass, and the
treble dampers are to be used separately, or together, as
may suit the taste of the performer. The scale is so well
regulated, that the force of the bass, cannot injure the treble, on account of the successive and gradual dimunition of
the weight in the ascent, that is from the middle G, the
progressive lightness ascends to the upper C, after which
the dampers are discontinued.

To give a just idea of the superior construction of this
instrument, it will be sufficient to state the fact, that after being transported from London to Trieste, and thence
on wheels to Modlin, it was opened, and found to be in perfect tune, already for the touch of the *Mighty Musician.*

On the harmoniac platform is the following latin inscrip-

"*Hoc instrumentum est
Thomas Broadwood, Londoni,
donum, proptu, ingenium illlustrisimi*
BEETHOVEN."

On the front plate in large letters of ebony, stand the name of BEETHOVEN, and underneath it, *John Broadwood & Sons*, Makers of Instruments to his majesty, and the princesses, Great Pultney Street, Golden Square, London. to the right, on the same plate, appears five names, of the greatest Peformers in London,

    Fred Kalkbrenner.   *J. B. Cramer,*
    Ferd Ries.   *C. Knyvett*
             C. G Ferrari.

In testimony of the transcendant superiority of the gift, it is pleasing to remark here, as a farther homage to talents and the arts, that no duties were exacted by any Custom houses through which this instrument had to pass.

JOHN WALL CALLCOTT.

JOHN WALL CALLCOTT, was born at Kensington Gravel Pits, on the 20th November, 1776. He was placed under the Care of Mr. William Young, where his progress was considerable for his age. At twelve years old, when he was removed from School, he had read much of Ovid, the greatest part of Virgil, and had begun the study of the Greek Testament. From this period, his acquirements, which were very great, were the fruits of his industry. His attention was addressed to music, at the period of his leaving school, (1778) when he obtained an introduction to the Organist of Kensington, and began to practice upon a spinett, which his father obtained for him. About the year 1782 he attended the service at the Abbey and the Chapel

Royal, and made some acquaintance with the heads of the profession. In this year he was also appointed assistant organist at St. George the Martyr, Queen's Square, Holborn, by Mr. Reinhold. He nearly at the same time, through the kindness of Dr. Cooke, obtained admission to the orchestra of the Academy of ancient music, and he sung in the chorusses of the Oratorios at Drury Lane Theatre. In the first of these years he began to bestow some attention upon the principles of vocal composition, and he finished his first to the words of Gray's ode " *O sovereign of the willing soul*," printed in Warren's 23d Collection. From this period he continued to improve in vocal harmony. During the year 1784 he had the pleasure to attend the commemoration of Handel, in Westminster Abbey. In the following year he gained three prize medals given by the Catch Club, and took his Bachelor's degree at Oxford, on the invitation of Dr. Philip Hayes. His exercise, on the occasion, was upon Wartons ode to Fancy. In 1786 he bore off two medals, at the Catch Club, and succeeded to several valuable engagements in teaching, through the interest of Dr. Arnold, by whom his glee, " *When Arthur first*," was introduced among the music of " *The Battle of Hexham*."—In 1787 he gained two more medals at the Catch Club. In 1788 he did not write for the prizes, though he still employed all his leisure in the study for voices. In 1789 he again became a candidate for the medals, and had the good fortune (the concomitant of his uncommon abilities) to gain all four ; a circumstance which never occurred before or since. He was elected organist of Covent Garden Church in 1789. The election was, however, strongly contested, and the business terminated by a proposal, on the part of Mr. CALLCOTT to divide the situation with Mr. Charles Evans. In 1790 the celebrated Haydn arrived in London. Mr. CALLCOTT was introduc-

16

ed to him, by Mr. Solomon, and received some lessons from
that eminent musician. He accepted the office of organist to the Asylum for Female Orphans in 1792, which situation he retained till 1802, when he resigned it in favor of
Mr. Horsely, the present worthy incumbent, afterwards his
son in law. In 1800, he took his degree of Doctor in
Music, in company with Mr. Clement Smith, of Richmond.
Mr. Horsley at the same time, took the degree of Bachelor. Dr. CALLCOTT first conceived the design of composing a Musical Dictionary in 1797, and he persevered in it
for some years after, but finding that such a work would
interfere too much with his business as a teacher, he laid it
aside till some future period of leisure and advantage, and
in 1804 and 1805 employed himself in writing the *Musical
Grammar*, one of the most popular works in our language.

The Grammar was first published by Birchall in 1806.
In the following year his various pursuits and incessant application brought on a nervous complaint, which compelled him to retire altogether from business, and it was not
till 1813 that his family and friends again had the happiness
of seeing him among them. He remained well till the autumn of 1816 at which, symptoms of his former indisposi-
tion again appeared. From this period his professional
avocations were wholly superseded, and on the 5th of May,
1821 he ceased to feel all further affliction.

The basis of Dr. CALLCOTT's fame rests upon his glees,
but he has written some songs that are unequalled in point
of legitimate expression, and which, as we esteem them,
are models for the formation of a fine English style. Such
an one is his " *Angel of Life.*" His glees certainly place
him among the very foremost of those who have cultivated
that species of composition. No man was ever more deservedly beloved than Dr. CALLCOTT for the gentleness and be-

nignity of his disposition, nor more highly respected for the extent of his various attainments in languages, literature, and in science.

MUZIO CLEMENTI.

Muzio Clementi was born at Rome in the year 1725, His father was a worker in silver of great merit, and principally engaged in the execution of embossed vases and figures employed in the Catholic worship. At an early period of his youth he evinced a powerful disposition for music, and as this was an art which greatly delighted his father, he anxiously bestowed the best instructions, by placing him under Buroni the principal composer to St. Peters, after which, and at the age of six years, he began sol fa-ing and was instructed by Cordicelli in thorough bass. At nine years of age he passed his examination, and was admitted as an organist at Rome. He next went under the celebrated Santanelli, the last great master of the true vocal school, and between eleven and twelve he went under Carpini, the deepest contrapuntist of his day in Rome. A few months after he was placed under this master, he was induced by some of his friends, and without consulting his Preceptor, to write a mass for four voices, for which he received so much commendation, that Carpini expressed a desire to have it. It was accordingly repeated in Church in presence of his master, who being little accustomed to bestow praise on any one, said to his pupil, after his dry manner, " Why did you not tell me you were about to write a mass, this is very well to be sure, but if you had consulted me it might have been much better."

At the age of fourteen a Mr. Beckford residing in Dorsetshire in England, then on his travels in Italy, was extremely desirous of taking him over to that country. The declining riches of the Roman church, at this period not giving much encouragement to the talents of the Father, he agreed to confide the rising talents to the care of Mr. Beckford.

The country seat of Mr. Beckford being in Dorsetshire, by the aid of a good library and the conversation of the family, CLEMENTI quickly obtained a competent knowledge of the English language. His efforts to acquire preeminence on the harpsichord, were in the mean time as indefatigable as they were successful, and at the age of eighteen he had not only impressed all his contemporaries in the powers of execution and expression, but had written his Opera 2, which gave a new era to that species of composition. The simplicity, brilliancy, and originality which it displayed, captivated the whole circle of professors and amateurs. It is superfluous to add what all the great musicians of the age have uniformly allowed, that this admirable work is the basis on which the whole fabric of modern sonatas for the piano forte has been erected. When Schroeter arrived in England, he was asked if he could play the works of CLEMENTI, he replied that they could only be performed by the author himself, or the devil. Yet such is the progress executive ability has made, that was once an obstacle to the most accomplished talent, is now within the power of thousands

After he quitted Dorsetshire, he went to London, and was engaged to preside at the harpsichord, in the Orchestra of the Opera house, where he had an opportunity of improving his taste by the performances of the first singers of the age. The advantages he derived from this species of study was quickly shewn by the rapid progress he made beyond his cotemporaries, either in the dignity of his style of execution, and in the powers of expression. This also he carried into his compositions and Dussek, Steibelt, Woelfl Beethoven, and other eminent performances on the Continent, who had no opportunity of receiving personal instructions from CLEMENTI, declare that they had formed themselves entirely on his works. His ability in extemporaneous playing, has perhaps no parallel. The richness of harmonic combination, the brilliancy of fancy, the power of effect, and the noble style of execution which he displays, make him stand alone in an age which has produced such a host of executive talent.

In 1780 at the instigation of PACCHIEKOTTI, he determined to visit Paris, where he was received with enthusiasm, and had the honour to play before the Queen, who bestowed upon him the most unqualified applause, the warmth of French praise, contrasted with the gentle and cool approbation given by the English, quite astonished the young musician, who used jocosely to remark, that he would scarcely believe himself to be the same man. Having enjoyed the unabated applause of the Parisians until the summer of 1781, he determined on paying a visit to Vienna. At Vienna he became acquainted with Haydn and Mozart, and all the celebrated musicians resident in that capital. The Emperor Joseph who was a great lover of music invited him to his palace, where in the latter end of the year 1781, he had the honour of playing alternately with Mozart before the Emperor and the Grand Duke Paul of Russia and the Dutchess. In 1782 he returned to England, and some time after he took John B. Cramer then about 15 years old, under his tuition. The following

year CLEMENTI returned to France, in 1784 he again came
back to England. From this period to 1802 he remained
pursuing his professional labours with increasing reputation ;
and wishing to secure himself sufficient time for the prosecution of his studies, he raised his terms to one guinea per
hour. His fame however was so great that this augmentation of pence rather increased than diminished the candi-
dates for instruction. The great number of excellent pupils which he found during this period, proves his superior
skill in the art of tuition ; the invariable successs which
attended his public performances, attracted his pre-eminent
talents as a player, and his compositions are a lasting proof
of his application and genius. About the year 1800, having lost a large sum of money by the failure of the well
known firm of Longman and Broderip, 26 Cheapside,
he was induced by the persuasions of some eminent mer-
cantile gentlemen, to embark in the concern.

A new firm was accordingly formed from that period and
he declined any more pupils. The hours which he did not
thenceforward employ in his professional studies, he dedicated to the mechanical and philosophical improvement of
piano fortes, and the originality and justness of his conceptions were crowned with complete success. The extraordinary and admirable talents of John Field, CLEMENTI had
cultivated with encreasing delight, and he had been often
heard to say, that such was his quickness of conception,
retentiveness of memory, and facility of execution which
this highly gifted boy possessed, that he seldom had occasion to make the same remark to him a second time. With
this favourite pupil in the autumn of 1802 he paid a third
visit to Paris, where he was received with unabated esteem
and admiration. From Paris he proceeded to Vienna,
where he intended to place Field under the direction of
Albrechtsberger, to which his pupil seemed to assent with

pleasure ; but when the time came, for CLEMENTI to set off for Russia, poor Field with tears trembling in his eyes, expressed so much regret at parting from his master, and so strong a desire to accompany him, that CLEMENTI could not resist his inclinations—they therefore proceeded directly to St. Petersburg.

In Petersburgh CLEMENTI was received with the greatest distinction. He played extemporaneously in the society of the principal professors, with his accustomed excellence, and to the admiration of his audience ; and having introduced Field to all his friends, soon afterwards left Russia, for Berlin and Dresden. At this place Klengel introduced himself to the acquaintance of CLEMENTI, and after obtaining some instructions, became desirous to accompany his master in his travels. CLEMENTI was so much pleased with his character, that he took him on to Vienna, where, during some months, worked very hard under his direction.

During the following summer CLEMENTI took Klengel on a tour through Switzerland, and returned immediately afterwards to Berlin, where he married his first wife. In the autumn he took his bride through Italy, as far as Rome and Naples, and on his return to Berlin, having had the misfortune to lose his wife in child bed, he immediately left the scene of his sorrows, and once more visited Petersburg. In this journey he took with him another promising pupil of the name of Berger, who is now the principal professor of the piano-forte at Berlin. At Petersburg he found Field in the full enjoyment of the highest reputation, he might be said to be the idol of the Russian nation. Here he remained but a short time, and went back to Vienna. Having heard of the death of his brother, he proceeded once more to Rome, to settle the affairs of his family, and afterwards arrived in England in 1810, and the year fol-

lowing married his present wife. His first publication after his return was the " Appendix," to his " Introduction
to the art of Playing on the Piano Forte," a work which
has been of infinite use both to the profession and to the
public, and the demand for which, has constantly augmented in proportion as its excellence has been discovered.
He next adapted the twelve grand symphonies of Haydn
for the piano forte, with accompaniments for the flute, violin, and violincello.   Afterwards he adapted " Haydn's
Creation," the oratorio of the " Seasons," and Mozart's
overture to Don Giovanni, besides various selections from
the vocal compositions of the same author.

We now come to mention a work, by which the author
must, have established his fame as a composer of the first
eminence, had he never written another note.   We allude
to his "*Gradus Parnassum*."   The public must anticipate
much pleasure from the knowledge that there are in press
several new compositions from the fruitful and unexhausta-
ble pen of the accomplished subject of this memoir.   We
must now close our sketch of the life of this extraordinary
man, whom we rejoice to see on the verge of seventy, retaining all the vivacity, freshness, and vigour of intellectual strength, and in the enjoyment of a constitution which
promises the musical world rich harvests still to come from
the fertility of his comparable genius.

G. J. JACKSON.

This truly scientific and very able professor, was born at Oxford, (Eng.) in 1745. At nine years of age he was placed under the superintendence of the celebrated Dr. Nares, with Drs. Arnold, Dupuis and Mr. Rayner Taylor of Philadelphia, of whom we shall have occasion to notice hereafter. Dr. JACKSON continued with Dr. Nares until 1773, when he was appointed a surplice boy at the King's Chapel Royal, on account of his natural taste for music, he was also one of the tenor singers at the grand commemoration of Handel in 1784, and received his Diploma from St. Andrew's College in 1791, and migrated to this country, in 1796. He arrived at Norfolk Virginia, where he remained a short time, and removed to Alexandria, visited the cities of Baltimore and Philadelphia. From thence he resided at Elizabeth Town, N. J. and subsequently at N. York, where he remained for many years in active and constant employment as a teacher and organist. In 1812. Dr. JACKSON removed to Boston, which city had been represented, as being a more desirable place for his profession ; immediately upon his arrival there, he was employed as organist at the church in Brattle Street, where he remained for some time, until he was exiled to Northampton, Mass. on account of being an Englishman, this country being then at war with Great-Britain. In 1813 Dr. JACKSON with Messrs Graupner & Mallet, commenced a series of oratorios, some of which were repeated at Salem. At the conclusion of the war in 1815, he returned to Boston, and was immediately engaged as Organist at the King's

17

Chapel, so called, in School street, after which he officia-
ted as organist, for several years at Trinity Church, in
Summer-street, and on the erection of St. Paul's Church
in Common Street, he was engaged at an extraordinary
high salary as organist, which situation he held until his
demise.

Dr. JACKSON was married in the year 1787 to the eldest
daughter of Dr. Samuel Rogers, Physician, London, by
whom he had eleven children. In recording some brief
particulars of this distinguished Professor, we are happy to
add our tribute of eulogy which appertains to his memory.
His professional erudition, solidity of judgment, and a cute-
ness of perception, were manifest on all occasions. As an
organist, he was pre-eminent. Any one acquainted with
the true style of Organ playing must acknowledge his unrivalled talents, his voluntaries were elaborate and replete with chromatic harmonies, embracing the most scientific and classic modulations. His interludes to psalmody
were particularly appropriate to the sentiments expressed
in the subject, and until his residence in the metropolis of
New-England, chanting the church service was little practised and less understood.

It is to this venerable professor, that this pleasing and
truly useful branch of church service was performed, and
its practice properly inculcated among the choristers of the
several episcopal churches in Boston, and to him, are we
indebted for a very valuable book of chaunts, canons, sanc-
tusses and kyrie cleisons. His compositions as a harmo-
nist, are of high rank, they possess a profound knowledge
of the science, and an originality of modulation wherein are
displayed a comprehensive view of effects, the result only
of deep and laborious study.

We are desirous to perpetuate the name of this erudite
professor, whose distinguished abilities as a teacher, many

of the first families in Boston have long and ardently cher_ished, and whose pupils have felt themselves fondly endeared, and whose memory will ever be appreciated.

Among the remaining highly talented professors, we presume this sketch will excite a sympathetic feeling, as it may lead those who are partial to the art, to enquire, whether the talents of professors in music are appreciated, or their endeavors properly rewarded? while we may with equal propriety inquire, whether we sufficiently value or reward those who are now laboring for our gratification and improvement ?

This subject is pregnant with interest, and we should rejoice, if our humble efforts would stir up a proper spirit, and more faithfully, both in sentiment and action, honour and reward what is at our command. We cannot help cherishing the hope, that the many respectable and highly gifted artists now domesticated among us, may yet more fully receive remuneration for their labors, and that when deprived by sickness, age or other casualty from their exertions, their talents and services may be recorded for posterity, by far more abler pens than ours.

JAMES BARTLEMAN.

Died on the 15th of April, at his house in Berner's street aged 54, after an illness of several years, Mr. JAMES BARTLEMAN. He was completely educated in music : he was a scientific singer, and learned in the various erudition of the English and Italian composers, particularly in the madrigalists, and the writers of sacred music. His bias was

decided towards those compositions which, even when he
first came into life, had already begun to be considered as
ancient music ; but all that lay in his own department, he
lightened of its heaviness by the brilliancy of his voice,
and animated by the energy of his manner. He carried
much dramatic effect into the orchestra, and he restored
the knowledge of Purcell's finest compositions, as well as
of Handel's finest opera songs. He was, of his own accord, and under the influence of his own disposition, rapidly infusing a new grace into *Base* singing, when the means
were afforded him by Haydn's character of Raphael, in
the Creation—by Callcott's beautiful songs, written on
purpose for him—by Pergolesi's " O Lord have mercy upon me,"—by Dr. Crotch's Palestine, and several other
things from Stevens, Webb, Callcott, and Horsley, of du-
rably impressing the stamp of elegance upon this point of
the art. The freer admission of ornamental passages, of a
cast between those employed by the bass and tenor, naturally followed, while the discontinuance of heavy divisions,
and the substitution of speaking, and beautiful melodies,
such as we find throughout the Creation—In Callcott's
Angel of Life—and in Horsely's Tempest, completed the
enlargement of the base singer from the imposing con-
straints of the former system. Nor has the pure and genuine eloquence of music, that just and forcible expression
which is the result of the happiest adaptation of sound to
sentiment, been abandoned or lost in the change. England
owes to the present generation of native composers, a combination of grandeur with grace, not to be matched, we
think, in the works of any other race of writers for bases,
scarcely excepting the author of the Creation himself.

Mr. BARTLEMAN was a member of the chapel royal and
other choirs, a scientific and erudite musician, and, as a
base singer, has raised the art of expression to a higher

pitch than any of his predecessors. He revived the music of Purcell, and supported the school of Handel—indeed the ancient schools generally, with a degree of energy, purity, and effect, for which the musical world may now look in vain. With this imaginative and energetic singer, the traditionary manner of such things as Purcell's "Let the dread engines," " The Frost scene in king Arthur," and " Saul and the Witch of Endor," will, we apprehend, be entirely lost. His voice had power and richness, yet these were joined with a lightness that is seldom met with in singing. He was perhaps, the first Englishman who endeavored to revive the mechanical effects, before this time considered inalienable, from bases ; and to form this part with spirit, fancy, finish, and a certain portion of elegance ; and he was perhaps as successful in the addition of these attributes to the native majesty and volume of tone, that are the foundation of base-singing, as any man ever was or ever will be. His style was strictly English, both in the formation of his tone, and in his elocution, which was highly animated, and full of effective transitions. The test of his peculiar excellence appears to be, that no one has succeeded in imitating his manner ; nor, indeed, has he left behind him any successor sufficiently strong to buckle on his armour.

In private life, Mr. BARTLEMAN was refined and well informed, lively in conversation, and enthusiastically fond of his art. He moved in a most respectable sphere in society.

SIGNOR & SIGNORA STORACE.

The former of these personages was a good Composer, and possessed a thorough knowledge of the science together with a wide range of acquaintance with the composition of foreign writers for the stage. He was a composer always natural, nervous, and generally polished, rarely however, rising to any high pitch of elegance or originality. There is said to be more merit contained in his concerted pieces than in his single pieces. His glees and chorusses are some of them beautiful and elaborate. The adaptation of the melodies of Italian composers to the words of new operas had been more general before this time than is suspected, but he enlarged the privilege, not indeed surreptitiously or covertly, but openly and fairly. This circumstance detracts very much from his originality, while we do not think it adds greatly to his reputation for taste.

Signora STORACE was a great accession to the English stage. She received an early instruction, had a masculine understanding, and was well trained to advance the grand objects of her brother's learning and taste, to the transference of the spirit of the Italian opera, and particularly of the comic opera to the English boards. She was a captivating actress, and possessed execution as a singer ; nor was it possible, to have found a woman so effective in the various tasks allotted her. The selections of this time, for the oratorios, were principally from the works of Handel, who writing for genuine basses, that is to say, for voices of great depth, weight, and volume, employed a style essentially different from what has since elevated the reputation of certain singers, enlarged the sphere, and even changed what appears to have been the most natural manner of composing for that sort of voice. The style of Handel, as exemplified in this species of music, is sublime and stately.

Signora STORACE was married to Dr. Fisher, with whom she lived but for a short time, when a divorce took place. It is said she was strongly attached to Mr. Braham, who was instrumental in improving her manner and style of performance, and to whom she bequeathed at her demise a considerable legacy.

MARA NEE SCHMELLING

Was born in Cassel in 1750, and it is stated on the authority of a foreign correspondent of Dr. Burney, that her early years were devoted to the study of the violin, which as a child she played in England, but quitted that instrument and became a singer by the advice of the English ladies who disliked a " female fiddler ; it may possibly have happened, that to this prejudice we owe the delight experienced from the various excellencies of the most sublime singer the world ever saw. Nor was the objection of the English ladies, the only prejudice Miss SCHMELLING had to encounter, for, on her arrival at Berlin, at the age of 24, Frederick the Great, king of Prussia, who affected as high a skill in music as in war, could scarcely be prevailed upon to hear her, his majesty declaring that he should as soon expect pleasure from the neighing of his horse, as from

German singer. One song, however, convinced him of
her ability, which he immediately put to the severest
trial, by selecting the most difficult airs in his collection,
and which Miss SCHMELLING executed at sight, as perfectly
as if she had practised each of these compositions all
her life. Her earliest singing master was an old man of
the name of Paradisi, and at fourteen she sung before her
majesty with the greatest success. From 1767 to 1783 she
passed through Germany and Switzerland, she visited Naples at a period subsequent to her appearance in England.
Although it is related that Madame MARA's first impressions
led her to songs of agility, yet her intonation was fixed by
the incessant application to plain notes. We know from
her own assurance that to confirm the true foundation of
all good singing, by the purest enunciation and the most
precise intonation of the scale, was the study of her life,
and the part of her voicing, upon which she most valued
herself. The late Dr. Arnold told the writer of this article, that as he had, by way of experiment, seen MARA
dance and assume the most violent gesticulations while going up and down the scale, yet such was her power of chest,
that the tone was as undisturbed and free, as if she had
stood in the customary quiet position of the orchestra.

The Italians say, that " of the hundred requisites to
make a singer, he who has a fine voice has ninety-nine."
Madame MARA had certainly the ninety-nine in one. Her
voice was in compass from G. to E. in altissimo, and all
its notes were alike even and strong ; but if it may be permitted to supply the hundredth, she had that also in a su-
per-eminent degree in the grandest and most sublime conception. At the early age of 24, when she was at Berlin,
in the immaturity of her judgment and her voice, the best
critics admitted her to have exceeded Cuzzoni, Faustina,
and indeed all those who have preceded her. Our age has

since seen Billington and Catalini, and we still believe that
in majesty and truth of expression (that term comprehend-
ing all the most exalted gifts and requisites of vocal science) the MARA retains her superiority. From her we
deduce all that has been learned or perhaps can be learned
concerning the great style of singing. The memory of her
performance of Handel's sublime work, " *I know that my
Redeemer liveth*," is immortalized, together with the air itself. Often as we have since heard it, we have never witnessed even an approach to the simple majesty of MARA ;
it is to this air alone that she owes her highest pre-eminence, and they who not having heard her would picture to
themselves a just portraiture of her performance, must image a singer who is fully equal to the truest expression of
the inspired words and the scarcely less inspired music of
this loftiest of all possible compositions.

But MARA was the child of sensibility ; every thing that
she did was directed to the heart ; her tone, in itself pure,
sweet, rich, and powerful, took all its various colorings
from the passion of the words ; and she was not less true
to nature and feeling in "*The Soldier tir'd*," and in the
more exquisite, " *Hope told a flattering tale*," than in " *I
know that my Redeemer liveth*." Her tone was perhaps neither so sweet nor so clear as Billington's, nor so rich and
powerful as Catalina's, but it was the most touching language of the soul. It was on the mastery of the feelings of
her audience that MARA set her claims to fame. She left
surprise to others, and was wisely content with an apparently (but not really) humbler style ; and she thus chose
the part of genuine greatness.

The elocution of MARA must be taken rather as universal
than as national ; for although she passed some time in
England when a child, and retained some knowledge of the
18

language, her pronunciation was continually marred by a foreign accent and those mutilations of our words which are inseparable from the constant use of foreign languages during a long residence abroad.* Notwithstanding this draw-back, the impression she made, even upon uneducated persons, always extremely alive to the ridiculous effects of mis-pronunciation, and upon the unskilled in music, was irresistible. The fire, dignity, and tenderness of her vocal appeal could never be misunderstood ; it spoke the language of all nations, for it spoke to the feelings of the human heart.

Her acquaintance with the science of music was considerable, and her facility in reading notes astonishing. The anecdote related above will prove how completely all music was alike easy to her comprehension. Perhaps she is indebted to her fiddle for a faculty at that time not very common. We have observed that all players on stringed instruments enjoy the power of reading and writing music beyond most others : they derive it from the apprehension of the coming note or distance which must necessarily reside in the mind, and direct the finger to its formation. The two branches of art are thus acquired by the violinist in conjunction, and to her knowledge of the violin we attribute Madame MARA's early superiority in reading difficult passages. MARA's execution was certainly very great ; and though it differs materially from the agility of the present fashion, it may be considered as more true, neat, and legitimate, inasmuch as it was less quaint and extravagant, and deviated less from the main purpose of vocal art—*expression*. Mrs. Billington once made this remark to us in conversation, and at the same time, with a modesty becoming her great acquirements, voluntarily declared that she con-

* A Pole can easily acquire and pronounce all languages, but no foreigner can pronounce the Polish tongue.

sidered MARA's execution to be superior to her own, in genuine effect, though not in extent, compass, rapidity, and complication. MARA's divisions always seemed to convey a meaning, such as we have before described under the name of *vocal declamation*, in our criticism on Mr. Vaughan : they were vocal, not instrumental ; they had light and shade and variety of tone ; they relaxed from, or increased upon the time, according to the sentiment of which they always appeared to partake ; these attributes were also particularly remarkable, in her open, true, and liquid shake, which was certainly full of expression. Neither in her ornaments, learned and graceful as they were, nor in her cadencies, did she ever lose sight of the appropriate characteristics of the sense and melody. She was by turns majestic, tender, pathetic, and elegant, but always the one or the other—not a note was breathed in vain.—She justly held every species of ornamental execution to be subordinate to the grand end of uniting the effects of sound and sense in their operations upon the feelings of her hearers. True to this principle, if any one commended the agility of a singer, MARA would ask " Can she sing six plain notes ?"

We place Madame MARA at the very topmost summit of her profession, because in majesty and simplicity, in grace, tenderness, and pathos, in the loftiest attributes of art, in the elements, of the great style, she far transcended all her competitors in the list of fame.—She gave to Handel's compositions their natural grandeur and effect, which is in our minds the very highest degree of praise that we can bestow. Handel is heavy, say the musical fashion-mongers of the day. This objection has been already largely discussed in our former pages. Milton would be heavy beyond endurance from the mouth of a reader of talents above mediocrity.   The fact is, that to wield such arms, demands the strength of giants. MARA possessed this heaven gifted strength.   It was in the performance of Handel that her finer mind fixed its expression, and called to its aid all the powers of her voice, and all the acquisitions of her science.

Here she still holds her seat in unblenched majesty, and still wears   " without co-rival
                      All her dignities."

MRS. BILLINGTON.

The paternal appellation of Mrs. BILLINGTON was Weichsell, and her mother, who was a singer of, some eminence died while her offspring, Mr. C. Weichsell, the celebrated violinist, and Mrs. B. were young. These children were trained to music at the earliest possible age, and even performed on the pianoforte and violin for the benefit of Mrs. W. at the Haymarket Theatre, at six years old at a time of life when they might have been well thought incapable of any acquirements deserving public notice.   Her first master was Schroeter, an excellent teacher of the piano forte, and her father superintended her musical education with a degree of severity, that could scarcely be justified even by the proficiency of the pupil.   Few persons have attained the perfection that Miss Weichsell reached upon this instrument.   At fourteen she came before the public as a singer at Oxford, and at sixteen married Mr. Billington, then a performer on the double bass, who carried her immediately to Dublin, where she commenced her theatrical career in the opea of Orpheus and Eurydice.

Here perhaps, for the only period of her life, she was doomed to some mortification, in the greater applause and respect obtained by Miss Wheeler, a singer much inferior to herself; and such was the effect on the ardent mind of Mrs. BILLINGTON, that it had well nigh been the occasion of her quitting the stage in disgust. The reputation of Miss Wheeler procured her an engagement at Covent Garden Theatre for three years; Mrs. BILLINGTON followed her to London, and no sooner had she arrived than Mr. Harris, the proprietor, and Mr. Lewis the manager, waited upon her with a proposal for her to play three nights. So short a trial she positively refused, expressing her desire to substitute twelve nights, under the apprehension that her too anxious solicitude to please her countrymen might defeat her first efforts. Such, indeed was her distrust that she considered this as a final experiment, and she had determined in the event of any failure either in the case of self possession or of deficiency of powers and attainments to quit the profession of an actress at once. They proceeded to discuss the terms of her engagement, and she desired a salary of twelve pounds per week, to which the managers objected as being the highest sum then given, and as the remuneration assigned to Miss Wheeler, whose reputation was so high and so established. The comparison was unfortunate, it irritated Mrs. B. and she instantly declined to enter into any permanent contract. She consented, however, to appear for the twelve nights, and was advertised for the part of Rosetta, in Arne's opera of " Love in a Village." She was announced for the Wednesday night, but the name of Mrs. BILLINGTON, late Miss Weichsell, having caught the attention of the King, his majesty commanded her appearance to take place two days sooner, a circumstance highly flattering as it was a solitary instance and contrary to the custom generally observed by the Sovereign.

It will readily be conceived that Mrs. BILLINGTON, whose habits of study and practice had been fixed by the severest exercise of parental authority, omitted no preparatory exertion to ensure her success with the public, under such high auspices. Indeed she laboured night and day, and nothing could be more complete than her triumph over the esteem of her audience and the rivalry of her former favoured competitor. Miss Wheeler was laid on the shelf as the theatrical phrase goes, and at the expiration of the twelve nights the managers again waited on Mrs. B. to renew her engagements on a permanent footing. They questioned her cautiously respecting her expectations, and she rather in jest than earnest demanded one thousand pounds and a benefit for the remainder of the season, with which to her astonishment, they immediately complied, and they afterwards voluntarily gave her a second night in return for the extraordinary emolument they had derived from the exercise of her talents.

During this season although her theatrical duties were unremitted, she never relaxed from the most sedulous general pursuit of the knowledge and practice of her art. She laboured incessantly, and received lessons of Mortellari, an Italian master of celebrity, at that time in England. The theatre had no sooner closed than she availed herself of the interval to fly to Paris, where she enjoyed the instructions of the great Sacchini, the composer. Thus, she continued from the first to fortify and enrich her natural gifts with the strength and ornaments of high science, an example to be followed by every student who aspires to the character of a polished and expressive singer.

At this time Madame Mara arrived in England, unequal-

led in the eminence she had attained. In 1785 the subject
of our memoir made her debut at the concert of ancient
music. Mara herself is said not to have beheld her reception quite unmoved, and some disputes even arose respecting place and pre-eminence in the seats of the orchestra, a
species of contention very unworthy the transcendant abilities of these gifted individuals.

Mrs. BILLINGTON's fame continued to spread while her
never ceasing ardour and assiduity were day by enlarging
her stock of knowledge acquirement and facility. She was a
constant performer at the concerts of the metropolis, and
she sung at the memorable Westminster Abbey performances. She remained at Covent Garden till 1793, when she
adopted a resolution to retire from public life, which she
vainly imagined she had firmness enough to adhere to. At
the instigation of her husband and her brother she was induced to make a continental tour, with a view solely to
amusement, and to this intent she declined all letters of introduction, intending to travel incognito. For some time
they succeeded and passed along without notice ; but at
Naples, the English Ambassador, Sir W. Hamilton, penetrated their secret and persuaded Mrs. B. and Mr. W. to perform in private before the King and Queen, at Caserto, a
country residence. The gratification they received induced
their Majesties to request Mrs. BILLINGTON to perform at
the Great Theatre of St. Carlo, then thought to be the finest
opera establishment in the world. She accordingly in May,
1794, made her debut in *Inez di Castro*, which was composed expressly for her, by the Maestro Francesco Bianchi,
who wrote an opera worthy the supereminent ability of his
primadonna. Her success was complete, for indeed her
celebrity had made her name known in Italy, and previous
ᐱ her quitting England the Venetian Ambassador had been

in treaty with her to accept an engagement, which however she broke.

Mrs. BILLINGTON's performance at Naples was interrupted by a sudden and affecting event. On the second night as Mr. BILLINGTON was seeking his hat, to accompany his wife to the theatre, he fell down in a fit of appoplexy and died in the arms of Bianchi, at the residence of the Bishop of Winchester. Nor was this the only circumstance that impeded her progress. About this time an eruption of Mount Vesuvius took place, and the superstitious bigotry of the Neapolitans attributed the visitation to the permission granted to a Heretic to perform at St. Carlo. Serious apprehensions were entertained by Mrs. B's. friends for the consequences of such an impression. Her talents, however triumphed, she renewed her performance, and no prima donna was ever more rapturously received in the country where the opera is best cultivated and best understood. Paisiello, Paer, and Himmel, successively wrote for her after Bianchi.

In 1796 she went to Venice, where, after the first performance, she was taken so ill that she could sing no more during the season ; and it is among the records honourable to human nature that the manager generously brought her the whole of her salary, which she compensated by playing the succeeding season without any other reward than the pleasure of reciprocating the liberality of her employer. Conceiving that the air of Venice did not agree with her, she quitted the place and returned. On her journey from Venice to Rome, she was earnestly entreated to give a concert at Rome, which she at first declined ; but a society of Cavalieri undertook the whole of the arrangement, and she and Mr. Weichsell performed to a very crowded audience.

Between this period and the year 1798, she visited all the principal theatres in Italy. In this year she married Mr. Felissent, and subsequently appeared twice only at Milan. In 1801, still retaining the name of BILLINGTON, she return ed to her native country.

No sooner was her arrival known than all the conductors of the public amusements were alike eager to engage her. The managers of Covent Garden and Drury Lane Theatres both made her offers, and the disposal of her services was at length referred to arbitrators, who awarded that she should appear at the two theatres alternately.

Mandane, in Arne's Artaxerxes, was the character selected for her debut, and the audience was struck with rapture and astonishment at her amazing powers. On this occasion she introduced a song from Bianchi's *Inez di Castro,* to the English words, " *lost in anxious doubts ;*" which being composed expressly for her, exhibited at one view her prodigious qualities, heightened by the delightful execution of her brother's obligato violin accompaniment. Perhaps no other singer could have sung this song ; very certain it is, no one has ever attempted it.

Engagements now multiplied upon her.—She sung at the at the Italian Opera in 1803, at the King's concert, at the Hanover-square Vocal Concerts, and at a round of provincial meetings from this time till 1809, when she finally retired.

Two remarkable circumstances attended during this period of her public life. On her re-appearance at the Opera, the Banti, then in the zenith of her excellence, played the character of Polifonte to Mrs. BILLINGTON's Merope, in Nasolini's opera of that name. Never was the house so crowded as on this occasion, the stage was so covered with ladies and gentlemen that the performers had scarcely room to move. The second occurrence was her performance with Mara on the 3d of June, 1802, the last night of that most distinguished singer's appearing in this country. They sung a duett together, composed to display their mutual accomplishments, and the contest excited both to the utmost pitch of scientific expression. Never certainly was such a transcendant exercise of ability. At length Mrs. Billington, having gained a competency, and feeling her health very sensibly affected by her efforts in the service of the public, she resolved to retire from exertions which, with a mind so keenly alive to the approbation of her auditors, and so devoted to the strictest execution of her professional duties, could not have failed to have shortened her prospects of repose, and even of existence. No entreaties were spared on the part of the noble directors of the ancient music, and of every manager of every public theatre or concert at which she had assisted, but her resolution was finally taken, and in 1809 she retired from all public performances, and was never afterwards induced to forego it, except on one occasion which she sung for the benefit of a charity at Whitehall, in the presence of the Queen, the Prince Regent, and other branches of the Royal Family.

She left England with her husband, in 1817, and died after an illness of a very few days at her estate, of St. Artien, near Venice.

ANGELICA CATALANI.

Madame Angelica Catalani was born in the papal dominions in or about the year 1782. Respectably, if not nobly, descended, she was placed in that genteel class of society which seemed at first to forbid her resorting to a professional life to ameliorate her fortune, which being but very small, like many other ladies thus situated, she was destined to take the veil.

The chaunting of the divine music in the church of Rome, is, perhaps, one of the finest criterions whereby to judge of the excellence of vocal powers. The voice of the youthful CATALANI was easily distinguished and admired as it ascended in delightful melody to the praises of the immaculate mother of our Redeemer. Friends and kindred united their persuasions that such intrinsic and wonderful harmony should not be buried in a cloister ; and she soon, even in her native land, carried off the palm of singing at the opera against veteran female performers. Her expressive and beautiful countenance, her youth, her excellent and graceful acting, all pleaded in her favor, and she was at that early period nearly established in fame, with scarce one rival competitor.

She visited the kingdom of Portugal ; and the then Prince of Brazil, now king of Portugal, with his Royal consort, particularly patronized her. She was engaged at the Opera-house at Lisbon for five years, and during her residence there, she improved herself by devoting her leisure hours to the study of music, and her singing became as scientific as it was melodious. Her allowance at the opera house at Lisbon was three thousand moidores per annum, besides a clear benefit. On her departure for Madrid, she was universally regretted ; and having enjoyed not only the patronage, but the esteem and confidence, of the princess of Brazil, she was furnished by that illustrious lady with letters of recommendation to the Royal Family of Spain, whose favor she experienced in the most ample degree, as well as that of all classes of people.

From Spain she went to Paris, where she married Monsieur Vallebraque ; she still, however, retained the name on which her celebrity had been founded, and by which her merits were known ; but she took the title of Madame, and dropped that of Signora.

The proprietors and managers of the Opera-house in the Haymarket,were eager to engage Madame CATALANI ; and in the year 1806, she consented to the offers they made her, of allowing her two thousand pounds annually ; and she appeared for the first time at the above theatre, in December, in 1806, in the part of Semiramide, where, to a crowded, most respectable, and scientific audience, she received those unanimous and reiterated applauses, which merit the most rare can only excite, and which imparted the most gratifying sensations to her own bosom.

Highly sensible of her very superior endowments, her emoluments were soon raised. In the year 1808, she was engaged to perform in serious operas, while Madame Dussek was to take the chief characters in those that were comic, if Madame CATALANI were indisposed. In 1809, Mr. Taylor, the manager of the King's theatre at that time, offered her six thousand pounds, with three benefits, payable in two equal payments, in 1810 and 1811, and this munificent proposal was for her performance for eighty nights, in serious opera. This offer, which, if made to any other than a CATALANI, we should call exorbitant, she thought proper to refuse. This conduct, which arose from the conduct of her brother not being engaged as first violin, together with the insolence and arrogance of her husband, M. Vallebraque, gave the public a kind of disgust, which though they yet highly estimated the harmonious talents of the lady, caused them to feel less of that warmth of friendship than they did at first, towards one they had so highly patronized. Her refusal of singing for a charitable institution was another cause of her loss of public favor ; but let no one judge harshly of Madame CATALANI on that account, since it is a certain fact that she sent privately, as a donation to that very charity, the sum of twenty guineas.

In excuse for that omission, it is stated that she had been attacked with one of those indispositions which the uncertainty of our atmosphere was continually bringing on her ; and who, especially a native accustomed to the pure and genial air of Italy, can encounter the fogs and frequent vicissitudes of the climate of Great Britain ?

When the late Mr. Harris opened his new theatre in Covent Garden, he engaged CATALANI to perform there occasionally. This engagement, was, however, totally done away by the O. P. affair. Having, therefore, no fixed salary, she performed at the grand music meetings at Oxford and Cambridge, and at several of the chief towns in the United Kingdoms, till she was induced to become the Directress of the Opera Comique, at Paris; a trust that she has fulfilled with science, with infinite credit to herself, and benefit to the concern. She has occasionally visited the Court of Vienna ; where her musical and vocal talents are held in very high estimation.

We cannot vouch for the late Emperor of France having much " music in his soul," but it is confidently asserted, that on his first hearing Madame CATALANI sing at Paris, he was so enchanted by the melody of her voice, that he sent her the next morning a present of two thousand Napoleons.

After an absence of seven years, she made her second appearance in England in July last, for the purpose of assisting in the vocal department at the coronation. She gave a concert, on Monday the 16th of July, at the Argyle-rooms, and was most enthusiastically greeted. Her voice is more beautiful, even stronger, than when we last heard her. In singing Rode's violin variations, an indescribable effect was produced on the audience by this extraordinary exercise of the human voice, which displayed at once her amazing rapidity, strength, and sweetness ; in fact, this must be pronounced the miracle of voice, and must be heard to be conceived. She looked remarkably well, and appeared highly gratified at seeing herself once again before a British audience.

Madame CATALANI gave another concert on Monday the 30th of July, the profits of which were given in aid to the funds of the Westminister General Infirmary, which at once displays the benevolence of heart, and must remove the unfounded prejudice imbibed by many, of her avarice, or that she will never exert her talents but for her own emoluments.

We have already said so much of CATALANI in our description of Mara and Billington, that our direct observations will necessarily appear shorter than they ought to be, and yet we shall find it impossible to escape tautology. The reader will therefore do us the justice to call to mind that our criticism has been, from a necessity incident to the subject, *comparative.*

In the first requisite—Intonation, CATALANI was as deficient as any pre-eminent singer we ever knew, a circumstance the more surprising, because we believe failure is more incident to thin voices, than to organs of such power, as Madame CATALANI's. Her *fausse note* was about Eb, we say about, for in the fluctuation of pitch to which the concerts of this country are subject, is impossible to fix a tone very definitively. Perhaps her general tune was affected by the force with which she was accustomed to sing, though it is hard to distinguish between her failure in the execution of passages, and in the more simple parts of her performance, because she excelled so far in the airs of agili-

ty, and indulged so continually in the introduction of most
elaborate and difficult ornaments, that she may almost be
said to have had no *cantabile* or plain style. Whatever
was the cause, she varied from the pitch frequently, although to common hearers the defect was lessened by the
prodigious volume and richness of her tone, and by the rapidity with which she skimmed along the liquid surface of
florid nototioc. We are inclined to suspect, that this lady
was seduced from the practice of plain notes too early, a
deviation, which all who are guilty of it, repent too late.
It is indeed a mistake that can never be atoned.

CATALANI was a singer for the Italian stage alone, and
fitted for no other department of vocal science. Her conception was purely theatrical, and when thus considered,
her style, as far as style was concerned, was certainly
grand and imposing. There are few instances of more vi-
vid intellectual expression, more chastely yet more effec-
tively embodied and delivered, than in some of the high
efforts of Madame CATALANI. Nor was her range confirmed to the great style, though there her forte lay. In the
lighter parts, such as *Susanna*, in Mozart's *Nozze di Figa-*
ro and *Aristea*, in *Il Fanatico per la Musica*, which were
alike excellent. The playfulness with which she could in-
vest the character of her ornaments contributed in no small
degree to the effect. She was a florid singer and nothing
but a florid singer, whether grave or airy, in the church,
orchestra, or upon the stage. But she could give an intellectual design, and set the stamp of mind upon these beautiful coruscations of her brilliant fancy, and nothing has
tended more to convince us of the possibility of marking
distinctly the passion, to illustrate which the ornament may
be applied, than the manner of gracing which CATALANI
could at pleasure adopt. It will not be stepping far out of
our way should we say, that the construction, boundless as

it is, of ornament, is more limited than the execution, and
that the manner of doing the passage, of accenting, retard-
ing, quickening, enforcing, or softening the notes, renders
it pathetic or pleasing at the will, and frequently according
to the physical powers of the singer.   Of such a kind do we
esteem the capital intellectual variety which Catalani exercised over this department of her art, and while she
bestowed her graces in more extreme and wanton profusion than any other singer we ever heard, there was nevertheless a general characteristic expression very delightfully defined, over almost all she did.   From this general
acknowledgment we must except the airs with variations,
which it was at once her honor and her disgrace to have
introduced into practice in England.   We use this phrase
of double interpretation, because her chiefest display of
agility was manifested in these efforts.—" *O dolce concen-
to*" and " *Nel cor piu non mi sento*" as she sung them, are
at one and the same time the most beautiful specimens of
simple, pathetic, and lively melodies converted into the
most exuberently florid songs of execution.   Such a means
of evincing her particular talent, shewed her extraordinary
facility, practice, and acquirement in the very worst possible way.   It was giving life to her execution by the com-
mission of a suicide upon her taste and judgment.   Madame
Catalani seems in this instance to have regarded the voice
as an instrument.   So poor a notion deprives the voice, of
its highest attributes, the voice being the finest of instruments, with the additional quality of giving force, feeling
and effect to all the images and passions which language is
able to convey.   Hence it happens that no application of
vocal power can be deemed legitimate, which has not the
expression of some sentiment or passion for its primary objects and impulse.   The selection of such airs as " *Nel cor*"
for such a purpose was therefore doubly erroneous.   It

degraded the vox humana to mere instrumentation, and it perverted and polluted the most exquisite specimen of genuine feeling to this vile purpose, when a harpsichord lesson or a fiddle concerto would have answered the purpose. Yet strange to tell, it was in these very songs that CATALANI drew more rapturous applause and perhaps more of the approbation of the entire mass of the public than from any other source.

Mere English critics are not competent judges of the power of CATALANI's elocution. No one indeed who has not resided abroad or been a constant attendant upon the Italian theatre, who has not mixed with the natives of that country, and learned to acquaint himself with their peculiarities of expression, can be a judge sufficiently skilled in the several requisites, or sufficiently liberalized, to pronounce upon her excellencies or defects in this essential particular.—Elocution in singing, rises infinitely beyond simple articulation, as it becomes the vehicle of mental impressions. English and Italian notions of the expression of various passions differ very materially, and we consider the ideas of this great actress not only to have been purely Italian, but also moulded by the Italian theatre alone. Upon the stage her personificaion was however more grand than touching. Her main defect in our eyes was the want of tenderness and pathos. She sometimes over-awed, but she never warmed or melted the heart. Mara was certainly the sovereign of expression ; Billington fell short of the grandeur and magnificence of CATALANI, but her deficiency arose out of the natural difference of voice ; the shade between CATALANI and Mara was intellectual ; CATALANI's natural organ we apprehend to have been more calculated for the expression of passion than that of Mara, but the conception ennobling whatever it lighted upon, was wanting. Her oratorio singing was the lowest of the three.

20

She literally had no apprehension of the true expression of English words, or the sentiments they represented. " *Holy holy Lord*," and " *I know that my Redeemer liveth*," from her lips invoked no warmer adoration, inspired no livelier faith in an English bosom. Yet CATALANI possessed strong feelings of devotion, and perhaps entertained the most extreme veneration for the Deity, the firmest belief and the most fervent piety of any singer that ever lived. She never entered a church or a theatre to perform without solemnly offering up a prayer for her success. When therefore we reason upon her failing to awaken the sympathy of her auditors we can only attribute it to the radical difference in the manner of expressing the same ideas that obtains between the natives of foreign countries and of our own. Mara was very early in life in England, and a large portion of the character of her mental acquirements is probably to be traced to that age ; CATALANI on the contrary had made all her associations before she came hither. Again, there may be, perhaps, a nearer approximation in natural constitution between the Germans and the English, than between the more ardent natives of southern climates, and the inhabitants of the " *ponitus toto divisos orbe Britannos*." All therefore that we must say specifically of CATALANI's elocution in singing, is that she was articulate, forcible, and powerful, occasionally light, pleasing, and playful, but never awfully grand, or tenderly touching to the degree that the art may be carried, or that Mara, actually with less power of voice did attain We consider CATALANI below Billington in the latter quality. In science she was so far inferior to both that the wonder among professors, is how she could possibly dare so much and succeed so well.

Many of our observations upon her execution have already entered into our previous pages. It was, however, certainly most extraordinary, while it had in it qualities that were peculiar to herself. Madame CATALANI with more velocity, more force, more brilliancy, and more variety than either Mara or Billington, was below them both in neatness, precision, and finish. Her facility seemed rather the effect of a natural aptitude or genius, than of study and labour. As a proof of this truth, she was far more dexterous in the introduction and execution of ornament, than in the performance of passages of agility set down by the composer. Her singing Handel amounted to a complete demonstration of what we assert. It wanted not a certain expression of her own, but it was for that very reason almost destitute of that of the author. Her divisions were not given with the vocal declamation, which we consider his mechanical passages to be endowed withal, at least we recollect no instance neither in her performance of his works nor those of any other composer, if we be allowed to except the bravura, " *Gratias agimus,*" which exhibited a wonderful example of force and rapidity combined. Her fertility in the invention of graces was richly abundant, but she took more satisfaction in producing pleasure through surprise than by any other legitimate method. The frequent introduction of triplets, arpeggios, and a succession of chromatic intervals was an effort of this description. At the same time the profusion was apt to cloy, and seemed to indicate [a propensity by far too common among artists] the desire to display every species of talent and acquisition as it were at once.

Distant spectators would have conceived that all the wonders CATALANI effected were wrought with so much ease as scarcely to deserve the name of effort. But such was by no means the case. It was perceptible to closer observers that the exertion was so vast as to excite the muscular powers of the head, throat, and chest into very violent action. In the execution of passages the under jaw

was in a state of continual agitation, in a manner too, generally thought incompatible with the production of pure
tone from the chest, and inconsistent with legitimate execution. This extreme motion was also visible during the shake,
which CATALANI used sparingly, however, and with little
effect. Indeed we must again remark that neither of these
great singers understood the value and importance of this
delicate and beautiful ornament but Mara. We call to
mind no other circumstances peculiar to CATALANI that can
enable our readers to form a better estimate of her powers, or tend to fix a permanent memory of the pleasure and
the wonder she raised, than those we have thus related.
We chose to compare these very high and gifted individuals because it is only by a comparison of great singing *in-
ter se* that criticism can be expected to establish any thing
approaching to a true standard of general or of indiviual
merit. There may be at the first glance an invidious appearance in adopting such a method, but it vanishes when
we recur to the impossibility of forming any accurate judgment of the merits of the one or the other, except by a
minute measurment of the several faculties, and a subsequent estimate of the relation they bear to each other.
We hope we have weighed them together justly and
truly.

The style of Mara was the great style, in its genuine application, and demonstrated by the natural faculties, and
the most elaborate and scientific acquirements. Mrs. Billington lowered the public taste a degree in the scale, by
the introduction of her power of grácing and execution, in
the place of grander elements ; and Madame CATALANI has
rendered little beside the substitution of power and agility,
for dignity still more universally agreeable. It is to this
last singer that we owe the execrably bad taste of degrad-
ing the nobler functions of the human voice, to the mere

province of an instrument. She first introduced airs with
variations similar to the piano forte lessons, in diametrical contradiction to the just and proper employment of
the most touching of all sounds, and to the utter annihilation of the sense and feeling imparted to music by words.
If we are to be required to listen to the tones of the voice,
and the tone only divested of the best attribute for singing,
to the *vox et preterea nihil,* let us hear execution displayed
in solfeggi or in a bravura.

Nor let us be considered as too severe in our notions
with regard to the propagation of such vile taste. To preserve these canonized airs untouched is, as it were, a part
of the religion of music. Every thing that tends to loosen
our attachment to pure expression is, as we esteem it, a violation of the great and fundamental law of vocal art, which
is, to combine the effects of sense and sound. To draw off
our attention and rivet it to mere sound, destroys the better half.

Execution is certainly a source of pleasure, inasmuch as
it awakens our surprise, and is agreeable and legitimate
when made subservient to the great purpose of singing.—
But here its effect stops, and in true science, is only to be
regarded as one of the means, and certainly not the most
forcible means of expression. We entertain no doubt,
from a careful examination of Handel's and Haydn's songs
of division, that these composers looked upon it as a mere
vehement manner of declamation. Handel indeed appears
to have used it more frequently than Haydn ; but there is a
mechanical structure in his passages, which seems to fit them
for the style of execution we have attempted to point out
as a separate and distinct species, nor do we recollect an instance were he employs divisions that are not in strict accordance with, or do not set off the words more expressive-

ly, than plainer combination of notes would have done.*

The error, therefore, of which we complain, is radical.—
It is not a redundancy of ornament, but an absolute contempt of words as unmeaning appendages, and the reduc-
tion of the voice to mere instrumental performance. We
consider the female voice to be the most affecting of any,
and consequently by this mode of applying it, the loss is the
more excessive. There is a sort of moral sense in music
as well as in poetry, and if there be a duty appertaining to
professional exertions beyond the acquisitions of gain, it
lies in the just performance of the obligation this sense imposes. Nor will such considerations, in choosing a line of
study and practice, eventually derogate from the reputation
a singer obtains, because, although he may for a time fail
to shine forth with the glare and glitter that always at first
surrounds brilliant execution, he will in the end secure a
much more high and lasting degree of fame from the feelings and the judgment of all persons of sensibility and sound
taste.

SAMUEL WEBBE.

In the annals of musical science the name of WEBBE has
long been eminently conspicuous, and the homage of amateurs and connoisseurs has alike been offered to his genius

* There are curious examples of this remark to be found in
Handel's most sublime works.

recording some few brief particulars attaching to a name beloved, and so respected, we are proud to add our tribute of eulogy to the universal pœans which have graced his memory.

SAMUEL WEBBE, Esq. by his general as well as professional erudition, his acuteness of preception, and solidity of judgment, the impressiveness of his language, his universal philanthropy, the simplicity of his heart, and the dignified amenity of his manners, excited the admiration and love of all who enjoyed the happiness of his friendship or acquaintance. He afforded the extraordinary instance of a well spent life, in the most unlimited sense of the expression, and exhibited an example that is not often presented to our knowledge. Mr. WEBBE was born in 1740, of parents of high respectability, and moderately independent fortune; to increase which, his father went to Minorca, under some Government appointment, while he was yet an infant of scarcely twelve months old ; and having settled his establishment there, had already written to his wife, with her child to join him ; when before the preparations for their departure could be completed, the voyage was awfully terminated by other letters announcing his sudden death. Independent of the shock on his beloved wife, the event was followed by some unfair proceedings, and by the diversion of property from its rightful descent on the part of those who had the power of controling the disposal. Mrs. Webbe was thus reduced to a state of comparative penury, which proved disastrous to the future fortunes of her infant son. She could extend to him little advantage of education, but being intent upon rendering him capable of providing for himself, he was bound apprentice to a cabinet maker, at the very early age of eleven years. This arrangement, however, was so little to his taste, that no sooner were the seven long years elapsed, than he determined to abandon the workshop, and contemplated with infinite regret what he regarded as a total loss of a considerable and valuable portion of his early life.

Within a year after his emancipation, for such he always termed it, he lost his mother, and with her was bereft of the little means of support derived from her slender income. Thus destitute of any visible means of support, and still under twenty years of age, he turned his attention to the employment of copying music, as connected with an art of which he was passionately fond, but with which as yet he was totally unacquainted. He obtained his principal employment from Mr. Welcher, keeper of a well known old music shop in Gerrard Street, Soho, through whom he became acquainted with a musician of the name of Karle Barbent organist to the chapel of count Haslang, the Bavarian Ambassador, a professor of no particular skill, but from whom he rapidly acquired the rudiments of music, which his own intense study and observation soon enlarged into a thorough knowledge of that delightful art. At the expiration of his engagement as Mr. Barbent's assistant, for four years, he applied himself sedulously and constantly to the acquirement of Latin, in which he did not allow himself to be interrupted even by the necessity of copying music for a subsistence, though when fully employed, he would sit till past twelve at night, and return to it by five in the morning, for many days in succession. He followed the Latin, by the study also of French, still appropriating every moment of intermission from those employments suggested by necessity, and excited by an anxious thirst for self improvement, to the ardent study of music, of which he had now determined to make himself completely master. His necessities were augmented at the age of twenty three, by the addition of a wife, and in the following year of a child to share his scan-

ty earnings ; having been married to Miss Anne Plumb, at
St. Mary le-bonne church, on May 30th 1763 ; but as difficulties increased, so seemed also to increase his exertion
and perseverance ; and shortly after the birth of his first
child, he furnished himself with an *Italian* master. About
this time he also ventured to become a teacher of music,
and his progress in the art, fully warranted this arduous
undertaking, though he was even then but twenty-five years
of age, and it was but six years since his first acquaintance with rudiments.

About the year 1776, Mr. WEBBE was elected organist
to the king of Sardinia's chapel, in London, and after a few years established a choir there, which he enriched with many of his own compositions, most of which were
published. From this period scarcely a single year passed
without producing the reward of one, and often two prize
medals, down to the time when the Catch Club desisted
from affording such liberal encouragement to that most delightful and social description of vocal music, glees, &c.
His literary studies were however subsequently enlarged
by the successive acquisition of the German, Greek, and
Hebrew languages ; in the reading and understanding of
which last, he was acknowledged by his master, a venerable and skillful Rabbi, to be equal to himself. Although it
may seem of minor importance here to speak of his bodily
graces, it may be in point to shew that in the vast
range of objects which his ardent industry embraced,
these coadjutors were neither forgotten nor neglected : and
in truth, he long excelled in the manly and graceful exer-
cises of fencing and dancing. But superior to all these
faculties of the mind, and these graces of body, were
those indescribable excellencies, the simplicity, the tenderness, the thorough goodness of his heart. His works
were extremely numerous, as well as infinitely varied, hav-

21

ing written largely for the Catholic Church, of which he
was a member ; while his anthems are also in use in almost
every protestant cathedral in the country. He composed
also two or three operas, many quartetts, and instrumental
lessons ; numerous songs, some of them highly distinguished as public favorites, as " The Mansion of Peace," &c.
and glees innumerable, and so well known as to require no
formal eulogium. As an English composer, he will always
rank with Lock, Morley, Purcell, Arne, and the most eminent of the British school, while, as a man and a scholar,
his transcendant qualities raise him high among British
worthies.

On May 26, 1816, at his chambers in Gray's Inn, this
excellent and truly worthy man terminated a long life of
usefulness in his 76th year , and no one within his sphere of
action has been more admired for public talents, or esteemed for private virtues. His compositions are almost innumerable, and are all characterized by taste,
simplicity, and feeling, as well as by a profound
knowledge of his delightful and delighting art. Many of his glees, for precision of harmony, beauty, and expression, obtained and deserved the highest popularity ; and
he was ever ready to contribute his professional exertions
in aid of benevolence or friendship, For some years past,
his infirmities had prevented him from visiting his friends :
but he was esteemed too much to be forgotten. He had
also for a long time declined all musical composition, and
chiefly amused himself with a friend at the chess board.
Thus closing a long career of fame and distinction, at
peace with God and man, and bequeathing to his family the
proudest of all legacies, the blessing and the memory of
their father's virtues.

To the memory of Samuel Webbe, Esq.

Written by W. Lindley, Esq. and composed by
LORD BURGHERSH.

———

Chant we the requiem, solemn, sad, and sweet ;
And muse awhile amid the festive throng,
   Be joy's inspiring song.
Strew we the cypress boughs, the muse's seat ;
For he the Father of the varying lay,
Of pain and sickness long the suff'ring prey,
Sinks to the grave, and leaves unstrung the lyre,
Silent each liquid note——extinct its sacred fire !
   List to that plaintive strain !
Was it " Thy voice, O ! harmony *" that sung,
Anselmo's magic lyre unstrung—
Ne'er on th' enraptur'd verse to burst again
Those chords so sweetly wild, so full, so clear,
It was " thy awful sound !"—the distant bell,
Beats slow, responsive to the anthem's swell
That pours the parting tribute o'er his hallow'd bier.
" When winds breathe soft †" where rests Anselmo's clay,
Round our lamented minstrel's shrine !
Shall " forms unseen ‡" the deathless wreath entwine ;
Soft warbling is the breeze the tributary lay !

———

* " Thy voice O harmony," with awful sound.
       Webbes Glees.

† " When winds breathe soft along the silent deep,
        Ibid.

‡ " By fairy hands their knell is rung,
" By forms unseen their dirge is sung."
        Collins.

MISS STEPHENS·

The Father of this accomplished vocalist was a Carver and Gilder in Park Street, Grosvenor Square, London. The first rudiments of musical instruction Miss STEPHENS received from M. Lanza a teacher, who proceeded upon the genuine Italian method of forming the voice, he initiated the pupil very slowly, but very surely, in the elements. At a subsequent period her studies were conducted with a view principally to the dramatic exercise of the art, and a deviation from the principles which best conduce to form a perfect orchestra singer were deserted for the practice which contributes to the efforts the stage demands.

Miss STEPHENS remained his pupil many years, during which time she was brought out at the Pantheon. Her Father had reason to think M. Lanzas attention too remiss, both for his own interest, and for those of his pupil. Mr. Welsh was applied to, who saw the promise, and exerted himself vigorously to bring Miss STEPHENS sufficiently forward to appear at Covent Garden Theatre, with brilliant approbation. Nevertheless, in spite of this success it was questioned whether the warmth of feeling and the fertility of imagination which are indispensible to perfect dramatic performance are inherent in her nature. It is thus probably that her talent was misdirected. In this particular there is a very curious difference between the Italian school of singing and the English. To train a singer for the serious opera is to count the highest attributes of the art. Such a code of instruction appears by the universal powers of almost every legitimate Prima Donna, to include the qualities of an actress as well as the highest cultivation of the vocal requisites The first woman of the opera must understand the full value of applying dramatic effect to vocal expression of the passions. Singers generally, on the contrary, who are trained for the stage, consider only one branch of the profession. If they vocalize well, it is they think sufficient, and they seldom care to remember that Singers who aspire to move the affections of their hearers must accomplish their ends very much by means which are common to acting as well as singing—in short, by dramatic force, dramatic fire, dramatic feeling, dramatic elocution—and all these refined by the highest cultivation, science and polish of vocal superiority. Miss STEPHENS' imagination if originally susceptible of the fiery impulses to which it is essential to train the conception of one who is to pourtray by regulated tones the workings of all the passions, has been cooled rather than heated in the tempering ; and whether she sings upon the board of the theatre or in the orchestra, her whole performance appears subdued somewhat below the point necessary to fine expression. The quality of her tone is full and rich beyond that of any other performer. In songs however of touching expression she seems to want tenderness, the liquid sweetness, that steals the sense away in passages of pathos and passionate ecstacy.

From this property of her tone, from what it wants as well as from what it possesses, it is to be inferred that the peculiar bent of her talent is towards ballads and songs of simple declamation,—in a word, towards that particular style which is generally esteemed to be purely English,though the formation of her voice may have been conducted upon principles of the Italian teaching. The chastity of her style, and the limitation she lays upon her fancy, confine our estimation of Miss STEPHENS' science to what she abstains from, rather than allow us to measure it by what she affords or introduces, her ornaments are correct and pleasing, but seldom for nought or surprizing. From the whole of her performances, there results a certain grateful sense of pleasure, somewhat analogous to the sensations experienced and the sentiments inspired by the conversation of a polished sensible and well bred person With these attributes she enjoys her full share of patronage ; and her title to the regard she earns so industriously and so honourably is supported by a purity of mind and character correspondent to her professional manner. Such characters as Miss STEPHENS prove sufficiently that the public exercise of talent is not incompatible with the grace, the ornament, and all the virtues of domestic life.

JOACHIM ROSSINI.

Was born in the year 1791, at Pesaro, a small town in the papal dominions, on the gulph of Venice. The only portion he inherited from his father was his musical talents, which had been in some degree cultivated by that father ; his education was confined, and he first went on the Italian stage as an *amateur ;* but though ROSSINI now sings with taste and spirit, he had no success then as a public singer. He composed, however, detached airs, which were handed about in company, and their style was original and sprightly. He was next engaged by two or three amateurs to compose an Opera. He was then but a mere school boy in appearance, and the manager of the opera house entertained but a poor opinion of such a composer : his pat-

rons, however threatened the manager that they would
withdraw their patronage, if he did not give the
youth encouragement : he therefore consented to bring
forward this first operatic attempt. This was *L'inganno
Felice ;* it was in the reigning taste but there were
in it a charming duo, and many bright flashes of
genius. Soon after ROSSINI composed those his master pieces, namely *Il Tancredi, L' Italiana in Algeri,* and *Pietra
di Paragone.* The opera of *Tancredi* in particular, circulated rapidly through Italy : but ROSSINI had a strong aversion to composing overtures, and actually did not compose
one for *Tancredi ;* this opera was therefore preceded by
one or other of the two overtures composed for the other
two operas. ROSSINI went to Milan, and there he assumed
the high rank he now holds among composers. It was for
the Milanese that he wrote *La Pietra di Paragone.* It was
at Milan he became a general favorite amongst the most
beautiful women ; and the ladies of rank dispensed with the
attentions of their noble cecisebos, and the favorite *Cava-
liere Servente,* was the young and engaging composer ; but
the most beautiful among them all made him her captive,
while he rendered her the first musician in all Italy ; and
we are told that when seated by her at the piano, love inspired him to compose the greatest number of those airs
since introduced in his operas.—When he quitted Milan he
went to see his family, for whom he always evinced much
affection ; he had never been known to write letters to any
one except to his mother, to whom they were addressed, to
the *Illustrious Signora Rossini, mother to the celebrated composer, &c. &c.* Certainly he has received homage for his
exquisite talents ever since he was eighteen, and must be
conscious of his own celebrity, though he often speaks jest-
ingly of his fame.

About this time that he visited Pesaro, he was exempted

from the laws of conscription. The minister of the interior proposed to the viceroy of Italy, an exception in favor
of ROSSINI, who, at first objected, but at length yielded to
the wishes of the public. ROSSINI afterwards departed for
Bologna ; there a very rigid dictatorship is exercised over
music, and he was reproached with violating the rules of
grammatical harmony in his compositions. ROSSINI acknowledged they were in the right, but that none of those
faults would have remained, if he had read his MS. twice
over. " But," added he, " I have only six weeks to compose an opera ; the first month is devoted to dissipation,
and it is but during the last fortnight that I compose every
morning a duo, or air, which is to be rehearsed on that very evening. How then will you have me perceive the minute errors in the accompaniment ?"

The musical rigorists still, however, made a great bustle about these sins of harmony, though they are scarcely
perceptible to the ear that is listening to ROSSINI's music ;
but it was envy at finding a handsome, indolent youth, of
about twenty, towering so much above them ; he was
doomed, however, to experience an attack of a very different kind.—His Milanese admirer quitted her splendid palazzo, her husband, her children, and her fortune, and one
morning rushed into the room then occupied by ROSSINI.
Scarcely had they met, when the door again opened, and
in came one of the wealthiest and most beautiful women in
Bologna ! ROSSINI, like Macheath, laughed at them both,
sung a lively air, and made his escape.

He was so successful at Bologna, that he received offers
from every town in Italy. He generally demanded for an
opera, a thousand francs, (rather better than forty pounds)
and he generally wrote three or four in a year. From
1810 to 1816 he visited all the principal towns in Italy: on his
arrival he was welcomed by the dilletanti of the place ; the

first thirteen days he devoted to his friends, dining out, and shrugging his shoulders at all the nonsense he was obliged to set to music ; for ROSSINI, as may well be imagined, with his good taste, was always an excellent judge of poetry. When he had been in town about three weeks, he would refuse invitations, and set himself seriously to study the voices of the performers. He made them sing at the piano, and when he had acquired an accurate knowledge of their vocal powers, he began to write. He generally rose late, and would pass the day in composing, while his friends were conversing round him ; but it was after returning from their parties at a late hour, that shutting himself up in his chamber, he has been visited by his most brilliant inspirations, these he would hastily put down on scraps of paper, and then arrange them in the morning.

The mind of ROSSINI is remarkable quick ; when he was composing his Moise, he was asked if he meant to make the Hebrews sing in the same way that they chaunt in the synagogues. He was struck with the idea, and when he went home, he composed a magnificent chorus, which begins with a kind of nasal twang, peculiar to the synagogue; but his facility in composing is not the most extraordinary of his qualifications. Ricordi, the principal music seller in Italy, has made a fortune, by the sale only of ROSSINI's works whose genius is fitted for the pleasurable ; for indulgence is often the ground work of his finest airs ; his great misfortune, however, is that he does not give sufficient dignity and plaintiveness to the passion of love, but treats it as an affair of common gallantry, yet it is his so often stooping to light and emphemeral graces that has rendered him such a favorite at the Parisian theatre.

Last year ROSSINI was to have presided at the king's theatre in the Hay-market, but his passion for Italy, or, perhaps, his natural indolence, there detained him. This year, however, he has crossed the Alps, and presides at Vienna. He is next solicited by the Parisians. He may perhaps, when exhausted by their admiration, try the opulence and patronage of the encouragers of musical talent in London.

Rossini has lately married, and, like many other men of genius, precisely the reverse to what might have been expected. The lady was Senora Colbrano, a Spaniard, but a singer by profession, beauty she was never possessed of, and has now lost her voice with her youth, for she is no longer young ; but since her marriage, she performed at Vienna, when Rossini directed the Opera ; her voice was so feeble that it was tuneless, and the proud Senora was in great danger of being hissed, but respect and regard to the husband saved the wife·

We have before spoke of the natural affection of Rossini towards his parents, and we cannot close this sketch without citing the following proof. In Italy, when Rossini presides at the piano forte during the first three representations of one of his operas, he receives afterwards his eight hundred or one thousand francs. He then rests himself a week or ten days ; he is then invited to a general dinner, given by almost the whole town, and then sets off with a portmanteau full of music paper, for another town. On the success of an opera, this affectionate man writes to his mother, and sends her and his aged father the two thirds of what he has received.

When this composer sets out upon his task ; he feels an importunate diffidence ; he invents, combines, separates, re-casts, and fails of excellence through excessive care. But as he advances, his work grows up around him, he becomes heated with his subject, his ideas multiply and he feels the God. In such moments he is freed from his shackles, he breaks out like the eagle from the cloud, and

feels the full strength of his wings. Rossini is little above
the middle height, very large in his make, and somewhat
corpulent, his countenance is open, grave, and intelligent,
his head is of extraordinary dimensions, his forehead finely
expanded and rising to a majestic height, but sloping a little backwards ; his eyes are a light brown, dull and medi-
tative, his whole appearance is far from common, yet does
not quite declare the composer of Othello. A Craniolo-
gist, without knowing him, spent one day in examin-
ing his head, and, at last declared " there was nothing particular in the organic construction, but perhaps, he might
have some inclination for music." He is frank and affa-
ble in his manners, easy of access to strangers, fond of
hearing and relating anecdotes, and best pleased with those
associates who will grant him as much talent in other subjects as in music. His health is not good ; he says himself
that in his youth he indulged too freely in pleasures from
which he should have refrained, and he complains of being
obliged to work for a livelihood, although his circumstances are generally understood to be easy. The facility
with which he composes, is astonishing. In a room half
full of people, talking to one, listening to another, he scrib-
bles on with twice the rapidity of an ordinary copyist, and
very seldom returns to consider or correct. He frequently
changes his sheet as though his ideas crossed one another ;
after writing ten or fifteen bars, a new vein of fancy opens
before him, and he seizes fresh paper to secure the happy
moment. There are persons in the world who laugh at the
raptures of the musician, and sordidly imagine that music
is merely a sensual gratification—Let them cast away such
belief.—Music is not sensual, it feeds the soul with one of
its purest aliments, and can infuse thoughts and feelings
which language cannot describe.

MRS. SALMON.

Few singers have appeared, who had the power to bestow such universal pleasure, without exciting any very deep or intense interest through the stronger affections, as this lady. She now takes rank with the very first of concert singers, and is confessedly amongst the most attractive to a general audience. There are few persons to whom her enchantments are unknown as a singer, so extended has been the fame of her talents, that there is scarcely a provincial meeting of any consideration at which Mrs. SALMON is not engaged to assist. As this has been the case for some seasons past, her merits may be said to be universally known.

An opinion has been entertained, that peculiar organization is in some sort hereditary, or at least partaken by various branches of the same family. Mrs. SALMON is a member of a family celebrated for vocal as well as general musical ability. Her first master was John Ashley, but time, practice, and observation appear to have been her most capable instructors. With all her acquisitions she certainly belongs to no school. She sings English and Italian with the same brilliancy of tone, and with the same facility, the two circumstances that form the characteristics by which every body sees the effects of this lady's performances.

Mrs. SALMON's intonation is very correct, though singing with male voices, it has in some instances been known to sharpen. It is however well known, that intonation inclining to be sharp rather than flat, bestows a superior brilliancy. It is analogous to the elevation of the general pitch of which instrumentalists are known to be always so desirous. In her tone lies the delight. Her voice possesses neither extraordinary compass nor volume, but it comes the nearest to the tone of musical glasses, if we can imagine that sound to be somewhat thinned and refined. "How," says a critic, " shall we find words to convey any notion of the syren who steals away the soul by tone so liquid, resonant, brilliant and delicious, that it leaves us scarcely any power to search beyond the pleasure we derive from the mere pulses of the sound."

Mrs. Salmon felictiously disables the severity of judgment. Clearness, beauty, rapidity, polish, invention, and taste are her attributes. Though never grand, and seldom, if ever, pathetic or touching, though never extorting the tribute of applause by sudden, powerful, and irrisistible appeals to the imagination or to the heart, she nevertheless captivates by sweetness, delicacy and uncommon ease.

MR. VAUGHAN.

Mr Vaughan is a native of Norwich, and he received the first rudiments of his musical education in the choir of the cathedral church. There were at that time subscription concerts upon a good scale, where the best secular music was performed under the direction of an amateur, and at these, young Vaughan sung with great applause. His voice, his countenance, and his manners, were alike prepossessing, and what adds interest to the relation, his father died and left him an orphan very young, at the very instant when the first notes of a concert for his benefit were performing. He was immediately befriended and protected. Dr. Beckwith, a very sound musician, then the organist of the Cathedral and St. Peter's and the most esteemed teacher of his day, continued to instruct him ; but he was still more fortunate in the friendship of a clergyman, deeply learned in the science and enthusiastically fond of it, who used such exertions to forward his promotion as belong only to warm disinterested affection. His merits aided by such assistance, soon translated him to the chapel of Windsor, and he has gradually gone on till he arrived at the eminent distinction of succeeding Mr. Harrison in the choirs and concerts of the metropolis. We have deviated from our tract into private anecdote, because we are desirous not to withhold what is so honorable to all the parties.

We are now to consider Mr. VAUGHAN in the high professional light he has placed himself. His intonation is mathematically correct and the clue to a precision so difficult to attain is to be found in the accurate knowledge he possesses of the extent of his power and in the rigorous austerity with which he limits his efforts to his faculties. The nice application of this rule of judgment is seen at the very commencement of an analysis of his qualities.—It will be found to accompany us at every step of our progress, and to predominate by its general bearing over every other element of his excellence, natural or acquired. Nature, exercise and taste, are all employed in the formation, preservation, and practice of tune, although it is very common to attribute perfection or approach to perfection in this particular to nature alone or to the ear as we familiarly say. But in truth ear is perhaps the least concerned at

last.   At first we regulate the scale by this faculty, but it is
exercise, that in the second stage confirms the organs of
sound and fixes them to just degrees by the force of habit ;
and finally is the knowledge of what stress these organs
will bear, that teaches us to confine the imagination within the bounds which nature has assigned to the functions of
the throat.   It will therefore easily be estimated for how
considerable a portion of knowledge, observation, and ability, we give a singer credit when we grant to him that his
intonation is mathematically correct.

Now we are about to aim at the description of Mr.
VAUGHAN's tone, we feel all the difficulty which the want of
precise terms, the necessity for a technical language of
sound, impose upon us.   We can call to mind neither
voice nor instrument that bears any resemblance to his.   It
is perhaps neither so rich nor so sweet as Mr. Harrison's,
but we should describe it as naturally more pure, if its being less modified may entitle it to such a distinction, more
free and quickly formed, less brilliant, though more
penetrating and various, not less ductile, certainly more
powerful, less adapted to tenderness, better fitted for the
expression of passion, deep pathos, and declamatory passages as well as for the rapid and forcible execution of divisions, and equally suited to light and delicate ornament.
Still we find that we can convey no definite and precise
idea of the voice.   If we say that we think it differs from
other tenor voices in the manner that Mrs. Billington's dif-
fered from those of the generality of female singers, or that
it partakes neither of the reed nor the string in any remarkable degree, we do not know whether we shall be
more exact, though we think the description is susceptible
of all these destinctions.   If adopting the fanciful illustrations of Sir Isaac Newton's supposition by a modern writer we should endeavour to assign a particular color as

analogous in its effect : we should not add a tittle to the
likeness. Our readers must therefore be content to perceive that we have not spared our pains in hunting for si-
militudes and to discover that words will not convey any
more precise idea of tone. We have, however established
already a standard of comparison and we shall go on to
complete the graduation of the scale by the notice of particular effects. The recitative and air " *Oh ! loss of sight*"
and "*Total eclipse*" from Samson, we consider to be the finest of Mr. VAUGHAN's performances, because the composition in itself is majestically simple though pathetic to the
very depths of pathos, and because there is nothing that requires so much elevated dignity of tone as well as conception and execution as this unadorned simplicity. If we regard the words they are the plainest but the most natural
and therefore the most touching description of the mental
suffering of the blind champion in servitude and chains.
This dignified simplicity it is that constitutes at once the
difficulty and the praise of singing Handel. The shades of
passionate enunciation are so nicely and intimately blended,
they melt into darker and darker hues from the first strain
of complaining sorrow to the climax of reproachful anguish
and misery in the exclamatory reflection,

" Why thus deprived thy prime decree ?
Sun, moon, and stars are dark to me !"

that there is no song within our remembrance requiring
more peculiar, more gradual, more delicate, nor more passionate expression of tone as well as general manner, than
" *Total Eclipse.*" Mr. VAUGHAN is here pre-eminently
great over all his predecessors and competitors. He exceeds Mr. Harrison in force and pathos, Mr. Braham in
dignity, temperance and delicacy. Mr. VAUGHAN is not a
singer that takes by storm. As a very fine female singer of
the present day and still finer judge of singing has been

heard to say of Madame Camporese, " she steals upon
you ;" he first possesses himself of your heart, and he afterwards satisfies your understanding. This is much the
work of tone. His is not the rapid, bold, irrisistible draw-
ing of Mortimer, but the finely-laid picture of exquisite
propriety, grace, feeling, and finish, where may be seen
the true taste and talent of the artist subdued and tempered by study and acquaintance with all the principles of the
art. The opening recitative of the Messiah " *Comfort ye
my people*," and the succeeding air " *Every valley shall be
exalted*," are entitled in our esteem to equal praise, though
dissimilar in the class of sentiments to which they are addressed. " *The Soldier's Dream*" and " *Alexis*" are alike
inimitable and inestimable in the chaste and beautiful cantabile style of tone, mixed however with sensibility, elegance, and delightfully chosen ornament.

A name appears to be wanting for Handel's songs of division—we mean such as " *Why does the God of Israel
sleep ?*" from Samson, or " *Thou shalt dash them*" from the
Messiah. The Italian term " airs of agility" fails us, because it does not imply the powerful expression which we
venture to call vocal declamation, and which forms the
characteristics of those compositions, for if lowered to
mere execution, they forfeit all their true and original design. Critics who deem these divisions to be merely of
mechanical construction, have never heard Madame Mara
in " Rejoice greatly," or Mr. VAUGHAN in " Why does the
God of Israel sleep." Mr. VAUGHAN images throughout
every note of the most harrassing divisions, the rapid and
impetuous thoughts which impel Samson to commune within himself, to raise himself up before his Creator, almost
to remonstrate, and to point the vengeance which is to
hurl his enemies to their destruction.

23

We consider Mr. VAUGHAN to be a genuine English singer ; his tone in Italian music is not transmuted to that of Italian formation, and therefore his singing may be thought to want the foundation of the style, he is thorought acquainted with the difference of the two styles, and though he executes Italian music well, in every other respect, we can but applaud the good sense that confines him to his proper excellence.

Mr. VAUGHAN realizes an image of perfection in the vocal art, which had begun to think was unnecessary and not to be found but in the hopeless contemplation of ideal possibility. His singing assures us that the chastity of English taste, the manly eloquence of English elocution and the genuine pathos of English expression may be combined with the purity and sweetness of Italian tone, and the grace of of Italian elocution.

N. STEIBELT.

N. STEIBELT, was born at Berlin in the year 1756. He very early displayed a great disposition for music, and the then King of Prussia being made acquainted with his de-cided ability for this science, placed him under the instruction of the celebrated Kirnberger, who was then at Berlin. Under this master he rapidly improved, and laid the foundation of future excellence.

STEIBELT's compositions for the Piano forte are excessively numerous. They consist of Concertos, sonatas,

pot pourries, and airs with variations. His fourth opera of
Sonatas are held in high estimation, and also his Studio
published in England.

While this Composer was at Paris he wrote *Le Retour de
Zephir*, a ballad and an opera called *La Princess de Baby-
lone*, both of which were performed at the Imperial Academy of Music with success. This opera was his last public performance previous to his departure for St. Petersburgh. During his stay he composed for the Theatre Fey-
deau, *Romeo & Juliet*, an opera which was received with
universal applause. While in London, in 1797, he performed with Viotti at the opera Concerts under the direction of Salmon. On the 26th January 1805, his Ballad *La
Latier e* or *Blanche Renine de Castile*, was performed at the
opera house, it was allowed to possess considerable merit.

STEIBELT finally went to St. Petersburg, where his ability received that encouragement which eminent merit demands. He died in the early part of the present year 1824.

RAYNER TAYLOR.

MR. RAYNER TAYLOR the organist and Composer ; One
of the most accomplished musicians in this or any other
country. Born, I believe in London, he entered at an early age, the Kings's singing school, as one of the boys of the
Chapel Royal : an institution that has sent forth much
valuable talent to the world. In this capacity he often
attended occasions which have since become historical
events, such as the funeral of Handel in 1759—That of

George the second in 1760—as well as the marriage and coronation of George the third and his estimable consort. Upon leaving the school, he was immediately in active employment as composer, vocalist, organist and harpsichord performer [Piano fortes not being there known.] Subsequently, for many years, he was established at Chelmsford, a large town in the county of Essex, where he was organist at the church and had an immense round of teaching, both at the principal female academies in private families. From this he was called to be the composer and director of the music to the Sadlers Wells theatre, a pleasing place of amusement, open during the summer months, which began to rise somewhat above the level of a mere show box for rope dancing, tumbling &c. and for which it was no less indebted to Mr. Taylor as composer, than to Lonsdale, who had assumed the office of author, as well as that of stage manager ; so that while the burlettas and pantomimes were formed upon some historical fact or passing occurrence, or had some classical allusion, eminent professors of music who visited this place of amusement to pass a leisure hour were astonished to find the little orchestra well disciplined, correct and effective, and were delighted with the pleasing yet scientific style of the music.

Mr. Taylor's song of " *A Sailors life at sea*," in a piece which represented the distress and return of the Guardian Frigate in most impressive dumb show,—and the ear tickling and the comic trio of " *Chin chet quaw*" sung in a pantomime exhibiting chinese manners and scenery received for several seasons. On every night, a certain *encore ;* and in a spectacle founded upon events then passing in France, the solemn and impressive solo and brilliant chorus that was sung upon the scene representing Louis the XVI. as taking the oath in the champ de mars constantly produced peals of applause.

About 1792, he emigrated with his family to America, and passed some time in the southern states ; but in 1793, he settled in Philadelphia where he has since remained, and where by age and infirmity, he has retired from public life.

Mr. TAYLOR's talents are various. As a composer, he stands upon the highest ground both as to science and originality, as well as to knowledge of effect, and in every respect is certainly highly entitled to public favour. But the best of his compositions were consigned to his shelves ; yet of those he published in this country. " *The faded Lilly,*" and the " *Beech Tree's petition,*" are delightful specimens of that melodious flow of air and harmony which formed the style of the last century.

As an organist he is second to no one. Any person acquainted with the true style of organ playing who has ever heard Mr. TAYLOR, will testify to this. Not his voluntaries alone, but each passing interlude to a common psalm tune was full of taste and ingenuity. But on various occasions, after church service, when he has obliged a favoured few who remained for the purpose, with extemporaneous effusions, a never failing strain of harmony and science would burst upon the senses. His ideas flowed with wonderful freedom in all the varieties of plain chant, imitation and fugue. Subject follows subject in quick succession, through all the mazes of modulation by the hour together. But I am sorry to be compelled to bear testimony to the fact, that his talents were not of the marketable kind. Scientific organ playing and shelves groaning under manuscript files of overtures, operas, anthems, glees &c. were neither productive of fame nor emolument to their worthy possessor· The drudgery of teaching and a scanty organ salary have been his only recompense.

As a vocalist, Mr. Taylor has not met with that approbation to which his talents so justly entitle him. This, in a great measure, is supposed to arise from his always selecting comic songs for his public exhibitions, and the circumstance of his singing not being in the fashion of the day. In short, many of his warmest admirers have regretted that so much talent should stoop to the performance of a Vauxhall ballad ; yet his merriment and vivacity in glees and catches of a humorous nature, have often added to social merriment. Sometimes among particular friends he would in perfect playfulness sit down to the piano forte and extemporize an Italian opera, giving no bad specimen, though a highly carricatured one, of that fashionable entertainment. The overture, recitative, songs and dialogue, by singing alternately in the natural and falsetto voice were all the thought of the moment, as well as the words which were nothing but a sort of gibberish with Italian terminations. Thus would he often in sportive mood throw away ideas sufficient to establish a musical fame.

T. S. WEBB.

This gentleman was a distinguished amateur in Music, and attained a high degree of celebrity, having been appointed the *first President of the Boston Handel and Haydn Society*, an institution under whose auspices, were laid a foundation which aspires to an eminent rank among the first of musical societies in this country.

Col. WEBB was the son of the late Samuel Webb. He was born in Boston, 1771, and shared the advantages of the public Latin School, by his rapid improvement, he became a proficient in the French language. Endowed by the bountiful Creator, with a mind above the common rank, the sweetness of his disposition, and the amiableness of his manners, while they procured for him the esteem of his instructors, and young associates, riveted also the parental affections, and strengthened the hope, that he would one day become both an ornament and a blessing to society.

The early buddings of his genius were soon discovered in the poetry of his youthful pen, and rewarded by the smile of approbation, which they excited. As an occupation congenial to his natural taste for mental improvement, he, at a suitable age, served an apprenticeship at the printing business in this city. Being thus qualified, he left the delights of home, and removed to Keene in New Hampshire, and thence to Albany in the state of New-York. He married a Miss Martha Hopkins of Boston, and had five children, three of which, with their mother died, after which, he married the sister of his wife. From Albany he removed to Providence R. I. where he acquired, from his personal activity and industry, a handsome property in a domestic cotton manufactory. With an intention to increase his wealth, he embarked a considerable portion of his property in machinery for the weaving of Cotton Goods, in the Western Country. He was about to settle in Ohio, hoping there to meet with greater success, where there was less competition, and to arrive at that enviable state of pecuniary independence which he had despaired of obtaining in New-England. He was on his way to Columbia, the place he had selected for his future residence, when he died.

Thus departed from the scene of his mortal labors and affections, a gentleman who was respected by the public,

honored by his acquaintance, and loved with the fondest
enthusiasm by his friends. In him were embodied a soul
of feeling and philanthropy : an understanding clear and
penetrating ; a disposition, kind and complacent, a taste,
exquisitely delicate and refined.

As a member of the masonic brotherhood, he was every
where known ; for those who had witnessed his personal
labors, had received the benefit of them, in the explana-
tions and illustrations which he published, and which are
received in most Lodges in our country as a manual of mo-
rality and religion. He had studied masonry as a science,
and found that it might be made auxiliary to the noblest
purposes, and his example was a powerful witness, that its
tenets might be incorporated with every action, and give
life, spirit, purity, and honor to the most exalted as well as
to the humblest occupations of man. He was not a free-
mason in theory only ; his daily pursuits were a practical
commentary on the usefulness and internal worth of the
principles he professed and advocated. His researches into the remote history of the fraternity were fruitful in the
production of information, instruction and amusement, to
others as well as to himself ; and he would have done violence to his urbane and social feelings to have kept for a
moment from his companions and friends a scrap of history, an anecdote, a maxim, or an observation which had afforded pleasure to himself. The continual advances he was
making in masonry as a science, and the facility and scru-
pulousness with which he applied every moral obligation to
practice, had procured him some of the highest distinctions
in the power of his brethren to confer. These honors
he wore with dignity and modesty ; not using them as
means to gratify ambition or disseminate the seeds of inno-
vation. His authority was exercised with mildness, and

those over whom he was called to preside were never made
to feel that office conferred power on the man, but they
saw that the man imparted honor to the office. Commendation from him was felt to be valuable, and admoni-
tion, whenever employed, was expressed in terms that commanded veneration, and strengthened the ties of affection.

To the other endowments of nature, the munificent author of good, added the gift and taste for music, which
from his early youth, began to make their appearance ;
and his succeeding life has shown that his whole mind and
soul was attuned to harmony, every chord of which, vibra-
ted at the slightest touch, and gave the softest tones of music's power.

To vocal and instrumental music both inclined ; the fife
and the flute were among the choicest companions of his
childhood ; they cheered his evening walks, and supplied
the place of a friend in retirement. To sing, ever gave
him the sweetest delight, and his personal exertions while
they have excited emulation, have also tended to enlarge
our ideas of a most pleasing and ennobling science. It
may be remarked with much truth, that his urbanity of
manners and persuasive conciliating disposition, as President of the Handel and Haydn, and Vice President of the
Phil-harmonic Societies, evinced powers of mind peculiarly calculated to the discharge of those offices. The ability with which he carried into execution the laudable objects of these meritorious institutions, must be universally
acknowledged, and to his endeavours may in a great measure be attributed their success. His influence in guiding the
versatile talents of their numerous members, and in commanding the good opinion of his associates, was unexampled. He possessed the faculty of surmounting difficul-

24

ties, of removing objections, allaying jealousies not unfrequent among musical men, and at the same time of securing the confidence, which he had once inspired. He was an affectionate husband, a kind father, and a fond brother. His associates in the musical part of the community will acknowledge the propriety of applying to his memory this just effusion of the bard.

" Each mingled chord, each wandering note,
His magic touch would oft combine ;
As dyes that o'er the azure float ;
Together in the rainbow shine !
If music now his soul inspire
Harp of the winds, thou art his lyre !

MISS BROADHURST.

To do that justice to the great professional talents and private virtues of this very estimable young lady which they so richly merit, is a task which none but those who knew her intimately should undertake.

Miss Broadhurst was born in London, and when very young became the pupil of Mr. Percy, a distinguished singing master and respectable composer. While yet a child she appeared at several readings and recitations which were then a fashionable amusement, and which were interspersed with music. Here she astonished the audience with her premature vocal powers. In a few years afterwards, when only in her sixteenth year she was brought forward by the manager of the covent garden theatre in the year 1791 among many

others as a candidate for public favour upon the departure
of Mrs. Billington for Italy. Here she seemed to be the
only one that succeeded.—She also accepted an engagement at the Lent Oratorios, a situation highly creditable to
the talents of even the oldest and most accomplished singer.
During her engagement at Covent Garden Theatre, a circumstance took place which, while it reflects high honor upon her professional abilities, proves that " music has
charms to sooth the savage breast," forms an event that
ought to be recorded in both musical and Theatrical history.

In the year 1792, when Covent Garden had undergone
some splendid alterations and improvements, the manager
raised the prices of admission and abolished the one shilling
gallery This caused a riot, and though not so dreadful as the
more recent one of the O. P. Dance, yet it was sufficient
for two or three nights to render each drama a pantomime.
The opera of the Duenna succeeded. Miss Broadhurst
was the Clara, and no sooner did she begin the delightful
song of " When Sable Night," than the sweetness of her
tones caught the attention of the audience. The desire to
listen rendered them mute—a rapturous peal of applause
followed with a loud and unanimous encore and which so
much engaged their attention, that in their profound admiration of the singer, they forgot their real or supposed
wrongs, and peace continued on that and every succeeding
evening.

In 1793, Miss Broadhurst, accepted offers from the
manager of the new theatre in Philadelphia to appear upon
his boards, and was for several years one of the principal
ornaments and most admired and popular characters of
that establishment. She also appeared in New-York, Boston, Baltimore, and Charleston, and at the latter place

was seized with the prevailing disease, where she left this for another and better world.

Miss BROADHURST was a regularly bred musician and independent of her vocal excellence was a respectable pianiste. Her voice was remarkably sweet and clear—her time, exactness itself—her intonation correct, rather inclined to sharp without being positively so, a quality said by some late critics to give great brilliancy of effect and which is ascribed by them to the present much admired English Vocalist, Mrs. Salmon. Her compass was about B. below the staff, to C. in alto. Her style of singing was various ; from the ballad to the Italian Bravura, she was equally excellent, and was an admirable singer of the airs of Handel which confessedly try the abilities of the best vocalist, and test their greatest powers. Perhaps her chaste and brilliant performance of Handel's " Sweet bird," with her bird-like shake, and Gillingham's accompaniment on the violin, were among the most delicious musical treats ever presented to an American public.

She was always eagerly engaged for every concert that took place in any city in which she happened to reside. Her concert singing was if possible, superior to her theatrical, and such was her popularity, that it was only necessary to announce her name to insure generally respectable assemblies. Her lady-like appearance in approaching an audience can never be forgotten, nor did it ever fail to inspire every hearer with peculiar pleasure. Exquisite as her singing was, it seemed to impart additional delight by her charming and modest deportment.

Miss BROADHURST was more fortunate than most dramatic vocalists ; Inheriting some property in the British funds, and always commanding from her high musical accomplishments, a portion of Scholars both for the piano forte

and vocal music, she was in a great degree independent of
the theatre, and invariably retired from dramatic engagements whenever terms, situation, or other circumstances
were not agreeable to her wishes.

In private life, Miss BROADHURST gave no indications of
the professional woman. Artless and amiable—cheerful
and engaging. In her deportment kind and communica-
tive, of a disposition as universally admired for its sweetness and urbanity, as her principles for their purity, liberality and correctness. She was an ornament to her sex.
Displaying a mind originally well formed and subsequently
refined and replete with various reading and knowledge of
the world. The tender and unceasing solicitude which, in
the midst of the most pressing duties she showed for an excellent mother, gave to her character that nameless combination of strength and softness so beautiful in woman. Nor
was her distinguished worth unknown or unappreciated.
She was no less the delight of the young than respected
and beloved by the more advanced. In every light in
which her virtues were displayed, they shed a lustre on all
around her. Happy would it be, did every instructor unite
in an equal degree, professional talents with moral rectitude,
and leave the same solid and purifying impression on the
public as well as youthful mind—and happy would it be
should her example be made a model for their imitation.

The early death of this " sweet singer," has not only left
a charm in the musical world difficult to be filled, but has
caused a deep and personal regret to every lover of that
" first of arts." Her public services will be remembered
with the liveliest gratitude by all who have derived improvement from her abilities, and her private character
will be impressed on the hearts of her numerous friends
while they can throb a tribute to virtue.

MRS. OLDMIXON.

Her maiden name was George. She was for several
years a brilliant star at the theatres Royal, Drury Lane
and Haymarket, as well as occasionally, at Dublin. Her
first appearance was at the summer theatre in the Hay-
Market, in the character of Rossetta, in Love in a Village,
when she was not more than fifteen years of age, and at
once became a universal favorite, both as actress and singer.
She soon after performed Mandane in Artaxerxes, a character universally supposed to be the criterion of good singing, and in which the young candidate for public fame acquitted herself equally to the honor of her own talent and
gratification of her audience. The success of Miss
GEORGE thus became more rapid and extensive than the
most sanguine of her friends had anticipated. The managers of one of the winter theatres [Drury Lane] immediately secured so desirable an acquisition to their boards,
and what was still more creditable to both her taste and acquirements, she was also engaged as principal soprano at
the Lent Oratorios. For a young female of the age of a
mere school girl to give so many convincing proofs of professional excellence, and to gain by her own acquirements
alone, such high public favor, may be regarded as a rare
circumstance in musical history. Nor was this evanes_
cent. It was no forced popularity by means of newspaper
puffs of influential friends.

Miss GEORGE always kept the high ground she at first stood
upon. Her line in opera, were the lively characters, and

Miss Phillips afterwards Mrs. Crouch, played the serious cast ; and often sung in the same oratorio with Mrs. Billington in Dublin, whither Miss GEORGE occasionally went and where she was a great favourite.

A circumstance occurred one evening which was highly mortifying to Mrs. Billington. In the Beggar's opera, a verse is sung by Polly [Mrs. B.] "Why how now Madam Flirt," and a second one to the same air by Lucy [Miss G.] " Why how now saucy jade." The latter in the thought of a moment, sung hers in alto. just one octave higher than Mrs. B. which produced a rapturous encore, and upon Mrs. B's coming forward to begin the song, the audience cried out " no, no,"—"GEORGE, GEORGE," and Miss GEORGE's verse was alone repeated. This circumstance innocently as it was intended, was never, it is supposed, forgiven by Mrs. Billington.

About this period, Miss GEORGE married and retired from public life, till she visited America, where she has performed with great eclat in the cities of Charleston, Baltimore, Philadelphia, New York, and upon one occasion in Boston.

Mrs. OLDMIXON's voice is of uncommon extent, being from B below the staff, to A in altissimo : that is, A upon the additional keys of the piano forte. Her tones are remarkably sweet and fluty, if I may use the expression, and her upper notes resemble staccato passages upon the flageolet. Her taste is exquisite—her ornaments are highly polished—and nothing can be more sweet and touching than her cantabiles. One great and striking excellence in Mrs. OLDMIXON's singing, is her oratory. Those who recollect her singing of Purcell's " Mad Bess," will easily discern why this quality is applied to express an excellence in vocal performance. Her Italian songs were

truly elegant, and proved that she had studied very deeply
the Italian mode. Her performance of Caroline in the
prize where she imitates an Italian Heroine, was perhaps
one of the highest combinations of great singing with great
acting, ever witnessed in this country. Nor was her exe-
bition of some of the sublimest of Handel's oratorios less
to be admired. Her manner of singing " Angels ever
bright and fair," was inexpressibly fine. She possessed a
peculiarly happy gift of dressing up a little rondo or
ballad in a manner altogether enchanting, and entirely her
own.

The dramatic talents of Mrs. OLDMIXON would alone
place her in a high rank, if she had never sung a note.
The Antiquated Dame or Lively Romp—the Lack-a-dai-
sical Lady of Quality, or Awkward Gawky—the Pert
Chambermaid, or Simple Rural Lass—the Irish Peasant,
or French Governante, were alike within the scope of her
powers. On the whole though it may seem a contradiction,
she acted too well ; for her talents were so various and
her utility so great in comedy and farce, that the manager
seemed to forget that he had in his company a first rate
opera singer. Talents like those of this lady, should be held
up and only brought forward in the most brilliant point of
view. By these means they would become a powerful
attraction—public taste would be improved—and new can-
didates for vocal fame be stimulated to exertion.

Mrs. OLDMIXON has for a number of years, retired from
all professional engagements, and in conjunction with
two highly talented and amiable daughters, has opened a female academy in Philadelphia, of the first respectability,
where several branches of education are taught by themselves in a highly approved style, and much to the credit of
those truly accomplished ladies who enjoy no small share of

the esteem and affection of a large circle of friends of the
first standing in society.

<hr>

MRS. OSTINELLI.

LATE MISS HEWITT.

<hr>

In the catalogue of Professional ladies, we know of no
one whose talents, demeanour, and general character,
ought so soon to invite our recollection of this principle, as
the young lady whose name stands at the head of this article ; they indeed conform most accurately to our pre-con-
ceived notion. It is not to be imagined, that merit is wanting where the progress to fame and universal acquaintance
with the public is slow. The task. that has devolved upon
us, is in itself very delicate ; in this instance it is rendered
peculiarly so, by the introduction of the name and talents
of a young lady, whose entrance into the professional life
she has adventured upon, has been attended with no small
share of success.

Mr. James Hewitt, the father of this young lady, has
been long known to the musical world, as a Violinist, Organist, Composer and Instructor ; he is eminent in science
and a gentleman of great experience and versatility of
talent ; to do that justice to his professional talents, which
they truly merit, is a task which none but those who knew
him intimately should undertake ; however inadequate
we conceive ourselves, we shall at some future period attempt it, when we have more leisure, and greater space to
our columns ; at present we have only to remark, that our
25

personal acquaintance furnishes us with sufficient matter
that will be interesting to the public, as well as satisfactory
to his family and connexions.

Mrs. OSTINELLI is a native of New York ; she commenced
at a very early age the study of music, under the care and
guidance of her father, whose extensive knowledge of the
science as well as general acquaintance with the most eminent musical literati, with which that city abounds, enabled
him from time to time, to bestow an invaluable benefit upon
his child, by placing within her power, the means whereby
she has obtained not only a genteel support for herself, but
has essentially contributed to the comfort of her parents
and family.

From the personal instructions of the father, together
with the occasional aid and assistance of other gentlemen
of talents highly skilled in the musical science, has Mrs.
OSTINELLI possessed herself of a sound musical education.—
Parents who look forward to this highest hope, must devote the hours of their children to application, nothing short
of intensity of study. No practice short of four hours daily,
continued for several years, will give a pianiste any superior title to be heard, as the art is now cultivated and understood.

At the early period of seven years of age, Mrs. OSTINELLI
for the first time was brought before the public, by her father at a concert given at the City Hotel New York ; from
this period to the age of twelve she occasionally appeared at
concerts and was always greeted with applause. In 1812,
her family removed to this city, at which time she was conceived capable, and obtained the situation of organist with
a handsome salary. After remaining here some time, Mrs.
OSTINELLI returned to New York, and was engaged as in-
structress of music at the celebrated Boarding School kept
by Mrs. Brenton. During this period till towards 1816,

she occasionally sung at the New York Oratorios, and often performed at the Concerts of the Euterpeian Society. It was at this crisis, her genius and powers of execution began to attract the notice of the gentlemen of the profession generally ; her studies were closely pursued under Dr. G. K. Jackson, and afterwards by Messrs. Ferrand and Moran, on the Harp and Piano-Forte.

In 1819, application was made to her by the government of the Handel and Haydn Society of this city, to return hither, when she received the appointment of Organist of that meritorious Institution, which situation together with that of Organist at Chauncey Place, and the addition of sundry pupils are the fruits of an early musical education.

The peculiar and proper distinction of this lady's performance is, that she posesses a brilliant execution as a Pianiste ; her playing is without the slightest mixture of constraint, but with energetic force and devoid of affectation. She indicates a becoming rigour of feminine modesty ; in the picturing of her imagination, as evinced in the intellectual dominion over the art, than an exuberant degree of enthusiastic imagination. Her playing is plain sensible and that of a gentlewoman ; she neither takes by storm, nor by surprise, but she gradually wins upon the understanding, while the ear, though it never fills the other senses with ecstacy, drinks in full satisfaction. There is never any thing to condemn, and there is always to be commended a purity and sobriety, a graceful and dignified reserve, which is at all times becoming. The excesses into which extraordinary genius is always betrayed, will often astonish, often enrapture, and almost as often endanger its supremacy by violence or disgust ; but there is a softness and sweetness, a delicacy, lightness, precision, and velocity, a charm truly persuasive and one that always pleases. Of this talisman, Mrs. OSTINELLI is the mistress.

With these attributes, this young lady is entitled to, and enjoys a share of public patronage ; her claim to the regard she earns so industriously and so honourably, is supported by a purity of mind and character correspondent to her professional merit. It affords us satisfaction to be able to point out the moral perfection of private worth and estimation with public utility, not so much because there are some instances to sully the reputation of the musical prosion, but because those examples are frequently most invidiously quoted, to the establishment of a line of demarcation between public and private life, most injurious to the former, and not perhaps without imposing painful restraints and privations upon the latter. The present instance proves sufficiently, that the public exercise of a talent is not incompatible with the grace, the ornament, and all the virtues of domestic life.

MISS EUSTAPHIEVE.

Notoriety is an indispensible condition attatched to the existence of *Genius*. It balances the account between *admiration* and its *object* ; and forms a kind of compromise in which accommodating nature offers something in the way of compensation for the exclusive privilege of enriching *one* at the expense of *many*. The same power which rresistibly calls for an acknowledgment of superiority, subjects this superiority to claims equally irresistible. Thus, unwonted talent especially as relates to the Fine Arts, is and always will be in some shape or other, emphatically, the property of the public ; the supposed qualification, that it is not professional, being, in fact only a *nominal* distinction without *real* difference. The poetic pencil, which en-endows the senseless canvass with the colors of life, breathing forth their spells before a crowd of admiring spectators, whether wielded by the hand of an amateur or a professor, is alike possessed, and gloried in, by the community at large. In cases of this description, so extraordinary as to justify extraordinary deviations, genuine modesty and humility may lose more by persevering in an impracticable retirement, at the risk of incurring the charge of affectation ; than by submitting at once, with honest consciousness and unshrinking candour, to the inevitable fate of a pre-eminence to conspicuous too elude the public gaze.

In announcing, therefore, so openly, the inspiring subject of these remarks, a subject too sensitive not to endure rather the full blaze of day, than the smallest shadow of subterfuge ; we are only impelled along like *consequences* in the train of *causes*, and the exercise of our right, as creditors in virtue of an implied contract, comes too late to assign " a name and local habitation ;" or even to give us the merit of expressing our own deep sense of the gratification we have with others so often experienced.

To exhonerate ourselves, however, from all possible imputation of premature officiousness, or breach of delicacy ; we fain would impress, on the too *scrupulous*, our own conviction, that we ought not to have sacrificed to mere punctilios so precious an opportunity to present to the lovers of harmony with an abstract yet grateful object of contemplation ; to encourage bashful talent by shewing how much may be accomplished, where such talents exist, without prejudice to other essential acquirements ; to produce a powerful example in vindicating the student from the charge of *frivolous* pursuit, and in rescuing the study itself from unmerited obloquy that mistakes its own paralizing effect for an extrinsic imaginary cause ; to fix upon a guide near at hand to aid us in illustrating certain positions relative to an art which labors as yet under the weight of local prejudices, and erroneously supposed to *debase*, when in reality it *elevates* the mind ; to cherish true taste, and discriminating love for the highest species of performance by holding up an unequivocal model of excellence ; to do honor to our native town, by proclaiming of what exquisite fruit on the tree of science it has been the nursery, an honor which, we venture to predict, will at no distant time be envied by the first capitals of Europe ; to satisfy legitimate public curiosity by directing it to a proper focus of vision ; and to discharge our own particular duty, in describing to the best of our abilities, [better late than never] a phenomenon, which falls so exclusively within our sphere of observation.

Our last, *not least,* motive is also to correct absurd, ridiculous, and contradictory notions, entertained of the progress of this favorite child of music, and arising no less from petty and perhaps unavoidable *jealousies,* than from *exagerating* as well as *depreciating* ignorance. A flame, whose own increasing brightness betrays its impotence of concealment, ought to be exposed entire, in all its unbroken unity; rather than be suffered, through inefficient partial obstructions, to emanate in undefined and often disadvantageous illusions. The most sacred veil of privacy had better yield to the respectful touch of removal, than to distort with false shadows the form of perfection, which it becomes too transparent wholly to conceal.

Mere assertions, arbitrary opinions, high pitched rhapsodies, fulsome panegyrics, or any other ingredients of contemptible puffing, must not be expected from us. Such

base things would as ill become our own character as
the dignity of our cause. Besides, we have no temptation to be guilty of an act of degradation, which
would be perfectly useless. Where even rigorous criticism is pleased to see its own sharpest arrows recoil in
harmless play ; or where fiction itself may fall far short of
reality, and truth appears but fiction ; bare facts alone are
to be preferred. We shall, therefore, adopt this plain
straight-forward course, pledging our accuracy for every
item, with the greater claim to confidence, as the smallest
error would expose us to immediate and mortifying contradiction. Neither shall we forget our intimation to make
such application of those facts, as will seem to us best calculated to promote the general utility of our labors.

We cannot conclude this introductory part without one
effort more to obviate all chances of complaint at the re-
sponsibility we have thus voluntarily incurred. We
thought we should proceed with much less offence by not
asking permission than by *disregarding* its refusal. We consider the young lady in the light of a collegian who is publicly announced to have obtained a glorious scholastic prize;
and therefore must still persist to justify ourselves in having
taken the same liberty with her name.

The uncommon musical capacity of this young lady was
very early displayed in a manner equally extraordinary.
When scarcely more than three years old, she was known to
catch, as if by inspiration, all the popular airs of the day, and
to sing them with such precision as to admit of free scientific accompaniment.

The first attempt to instruct her, at the age of six, was
after a few trials, abandoned as too onerous. The second,
only a year after, proved decisive. Her talents unfolded
themselves with a rapidity that, at the first onset, outstrip-
ped the regular pace of tuition. Every new lesson was

learned with such expeditious ease, as to render indispensible the intervening burthen of home instruction, which placed her several pages in advance of the ensuing lesson, and which daily increasing, made it at last an act of justice to unite the credit with the labor. Accordingly she became exclusively the pupil of her own father, who found himself thus unexpectedly compelled to teach, while he himself had yet to learn ; the piano-forte not being an instrument on which he is a distinguished amateur.

When she was entering upon Pleyel's sonatas, Mr. Etienne made a professional visit to Boston ; and by his liberal conduct proved that sympathy between talents, and their reciprocal homage, are not imaginary. At a glance he perceived the kindred gem as yet in its native bed, and unable to watch over it in person, he left behind him such advice as powerfully aided in its progressive polish. The lustre which it has since acquired, probably surpasses his utmost anticipations ; but the mode and course of instruction which were adopted at his recommendation, entitle him to that strain of eulogy and gratitude in which he is generally spoken of by the family.

In the year 1817, having occasion to visit St. Petersburg, where Steibelt and the much celebrated Field resided, Miss EUSTAPHIEVE's father took her with him for the express purpose of hearing those great masters, and, if possible, of profiting by their instructions. But this purpose, in a great measure, though not wholly, was defeated by the circumstance of her being obliged, sooner than was expected, to return to Boston. She left the imperial capital after staying there only two months, just long enough to make both these eminent characters regret her departure.

Thus, guided chiefly by the general taste of her paternal instructor ; without the opportunity of hearing great performers either late enough, or often enough to derive benefit, being removed from all competition which might excite laudable emulation and a necessary portion of ambition; with no association even to relieve her daily task, which must have appeared to her without a definite object and therefore more tedious than that of Penelope ; bereft of all inducement voluntarily to prolong her practice which never exceeded five out of twenty-four hours, and which decreasing, as other studies interfered, is now reduced to about one half of the time; she nevertheless in the progress actually made, excels the European student as much as he does her, in the possession of all these superior means, and positive advantages.   Such is the triumph of genius !

To convey some idea of her masterly performance, would be impossible without violating our pledge, not to advance any thing, in the form of opinion ; but we are fortunately in the possession of some well known facts, which can be adduced even on this point apparently incapable of demonstration.

At the very commencement of her ninth year, she astonished a numerous audience at the Philharmonic Society, and in private assemblies, by a successive, rapid, brilliant, and in the strictest technical sense, faultless execution of " The Battle of New Orleans," " Viotti's Concerto," " The Conflagration of Moscow," the " Storm Concerto" and the like compositions. Having since passed with the same success to the master pieces of Kalkbrenner, Ries, and the gigantic Beethoven himself ; having frustrated the utmost efforts of science to arrest her career by an accumulation of difficulties, and exhausted the moderate means of supplying her with new music, she is now literally confined within the circle of her own musical library, which though not the largest, forms perhaps the choicest private collection in the United States. Every page is at her command at a moment's notice, yet every page to be mastered, requires powers at least equal to her own.

A genius like this, would have had in Europe, the invaluable privilege of exercising itself in the well-supplied stores of music without additional expense ; yet, though deprived here of this advantage so essential to make a good reader, or sight player, how much she excels even in this highly artificial branch, may be known from the concurrent testimony of our professors who witnessed, and often accompanied her on such occasions.

In the art of accompaniment she had still less practice; yet, with what taste and dexterity she can even here acquit herself, we appeal with confidence to all those who have heard her accompany " The Creation" or the " Mount of Olives" and particularly to the late eminent musician Doct. Jackson, who was very justly placed at the head of this scientific department.

Such is her confidence in herself, arising from the modest, yet full consciousness of her powers ; that spirit of her performance, instead of being abashed, invariably rises in proportion to the number of her hearers qualified to form a critical judgment. It is particularly worthy of remark that she has never been known to commit one single mistake, such as would attract notice, or make correction necessary in any of the great number of pieces which she was called upon to play after ever so slight a preparation.

Such too is the accuracy of her ear, that, like the celebrated Master Crotch, she can, with her face averted from the instrument tell every single note, or a group of notes, soon as the keys are touched by another person. This she can do even on instruments with which she is totally unacquainted ; a gift very rare even among the first rate veterans.

She has never yet failed to exceed the highest expecta-

tions and to subject the eye so much to the novel illusion
of the ear, that one does not even suspect himself to be in
the presence of any other than an eminent, mature, professional performer.   All these positive, though extraordinary
facts, and they will be acknowledged as such, by all those
who have enjoyed an opportunity, and possess the necessa-
sary requisites, to form a correct opinion, are recorded of
Miss EUSTAPHIEVE.

We might be expected to notice, by way of comparison
several remarkable instances of musical precocity, which
have come to our knowledge, and have appeared at
different times in various parts of the world ; but it
would be an useless waste of labor, as, with the exception
presently to be made, none appears fairly entitled
to stand in the list of competition.   We must ex-
clude even Master Crotch, because, as Dr. Crotch, he has
since made no great figure ; and was celebrated only for a
gift valuable on the score of curiosity, but uncon-
nected with any merit of acquirement ; a gift, which, as
we have already shewn, is fully possessed by Miss EUSTA-
PHIEVE, without any importance being attached to it either
by herself or her friends.

There remains only Mozart : not the Mozart at the prime
of manhood, matched, and perhaps excelled by Haydn and
Beethoven, but the *infant Mozart* who never had, and, in a
certain sense, never may have his equal.   To yield to him,
and him alone, is to excel all that have appeared since his
time.   The most craving ambition cannot wish for more.
As regards, however Miss EUSTAPHIEVE, he is rather a subject of contrast, than of comparison.

Mozart was born and reared in a part of Europe, the most
celebrated for musical science ; his father was an eminent
composer and profound teacher of harmony ; his associates, visitors, almost the whole community in which he liv-

ed, even his play-fellows, were, more or less, zealous culti-
vators and admirers of music : he may be said to have imbibed harmony with his mother's milk, and inhaled it from
the very atmosphere he breathed : the reverse of all this
has fallen to the lot of Miss EUSTAPHIEVE. Mozart lived
among friends, relations, countrymen, interested in the fame
and progress, and attached to the pursuit itself, which they
deemed honorable and dignified ; Miss EUSTAPHIEVE on
the contrary, has been placed amongst strangers, some of
whom, are only so far interested in her talent as to endeavor to bring it into discredit and array against it the
whole formidable host of local prejudices. Mozart's genius is transmitted to us, as regards details, through the
medium of history, mellowed by distance, consecrated by
death, placed beyond the reach of detraction, magnified,
or at least embellished by the endearing touches of surviv-
ing enthusiasm, cherished and guarded by the most faithful
of centinels, *national pride,* which frowns on the smallest
attempt to examine, with the critical eye of incredulity,
the flowers upon his grave.

Thus we might fairly insist on a rational deduction from
the wonders recorded of Mozart ; but we have neither inclination nor interest to disturb the ashes of that great
man ; and will rather run the risk of acquiescing at probable exaggeration, than of committing injustice.

Mozart, as a composer at thirteen years of age, a fact
which we will not question, must therefore enjoy his superiority for ever. In this respect we acknowledge him unrivalled, without the smallest qualification to be drawn from
a retrospective glance at the superior advantages of education which it was his good fortune to enjoy. We may,
nevertheless, consider it is an obvious inference, that the
very same cause which so early prompted him to compose,
would now prevent him from making the attempt. The

piano forte compositions at his time were so few and mea-
gre, that his genius, naturally dissatisfied with so poor a
fare, sought to supply the deficiency from its own resources ; but Miss EUSTAPHIEVE has now to contend with the
opposite difficulty, which consists not in the want, but in
the choice and mastery of the astonishing productions
which have, since his days, enriched and ennobled that instrument, itself greatly improved. The very study of these
master pieces must necessarily, and very profitably, employ
the whole space of that early life which otherwise might have
embraced the art of composition. To compose tolerably
well, was a great merit, while there was none greater, [we
speak exclusively of the piano ;] but to acquire such merit at this stage of improvement, one must be a full grown
giant in composition, or nothing. We are quite sure that
Miss EUSTAPHIEVE, for the very reason that she has acquired a taste for the greatest productions extant, will never
compose, unless she can equal them ; a thing absolutely
impossible at her time of life, since it was impossible even
for Mozart himself at any period of life ; his best and lat-
est compositions, with all their undeniable beauties, being
inferior to those we have mentioned. It was good policy
to encourage him in the career of composition, as it was
evidently superior to that of his cotemporaries ; but it
would be downright impolicy to give the same direction
to the scholar of the present day, whose premature
vanity, as a composer, would not fail, for it has never yet
failed, to divert him from the great masters, before he has
sufficiently studied them, and reduce him to be the constant
retailer of his own comparatively worthless trash. Many
a performer of promise, that would have arrived at the pin-
nacle of excellence, has been ruined by this mode of proceeding. The scholar must now learn to curb his impa-
tience, and for a long time console himself with the con-

sciousness that in music the distance, between the projecting head and executing hand, is not near so great as in some
other arts.   Genius can alone give utterance to the sounds,
which genius has originated.   The great performer submits
to be guided by the great composer only to become a guide
in turn and be the first to inform the latter of the effect of
his own combinations. The independence which exists between the dramatic author and the actor, the former having the power to present himself to the public without the
intervention of the the stage, is impracticable in the science
of music, unless both the characters are united in one
person.   *Theseus*,   the   groping hero, and *Ariadne* the
tutelar spirit leading him out of the labyrinth, present a
just emblem of that close alliance which subsists between the great composer and the great performer, and
which elevates the latter far above the mere mechanism of execution.   Nay, a composer of moderate reputation is absolutely inferior to a performer of rare, but acknowledged merit ; as it requires much less genius to constitute the one, than seize, as. does the other, the master-
key of witchcraft, to wield the mysterious machinery, and
to put in motion the whole mighty creation with the dark
towering spirit of a Beethoven !

The proper question, then, is, was Mozart, as a performer on the piano, equal at the age of twelve, to the young
lady of the same age, whom we are describing ?   We answer without hesitation, no : not even at a far more advanced
period of life.   A presumptive as well as a positive evidence are both on our side.   Whatever skill he may be
supposed to have evinced in encountering the masterly and
scientific works of other composers of his day ; the pau-
city and almost the non-existence of these, render such a
supposition quite gratuitous.   The whole extent, therefore,
of his powers of execution, may be infallibly traced in his

own works transmitted to us entire, and placed at once within the scope of our own judgment. They present, it must be confessed, strong proofs and no ordinary trials, but by no means equal in magnitude to those which Miss EUSTAPHIEVE has already sustained with so much credit.

We have, therefore, a right to conclude, that as a performer, she has never yet been excelled or even equalled by any of the same age ; and that in applying to her the word *prodigy*, we restore the word itself to its legitimate owner, and rescue it from the profanation to which it has so often been subjected.

END OF BIOGRAPHICAL SKETCHES OF VOLUME ONE.

THE LOGIERIAN SYSTEM.

——

Mr. Logier, (a German by birth, but who has resided for fifteen years in England,) teaches the piano forte, together with the principles of harmony, on a new plan of which he himself is the inventor. The most remarkable feature of this new system is, that the pupils, who frequently amount to thirty or forty in number, all practice their lessons at the same time. Mr. Logier has written three volumes of studies, all grounded on a simple theme, of five notes to each hand, and advancing progressively to the most difficult combinations.

While the beginners play merely the *Thema*, the more advanced pupils practice variations more or less difficult. It might be supposed that the confusion arising from this method would render it impossible for the master to detect the faults of his pupils, but as all who practice the same lesson are ranged close to each other, the master when near them is capable of judging of their performance without being disturbed by those who are playing other lessons. He occasionally orders one half or all the scholars to stop, while he directs his attention to each individual. For be-

27

g inners he employs his Chiroplast,* by which the children, even in their earliest lessons, acquire a proper position of the hand and arm. It cannot be denied that this machine is admirably adapted for the object it is intended to fulfil ; and it of course affords vast assistance to Mr. LOGIER in superintending a number of pupils at once. It might also be advantageously employed for learners in general ; for although at the period of giving a lesson, the master has the opportunity of pointing out and correcting bad habits, yet children when abandoned to themselves, are but too apt

* The several ingenious contrivances to whic hthe learned appellation of Chiroplast is given, are, *The Gamut Board, The Position Frame, The Finger Guides* and *The Wrist Guides.* The " Gamut Board" is to direct the pupil how to find the proper key for every note, and consists of an oblong board, which on one side has drawn upon it two staves of five lines each, one for the treble and the other for the bass, exhibiting the notes so written, that, when slid over that part of the piano forte which is immediately behind the keys, and which generally shows the makers name, each note, with its name, will be exactly above its corresponding key.

"The Position Frame," consists of two parallel wooden bars, covered lengthways over the whole board, so as to be before it, and admit the hands passing between them nearly as far as the wrists, by which means the hands can move horizontally.

" The Finger Guides" are two moveable brass plates with five divisions, through which the thumb and four fingers are introduced The divisions correspond perpendicularly with the keys of the instrument, and may be moved and screwed fast to a brass rod, on which they are made to slide.

" The Wrist Guide," is a strong brass wire projecting from the finger guide, so as to confine the wrist in a proper position, and to prevent its being inclined outwards.

It would therefore appear that the Chrioplast is a musical stock, in which the hand, and fingers are so confined as to preclude the possibility of faulty action or motion.

to contract awkward positions of the hand and arm in the practice of the piano forte.

As soon as the pupils are so far advanced as to know the notes and keys, the machine is removed first from one hand, and then from the other, and they are next taught the proper motion of the thumbs, and to run up and down in the different keys ; these runs are performed by the pupils all at once, and with the strictest accuracy as to time. When a certain class is advanced to a new lesson and cannot all play it with equal rapidity, they strike only a few notes in each bar ; the difficulty, however, it may readily be supposed, is soon overcome, and in a short time the new lesson is played with as much facility as the old one.

Another advantage of Mr. LOGIER's system, is, that he instructs his pupils in the principles of harmony along with the first practical lessons on the piano forte. How this is done I know not : it is a secret, which, for the payment of 100 guineas, he communicates to those teachers who choose to adopt Mr. LOGIER's system, as evinced by the progress of his pupils, is most astonishing. Children of from 7 to 10 years of age, who have been learning not more than four months, solve the most difficult musical problems. I wrote down a triad on a tablet, and mentioned the key into which I wished it to be modulated, and one of the youngest girls after a little reflection, noted down, first the figured bases and then the upper notes of the chords. I repeated this proposition in the most difficult ways possible, requiring that the scholars should modulate it into the remotest keys, where the harmonic changes were necessary, and in no instance did they commit a fault. If one pupil hesitated, a second wrote down the notes, and her figured bass was again corrected by a third, while, at the same time, they pointed out to their master the fundamental bass of all the chords.

MAELZEL'S

Metronome or Musical Time Keeper.   The Metronome in point of correctness and practical utility, claims a decided preference over all the numerous attempts at Chronometers that have been made for a century past.   It is a portable instrument, which beats both the vibrations to which it is set, and the scale of which being deduced from the divisions of time into minutes, is universally applicable and intelligible in every country.   The principal part of the Metronome consists of a flat steel rod, of the breadth of a small pea, the thickness of the back of a penknife, and the length of about eleven inches.   Supposing this rod placed upright, its lower end is fixed to an immoveable round weight of the diameter of a shilling ; at the distance of about four inches upwards, a steel pin is fastened to the back of the rod,   On this pin, as on an axis, the rod is suspended vertically, so as to swing sideways to the right and left, in the vibration which it thus makes are produced by an escapement, two wheels and a main spring, wound up like that of a watch.   The upper and longer part of the rod or pendulum, (i. e. that which is above the point of suspension, and measures about seven inches,) has attached to it a counter weight, which slides from the before mentioned point of suspension to the upper extremity of the rod.   Immediately behind is a scale similar to that of a Thermometer beginning at the top with the number of 50,

and proceeding downwards, with the omissions of some in-
termediate numbers, till it ends near the axis of the rod
with the number of 160. By means of a small spring in
the sliding weight, and small notches in the rod, the sliding
weight can be stopped precisely opposite to any of the numbers on the fixed scale behind.

All these numbers have reference to a *minute of time* so
that at 50 the pendulum will vibrate fifty times, at 80 eighty
times, at 160 one hundred and sixty times per minute, &c·
&c. ; and by a particular contrivance in the mechanism,
these vibrations are not only visible, but audible, so as to be
distinctly heard even in a room adjoining. The whole of
this apparatus is confined in an elegant little obelisk of
about a foot in height.

The object of this invention is as Mr. Maelzel states, two
fold :

1*st*. " It affords to composers of every country the means
of indicating, in a simple, and decisive manner, the degree
of quickness with which their works are to be executed."

2*d*. " It accustoms the young practitioner to a correct
observance of time, which it beats with unerring precision,
and according to any velocity required, during the whole
performance."

With respect to the first of these two objects, every
musical man has for this century past felt the insufficiency
of the vague Italian terms, *adagio*, *allegro*, &c. for this purpose ; and if there were a doubt on this point, Mr. Maelzel's observations, and his quotations from classic works,
not only tend to remove it but actually create a degree of
surprise at the patience with which these Italian terms have
been so long endured. This, no doubt, was owing to the
want of a universal scale for musical time, and this universal standard measure being now obtained through the Metronome, we should hope that in a short time no sensible

composer will risk the proper execution of works, and consequently his fame, on these Italian terms alone—terms, which mean nobody knows rightly what. In this hope we are fully confirmed by the strongest testimonials of approbation on the part of the first rate composers, who by their declarations, have formally pledged themselves to time all their future works according to the Metronomic scale. The universal standard measure proposed by Mr. Maelzel is, as we have before stated, deduced from horary or clock time, which is the same all over the world: his Metronome enables the composer to prescribe to the player how many crotchets or quavers, &c. in the piece ought to be played in *one* minute, while it puts it in the performers powers instantly to adopt his play to such prescription. Thus in a country, even where the Metronome is not known, and in future ages, in the event of the Metronome being no longer in existence, the signatures founded on the Metronomic scale will serve as a record to trace the proper quickness of a composition, as long as the sun keeps true to his present daily career. Would to heaven we now knew how many notes of a certain value go to a minute in the performance of all the works of Handel, Haydn, Mozart, Beethoven and Pleyel. This consideration alone must render the superiority of Mr. M's standard measure, founded as it is upon the universally adopted division of time, obvious and indisputable ; and under this point of view, his Metronome combines the two-fold merit of assuming that standard, and of furnishing the means of applying this measure in a manner the most convenient and instantaneous. While we thus consider the attainment of a universal standard measure of time the principal merit of Mr. M's invention, we are, at the same time, fully sensible of the advantages which the Metronome holds out in the instruction of young beginners ; and we are equally ready to admit, that this instrument not only demonstrates the advantages in a manner absolutely unanswerable, but also indicates the way and proper method of obtaining all the benefit to be derived by the exhibition of true time in the tuition of music.

CHURCH MUSIC.

The following essay on *Church Music,* has lately appeared in the London Quarterly Musical Magazine and Review,—and when divested of its local application, will be found to contain much that is instructive and useful to the Musical community in this country.

" Let us sing to the praise and glory of God."

Church Music has, or ought to have this proud distinction above all other : it is destined to the " praise and glory of God." Until this principle is fully recognized by all who have the management or control of this delightful portion of divine worship, by all organists and their assistants, by all singing men, singing women and singing boys, it will never emerge from that deplorable state of degradation in which it is now too generally found. Independently of all secondary considerations, what other motive so sublime, so calculated to awaken all the best energies of the soul and almost etherialize the grosser portion of our nature ! What so calculated to inspire that holy and chastened enthusiasm in which genius delights to revel ? What so calculated to rouse the " fine phrenzy" of the mind and

28

to elicit the noblest productions of refined intellect ! What
calculated to sublime and purify the imagination from the
crassitude of earth, till we seem to enter the heaven of heav-
ens, and fall prostrate before the throne of God himself !
Where else can a motive be found which shall at once so
stimulate, so exalt, and so ennoble the affections of humanity ?
Compared to this, how low, how grovelling the two common
substitutes, " love of fame," or, as elsewhere called, "vain
glory." How poor, how humiliating, how transitory the
gratification it affords !

How are we to account for the indifference which seems
to pervade the clergy on this subject ? Surely, out of a
hundred sermons each per annum, they might bestow *one*
upon this important part of the devotions of their congre-
gations. How is it then that the whole duty of exhorting
the people to a proper performance of this prominent part
of Divine Service devolves exclusively upon the Clerk,
who, as if by instinct, discharges it uniformly in the same
words, " Let us sing to the praise and glory of God !" If
it be true that the object of preaching is to point out the
way in which the Deity is to be worshipped ; if it be true
that " God is a Spirit," and that " they who worship him
must worship him in spirit and in truth," surely it would
not be a great dereliction from the line of a minister's duty
were he occasionally to admonish his hearers to " sing with
the spirit and with the understanding also," and to inform
them, in as polite a manner as he pleases, that otherwise
they " sing to the praise and glory of " any body but their
Maker.

Church Music is either instrumental, or vocal, or mixed;
which latter indeed, being a compound of the former two
is that in most general use. Music purely instrumental is
seldom employed excepting as produced from bells or organs. The former when we enter the church are supposed
to be silent.

But before we proceed directly to the consideration of
the music itself, it will not be foreign to our purpose to bestow a few words upon that noble instrument, the organ,
which is universally acknowledged to be the most majestic
and is undoubtedly the most beautiful musical instrument
which the wit of man has hitherto devised. It is,
as if by common consent, almost exclusively devoted
to the service of the sanctuary. This seems its proper
place in more respects than one. As being the best,

and as being of such magnitude as few other edifices could conveniently contain, and of such value as little less than the resources of a multitude could provide. Of the period and merits of its invention, nothing needs here be said. Whether it has reached its highest point of perfection or not, time will show ; but it seems still susceptible of a great degree of improvement.

THE ORGAN.

The organ is usually placed in a gallery. In the old churches this is judicious. The roof reverberates the tone to the floor, and the floor returns it to the roof, and thereby the general effect is improved. In modern churches, wherein, from the presence of large galleries, and the other causes before mentioned, there is little or no reverberation, the organ would perhaps stand better on the floor ; because thereby a greater height would be allowed for the large pipes, and because also, it would be more distinctly heard by the whole congregation. The common defect of organs is a want of bass. The majesty of an organ lies in the lower notes of the diapason. If these be defective the want cannot be compensated. This is an organ builder's great temptation. He cribs a few hundred weights of metal, but spoils what might otherwise be an excellent piece of workmanship ; yet the evil has not originated exclusively with the Organ builders. They are generally assigned so much room in feet and inches : and this space they must not exceed.

It is worthy of remark, that modern instruments are deficient in imitative stops. It is not intended to describe minutely the various parts of which an organ consists, but merely to afford a tolerably correct idea of the whole. More circumstantial knowledge may be obtained from other sources. The principle of the common whistle is that on which this magnificent instrument is constructed. As Milton expresses it, the sound board, which is that part of the organ on which the pipes generally stand, breathes into various rows of pipes or whistles, at the motion of the or-

ganist's fingers : and is itself supplied by bellows, sometimes not widely differing, otherwise than in magnitude,
from the common blowing article of kitchen notoriety : and
thus is produced that sublime effect which can be derived
from no other instrument, or collection of instruments under heaven.

A good church organ is usually divided into three parts,
or distinct sound boards ; the great organ, the choir organ,
and the swell ; which last is of inferior compass, or extent,
but of superior power of expression, to the other two.
The great organ is of course the largest and the loudest,
and should be the best part of the instrument. The choir
organ ; as its name implies, is intended to be used for the
accompaniment of the singers ; and is therefore voiced
soft. Sometimes it is built in the same case with the great
organs ; sometimes it forms a part of the chorusses, and
sometimes it is altogether detached from the main body. It
is very essential to the light and shade of music. Contrivances for moving the stops by pedals are too often introduced as a succedaneum, but after all, a church organ,
destitute of it, is like a coat without sleeves, or a dinner
without salt. The swell, or gradual increase of sound, is
produced by opening the door of the box in which this part
of the organ is enclosed. For this purpose a pedal is provided, having a communication with the sliding door, and by
which it may be easily moved up or down with one foot.
There is sometimes a fourth division for the pedals ; a set
of keys with corresponding movements, sound board and
pipes, performed upon by the feet, and this division constitutes the grandest part of the organ. Till within these few
years, pedals were scarcely known in England, and even
now are generally what are termed " sham ;" *i. e.* they are
only a range of sticks for the feet, connected with the keys
of the great organ. Even these are of such use, that a
person accustomed to them can scarcely endure the empti-
ness of the performance, which is manifest when they are
wanting. They enable the performer to double his *bass*,
without being under the necessity of deserting the *tenor*,
to which the left hand should be almost exclusively devoted.
Indeed an organ, played with pedals, is as much superior
to an organ played without them, as the grand piano forte
is to the spinnett of our great grandmother. There will
be a time when it will be esteemed disgraceful for an organ

not to possess them, and an organist not to know how to use them.

In each of the divisions before mentioned there are various longitudinal rows of pipes ; which rows, with the movements connected with them, are called *stops*.

A large organ contains from twenty to forty of these stops; and as there are commonly between fifty and sixty pipes in each stop, the whole number of pipes is very considerable. The organ in St. Paul's cathedral, contains 1976, of which the largest is sixteen feet, and the smallest about half an inch long, measuring from the mouth ; yet such is the order in which they are arranged, that an experienced organ builder knows every individual by name ; and upon the occurrence of an accident with one of them, can instantly distinguish which is in fault. Of these stops the most valuable is the *open diapason*. These are the pipes usually seen in the front. There are commonly two in the great organ ; if good, they will cover a multitude of faults ; but if defective, the whole is imperfect. By the compass of this stop is that of the whole organ ascertained and expressed ; so that if the largest pipe measures eight or sixteen feet, it is usual to call it an eight or sixteen feet organ. It is much to be wished that some definite standard of compass were adopted, and that all organs should be constructed to terminate at a particular note, varying one from the other only by complete octaves ; for this purpose C seems most proper, never omitting the C sharp above it. For a small place eight feet is sufficiently large ; for a moderate sized church sixteen feet, and for a large cathedral not less than thirty-two feet C ; this would be a good basis for a first rate organ. What is called a *double diapason* all through, comes recommended by the sanction of parties, to whose taste and discrimination much deference is due ; but some cannot help being still of Dr. Burney's opinion that it gives " a clumsiness to the melody, and has the same effect as if the treble part in a concert, were played by double bases." In the bass it has undoubtedly a fine effect ; and if made to draw in two parts, the treble part may be omitted at pleasure. Many other of the stops are *harmonies* of the original notes ; as, for instance, the octave, [principal, clarion, flute, &c.] twelfth, fifteenth, seventeenth [tierce], nineteenth [Larigot], and twenty-second ; these, when well proportioned—that is, subdued to proper dependence upon ground tones, to effect which requires the utmost delicacy and precision—add a vast brilliancy and richness to the sound ; but when predominant, as is too often the case, they tend only to insufferable noise and ear rending confusion. Three, four, and even five of these harmonies, are bundled up commonly into one stop, (as the sesquialtera, mixture, and cornet for instance,)whereby of course the performer is compelled to use all or none. Were every rank to draw separately, there would be much more room for the exercise of taste and ingenuity on the part of an intelligent organist than the present arrangement affords, and a bungler might draw them together as at present.

The remaining stops are diapasons of various qualities of tone, arising from a difference in their shape and texture, *c. g.* the *stopped diapason*, of wood but far inferior to one of metal ; the *dulciana*, an open *diapason* on a small scale, producing a remarkably sweet and pleasant tone ; the *trumpet*, in which the sound is produced by the vibration of a small tongue of brass (called a *reed*, at its lower extremity, and other imitative reed stops, in which department of organ building there is ample room for the exercise of ingenuity.

Of the interior of the organ a very brief description has been given ; it remains to consider as briefly, the exterior. Here the disproportion often times manifest is very striking between the decorations and the useful furniture of the instrument ; and the next, the frequently utter incongruity of those decorations with the general character of the place in which they are displayed. The one, if not the other, undoubtedly lies within the compass of the subject of this essay, as having a direct tendency to lessen the sum which would otherwise be expended on the proper apparatus of an organ. It would argue a sad want of taste to deny that, in many places, the organ forms a splendid and appropriate ornament ; but in many others, it must be allowed, that it has the effect of disturbing the uniformity and design of the building. It stares us in the face like some huge gilt gingerbread toy, and there can be but little doubt that the same feeling, a love of show, has given rise to both.

How common is it in a venerable gothic edifice, to see the case of the organ decorated with Corinthian Capitals, and other incongruities, and how universal the custom of covering the front pipes with a load of hypocritical gilding.

constituting a very unseemly set off to the solemnity of the
rest of the structure. The natural colour of the metal of
which the pipes are made [a mixture of lead and tin]
would at the same time harmonize better with the character of the place, generally speaking, and with the spreading
spirit of economy and retrenchment, of late years so loud-
ly preached and so generally practised. If the metal will
not retain the brilliancy of its colour, let it be varnished ;
or if a superinduced colour be absolutely indispensable,
which is much to be doubted, let it be that of Silver. Although this custom of gilding is now so general, perhaps a
better taste may prevail ; and then it will never again happen that the case and gilding cost just much as the organ
itself. The fact is, that a judicious arrangement of its
component parts only is necessary to produce a very pleasing and tasteful appearance, to the exclusion of gewgaws
with which it unfortunately is generally caparisoned. Had
this principle been universally acted upon, there might be
less of glitter, but there certainly would be more of music.

THE VOLUNTARY.

Almost the only species of purely instrumental music
now employed in our churches is the organ voluntary.
Even this is getting into disuse. The term is usually confined to signify an interlude between the psalms and the
first lesson. By what authority it was originally introduced
is not easily ascertained ; it stands now by prescription,
and may therefore be concluded to be of high antiquity ; at
least " the memory of man runneth not to the contrary,"
which is sufficient to constitute it a valid custom, and in
cases of its interdiction, perhaps to enforce its readmission
into the service. As organists are generally a peaceable set
of men, and as moreover they commonly hold their office
by a very precarious tenure, there is no danger of their
acting upon this suggestion

A voluntary is generally understood to signify an un-
written or extemporary piece of music as distinguish

ed from the execution of a copy.* This is a species of performance for which the organ is peculiarly adapted, and which is susceptible of more of the impress of genuine feeling than any other description of music. The imagination, unchecked by the fetters which the act of writing necessarily imposes, gives life and vigour and maturity to its creations, even in the very moment of their conception. Emotions of the soul which cannot be embodied in language, become by the medium of melodious sounds, transfused into the breasts of the hearers, communicating a sensation not to be expressed, and imparting a tranquil pleasure but rarely otherwise experienced.† By the glow of enthusiasm passages which reflection could not furnish, nor memory retain, have been elicited, warm from the heart, and almost imbued with a principle of vitality; and in the same moment like the evanescent beauties of a summers evening, have passed away for ever.

The voluntary has therefore precisely the same advantage over a written piece of music, as an eloquent extemporary sermon over the dull reading of a precomposed harangue.—From neither is previous meditation and study excluded; on the contrary it is absolutely indispensable that the theme or subject be accurately digested, and perfectly well understood, leaving only the particular expression, unrestrained by the shackles of definite notes, to be qualified at the moment of delivery by the genuine feeling of the heart. But laziness has crept in here as elsewhere, and it is now as customary for a voluntary to be played from a copy, as it is for a sermon to be read from a book.

However, as the production of a good voluntary requires a degree of talent, which in the present state of musical knowledge every parochial organist cannot be supposed to possess, and a frame of mind to which some charitably suppose most of the profession to be entire strangers; it is prudent to permit the introduction of written music in its stead, and which usually passes by the same name, as some-

* Although one says, " The voluntary derives its appellation from the license formerly enjoyed by parochial Organists of performing or omitting such interlude at pleasure."

† It was a voluntary which David played before Saul when the evil spirit was upon him, and the consequence was, that " Saul was refreshed, and was well, and the evil spirit departed from him."

times do also the other parts of an organist's duty, " called playing in" and " playing out," which might with great propriety be termed prelude and postlude. All three require much the same style, excepting that it may be allowed in " playing out" to employ occasionally a somewhat brisker movement than in the other two.

The purpose of the whole is evidently to enliven and embellish the service, to relieve the minister and the congregation, and to afford to the people an opportunity and excitement to serious meditation ; and this purpose should at all times be steadily kept in view by the performer. He should recollect, and let the impression be constantly upon his mind, that he is not playing in a theatre to excite the vain applause of the silly multitude, but in the house of his Maker, in whose immediate presence he is, and to whose " praise and glory" all his efforts should be directed. By this reflection he would find himself relieved from many distressing embarassments, his mind free from the petty anxieties which on other occasions are so apt to distract it, and all his energies at perfect liberty to be concentrated upon the simple object before him. His music would be solemn yet cheerful, and strictly adapted to the circumstances of the occasion ; too varied to excite weariness, and too consistent to promote levity ; sufficiently learned to please the ears of the most fastidious, yet not so recondite but that in it the most uninformed might experience satisfaction ; to which men might listen with delight, and even angels with complacency.

In the voluntary there is the most unlimited scope for the exercise of taste science, and ingenuity—reference being always had to its sacred objects. Diapason pieces and andante movements seem best to suit the commencement and middle of the service, and fugues of sober character, whether *ex tempore* or otherwise, are admirably adapted to the close. There are no organ passages more deservedly popular than those performed on the swell ; when judiciously employed they have a wonderfully captivating effect ; but they are liable to a very serious objection, viz. that as the organ is at present constituted, they necessarily abstract one foot from the service of the pedals. Great length should be most carefully avoided, as should also long dwelling upon any particular series of notes or combination of stops ; and when the close arrives, it should come de-

29

cidedly, and not leave the minister or the congregation in
suspense as to the actual termination of the piece. An
awkward cadence may thus in one moment, by exciting a
feeling of anxiety, deface the impression which the foregoing performance had produced, and spoil the cordiality
of the whole service, as an accident towards the commencement generally destroys the harmony for the remaining time of meeting. In the concluding voluntary, of
course greater latitude of time may be allowed, as those
who are weary are at liberty to depart. In some churches
in Holland, it is said to be customary for the organists to
continue playing for a full hour after the conclusion of the
service, and that not to empty pews, as the greater part
of the congregation is found to remain.

Connected with this subject, a pleasant anecdote is told
of the celebrated Handel, who excelled in performance as
in composition. In a country church he once asked the
organist to permit him to play the people out ; to which
with a politeness characteristic of the profession, he of
course consented. Handel accordingly sat down to the
organ, and began to play in such a masterly manner as instantly to attract the attention of the whole congregation,
who, instead of vacating their seats as usual, remained for
a considerable space of time, fixed in silent admiration.
The Organist began to be impatient, (perhaps his wife was
waiting dinner,) and at length addressing the Performer,
told him that he was convinced *he* could not play the people out, and advised him to relinquish the attempt ; which
being done ; a few strains in the accustomed manner operated like the reading of the Riot Act by instantly dispers-
ing the audience.

With reference to every subject, there are degrees of
sympathy or antipathy, veneration or aborrence. So in
music ; one thinks it absolutely indispensable to the
celebration of Divine worship, another is indifferent
about it, a third objects to particular sorts or kinds,
a fourth asserts the whole to be a superstious ad-
junct and altogether foreign to the genuine spirit of
Christian religion, and a fifth declares it a devilish machi-
nation which ought to be altogether banished from civilized society.

Our present business is with those only who object to instrumental music, particularly the organ voluntary. What
is sufficiently remarkable is, that the parties so objecting

are generally, if not universally, found to be of the class usually called Evangelical : not, it is imagined, that there is any necessary connexion between Evangelical religion and a dislike for music ; for if so, what a heathenish place heaven must be !

The objections brought against this ceremony are principally the following : That as instrumental music only, it expresses no sentiment and consequently is of no use ; that it adds to the length of a service, already sufficiently extended ; that it distracts the attention, which should be fixed on better things ; and sometimes, with great propriety, that it is abused to a mere display of dexterity. Of these in their order.

If the religion of Christ were a system of pure sentimentalism, if it had *only* to do with the head and were not intended to affect the heart, if the spirit only were to be engaged and the body to operate upon it as a mere clog, then indeed the first objection would be fatal. But such is not the fact, religion has more to do with the heart than the head, with the affections than with the understanding ; and upon the very same part of our nature, has music also its most powerful hold. Harmony is not addressed to the intellect, but to the feelings ; that it is therefore of no use, is far from self-evident ; it only follows that it is of no use to those who have no feeling for it, and who are on that account, provided they thrust not their stupid insensibility in the way of the enjoyment of others, to be rather pitied than contemned. They want a sense.

Concerning the *time* which it is said to occupy, it may be urged that a few minutes* do not seem of any very great importance; but if they should be so esteemed, perhaps there is some other part of the service from which more than an equivalent may be subtracted, without serious loss or inconvenience. At all events, the objection does not apply to the voluntary before or after service. The former would evidently have the tendency to produce a more punctual attendance [of the musical part of the congregation at least,] than is now at all times observed ; and the latter could not possibly interfere unpleasantly with the time of any, because none are under the slightest obligation to remain to hear it.

* The voluntary should not exceed five minutes,

But the objection to which most weight is by a certain party uniformly attached is, that it takes off the attention from better things ; or with reference to the "playing out," that "it drives the sermon out of the people's head," A serious charge certainly ; but to support it, it should first be proved that the sermon would otherwise *remain* there. If sit so loosely as this assertion supposes, is it not more than probable that the act of walking home, or at least that of eating a good dinner, produces precisely the same effect ? and if such be the case, is it not better that the sermon be displaced by what does partake somewhat of a sacred character, than by that which is altogether secular ? If there were any weight in this objection, it would follow that the prayers are in like manner " driven out" by the sermon, and consequently that the latter should be conscientiously interdicted.   But in a mind of common capacity, when religiously disposed, neither the one nor the other effect takes place.   With such an one, an appropriate voluntary (and only such are here defended) has the tendency to fix the impression which the preceding discourse may have produced, in the same manner that a good varnish preserves the colors of a painting.   But were the objection, ever so valid, it applies with very small force to the voluntary after the psalms, and with none at all to the prelude before the service.

To the more mighty objection drawn from the abuse it must be conceded, that voluntaries have been heard, in which, apparently, the only effect was to get over the greatest number of notes in a given space of time, or to educe as much noise as the utmost powers of the instrument could furnish, or most effectually to remove all serious impressions from the minds of the hearers by light and trifling airs, and even sometimes by the music of well known profane songs, so as infallibly to call up gross and wanton ideas.   It is not pretended that the language of the confession, "*We have left undone those things which we ought to have done, and we have done those things which we ought not to have done,*" is not as well adapted to the race of organists as to any other class of human beings.   But what of all this ?   Must it be repeated, for the millionth time, that the abuse does not disprove the use ? or are only those things to retain their rank which have never been abused ?   What then will be left to us ?   No psalms, no hymns, no voluntaries ; no prayers, no speeches, no sermons ; no music, no painting, no poetry ; none of the arts of civilized, none even of savage society.*

True, the voluntary has been abused. Now if this be the real objection, let it be candidly stated, and let the transgressing organists clearly understand that there is not sufficient confidence reposed in them to discharge their duty with becoming decorum ; and let them be cashiered as inefficient ; and let this stigma remain indelibly affixed to their characters. It is more than probable, that in the event of the adoption of such a measure, the next generation of professors may renounce the folly of their predecessors, and so the good old custom be completely re-established.

The marks of design, manifest in the formation of those parts of the human system which are destined to the production of articulate and melodious sounds, are abundant proofs of the divine origin of the art of music. That there is a charm in the powers of the human voice, far surpassing the sweetness of the most exquisite musical instrument, is a position, the truth of which is incontestible. These have such a ductile flexibility and ineffable energy of intonation, as alone to constitute it a machine of truly wonderful expression ; but, as combined with the faculty of speech, leave every other at an immeasurable distance.

VOCAL MUSIC.

There are, who commend the voice to the disparagement of instruments ; and there are also, who unjustly exalt the value of instruments, and utterly disallow the pretensions of the voice. Both are in egregious error. Neither the one kind of music, nor the other, is exclusively good. Much as the one excels the other in pathos, and the excitement of the softer feelings of our nature, it is equally behind it in power and compass and consequently in the development of the grandest harmonic combinations. But when conjoined, the defects of both are supplied. Each derives addi-

* " Nihil prodest quod non lædere posset idem ;
Igne quid utilius ?"

tional beauty or effect from the connexion with its rival;
and hence they present a not unapt resemblance of the
connubial relationship. The majesty of the organ is thus
blended with the sweetness and expression of the human
voice ; it lends a richness, a brilliancy, a fulness, and even
a solemnity which the voice otherwise could never acquire;
but receives in return an animation, an impress of mind, a
glow of devotion, to which merely instrumental music can
never approach. Besides all this, the voice is actually indebted for its perfection to the use of the very instruments,
which some would banish from our places of worship, as so
many ambassadors from " the prince of the power of the
air." It is universally found that accuracy and precision
of execution, not to be met with under other circumstances, are results of a habit of singing to a good instrumental
accompaniment ; so that in the very instances wherein vocal music only, to the exclusion of instrumental, has been
commended, it will be found to have been the case that the
parties performing have acquired their correctness from
previous constant, or at least occasional, accompanied practice ; and it may be at almost any time observed, that in
those places where instruments are never allowed, the
singing partakes of an unsteady, disorderly, pot-house quality, resulting from the natural defects of the human voice,
aggravated tenfold by the want of cultivation. How should
it be otherwise ? How should a school-boy learn to write
straight without lines ? and *in music*, what is any congregation, taken collectively, but a mob of children ? Is it
seemly, is it right, that the Lord of the whole earth should
be thus put off with stuff, misnomered, singing, such as if
heard in a common parlour would excite only ridicule or
disgust ? and this too from choice. Surely whatever we
offer to the Deity should be the best we can procure. But
congregational singing never will be, never can be, even
tolerable to but half instructed ears, till led by some steady
guide, which shall gradually accustom the voices to a degree of order and discipline, and on emergence be in readi-
ness to correct extravagancies.

Vocal music is either congregational or choral : that is,
adapted to the use of the whole, or of a part ; of the merits
and uses of each of which, more will be said hereafter.

It may not be amiss here, before we enter minutely upon
the various kinds, to advert to its general attributes.

Unquestionably then, all church music, as well vocal as

instrumental, should partake of the character of the place
and occasion of its performance. It should be solemn, yet
not gloomy,—learned, yet not abstruse,—appropriate to
the occasion, yet not affected, got up in the best manner,
yet with no view to the gratification of vanity or conceit.
If none can act quite up to the letter of such instructions,
they may yet not do the worse for keeping them in view.
No one can err by fixing his standard of perfection too
high.

The works of nature are infinitely deversified, and the
species into which they are artificially divided, exceedingly numerous. The shades of difference between one species and another are so minute, that it is often difficult,
sometimes impossible, to decide, concerning an individual,
to what class it belongs.

Even so is it with the objects of the doctrine of sounds.
It is impossible to ascertain precisely at what point *saying*
terminates, and *singing* commences.—Singing indeed is only a melodious saying, and saying an irregular singing. In
common unaffected speech or conversation, the inflection
of voice employed by persons not at all connected with the
study of music, is a field of most curious and interesting
observation. The number of distinct sounds, so produced,
in a very short space of time, any one of which, continued
for a moment, would be found to admit of musical admeas-
urement, is truly astonishing.

"Musical harmony (saith the judicious Hooker) whether by instrument or by voice, is but of high and low in
sounds a due proportionate disposition." in conversation
this is not sought ; in singing it is. But where is the standard ? What is a due and proportionate disposition of
high and low sounds ? Herein music labors under peculiar disadvantage. It has not, like painting, a direct appeal
to any model in nature. It is the pure offspring of the
imagination and of the feelings—a creature of taste.

Unquestionably there is music in speech ; but it has not
been subjected to rule. The intervals it expresses are almost infinitely small, and human ingenuity has not yet discovered a method of confining and embodying them in
any system of notation. Nevertheless, it may be remarked that every speaker has what may be termed a key-note,
and his pronunciation is said to be pleasant or unpleasant,
according to the manner in which he manages the modulation or progression about this fundamental note or sound,

Accordingly, it may be noticed, that no two persons do or can pronounce the same words precisely in the same manner.   Independently of the different qualities of tone or sound, and the pitch of the key-note of particular voices, each has a peculiar method of inflection.   In various parties, this is done in dissimilar ways, to the production of widely differing effects.   Hence one man shall speak as "having authority," and all shall attend to his admonitions with the deference due to a superior being ; and another shall repeat the very same sentences, and his words shall pass unheeded.   The sound of the voice of one shall so captivate his hearers, that though on an errand of blood, their purpose shall be arrested ; and the effect of the speech of another, though intended to melt the very soul, shall be only to move to laughter.   The reason is to be sought in the constitution of our nature.*

At first all this may seem foreign to the subject, but a little consideration will induce a different opinion.   If what has been advanced be correct, it will follow that no two persons can speak or read together, in the ordinary way without producing an unmusical dissonance, which will be proportionally augmented by an increase of the number of the parties so engaged.

But let the same number of individuals read or repeat in one even tone, which may be accomplished almost without effort, and the most fastidious ear needs not to be displeased.   To effect this is only required a Precentor possessed of a strong, clear, tenor voice, which may be distinctly heard of all present.   Such a Precentor in parochial churches is, or should be, the clerk ; who is to officiate as bellwether to the flock.   As has been premised, it is necessary that he read in a continued even tone, seeing that otherwise it is absolutely impossible for the people to follow him, and the harsh discord which is the inevitable consequence of a different method of proceeding, is obvious to the most unmusical ears.   Some parish clerks, as though infected with the would-be-reforming spirit of the age, have recently modified this part of their duty, and betaken themselves to a style of reading, to speak the most respectfully of it,

---

* Doubtless the remote cause of this diversity is, that some feel the force the language which they express, and others do not ; and even if those who do, each in a different degree : but a consideration of this subject would lead a long way about, and therefore it has been thought proper barely thus to glance at it.

highly inappropriate. Where the people do not take the trouble to repeat the parts of the service allotted to them, which is shamefully the case in many places, it matters not much in what manner the clerk conducts himself ; but where they follow the directions of the Rubric, his demeanor becomes a matter of considerable importance. When he reads in a full steady tone, the people naturally repeat in the same, or in some other, having a musical relation to it ; but when he turns one word up and twists another down, now exalting his voice, and now depressing it, after the similitude of a certain animal as notorious for his musical taste as for his exemplary patience—the undisciplined and unrestrained voices of the multitude run into a mass of jarring sounds, a chaos of noises, in which nothing is to be discerned but discord and confusion. The one may be compared to the march of a veteran regiment, the other to the scamper of a tumultuous mob.

ON CHANTING.

Reading in an even tone is the first step to chanting. It is the lowest species of church music, and one in which it may be reasonably expected that every one should join. The monotony, of which some might feel disposed to complain, is relieved by those parts assigned to the minister alone, and who as reading singly, of course very properly takes advantage of all the means of expression in his power. The pitch should not be so high, but at most might comfortably reach it ; nor so low but that those who felt so disposed might make use of its octave.* But some may

* It may be proper to remark, that it is not intended that very part of the service should be read in the same pitch or elevation of voice. There are some parts wherein a lower, and some wherein a higher tone is desirable ; as for instance the Confession, which is directed to be said " with an humble voice," and the Lord's Prayer, which, when occurring the second time, is ordered to be said " with a loud voice." Common sense will supply other varieties.

object that this will utterly prevent the giving of proper expression to the words.   True, it may remove one kind of expression, but much is left.

Emphasis and accent not only depend upon the relation to a key note, but upon the quantity or intensity of sound, the duration of time, and other circumstances, connected with the pronunciation of any particular word or words.   Only one sort of expression therefore is debarred, and that to prevent a confusion in which none at all can be distinguished.   This point is so clear that it seems needless to dwell upon it ; yet it is strange how the prevailing practice outrages all sense of propriety.   May not this be one reason why the service itself is, in many parts, suffered to slip by as an idle ceremony, in which the people are no more concerned than the particles of dust upon the floor. Where by adding his voice each only adds to the mass of confusion, what better than silence ?   Who endued with but a particle of musical feeling, could, but by an act of self denial, join in a ceremony which, as too often conducted, partakes only of the nature of horrid noise, as ungrateful to one sense as the most loathsome stench to another ? When it might be so easily corrected, who but must deplore the existence of such an evil ?   In the name of decency, of order, of decorum, and of that uniformity at which the Episcopal Church aspires, let the good old custom be restored.

If after reading steadily through some verses, a slight deflection of voice be made on the penultimate syllable, there will be produced a very agreeable musical effect. Hence originated the old ecclesiastical chant, which consisted of but few notes, and was sung of the whole congregation in unisons.   This is music of the simplest description, but such as is capable of association with the true sublime.   What is much to be regretted, it is rarely to be heard, excepting in some parts of the cathedral service, and there but sparingly ; the reason of which may be, that to give it its best effect, it is requisite that it be performed by a vast number of voices.

The next degree of church music is constituted by the addition of other sounds, at harmonic intervals, with the former or principal melody, that is—making what is called a chord with it.   It is hardly possible for a person possessed of an ear for music to attend to any single sound, long

continued, without imagining another bearing a relation to
it. Indeed, in the nature of things, one sound always gene-
rates more, only they are not always perceptible. In the
sound of a large bell there may be distinguished many different tones, all springing from the original note as their
common parent. The harmonic simultaneous sounds can
be produced by human voices more perfectly than by any
other means, and are said to have been invented and introduced into the Christian Church by Guido, in the beginning of the eleventh century ; from which period almost
up to the present time may be dated a progressive improvement in Church Music.

That to which this remark principally refers is the singing of the Responses or certain short petitionary and other
sentences, occurring in various parts of the common prayer, without an instrumental accompaniment. This, as requiring considerable skill, can scarcely become congregational, and, therefore can hardly be wished to be universally introduced ; yet it is so heavenly in its effect, that none
but a vandal could talk of its total expulsion. It is at present nearly confined to the cathedrals, where it may be occasionally heard to great perfection. Its beauty consists in
the peculiar sweetness of which concords, formed entirely
of well regulated voices, are susceptible, and which derive
additional attraction from the situation in which they are
heard.

Of the same description with these sentences, but of much
easier performance, is the word of so frequent recurrence,
the emphatic Amen, with which, in the form of a simple
cadence, much beauty can be associated. The Amen in
in the primitive church, we are told, was wont to come
forth like a clap of thunder ; but alas ! that thunder has
long since ceased to call. Where the word now makes its
way out, it is often times rather like the muttering whisper of some little urchin, fearful that his master will over-
hear and punish him for breaking silence. The reason of
this has been already surmised.

There is daily an increasing want of a standard or guide,
and those who are not silent from other considerations, or
the want of them, find it better to be mute than to add to
the uncertain sound, another particle of discord. But besides this, there is another fearful point on which multitudes
are at issue. One repeats the bold, round, English *Ah !*

men ; another the more refined and delicate *Ai* or *Ae*-men, and a third fllies to the opposite extreme and cries *Au*-men. Which is the orthodox reading ?　Even the learned are divided ; only it may be noticed, that the *Ai*-mens are increasing, which may be perhaps accounted for by the remark, that that is the pronunciation generally adopted by the ladies.

Whichever way this question may be ultimately disposed of, if resolved *musically*, it will be settled in favour of the plain simple A. neither dwindled into the meaner mincing sound of Ai, nor spread out into the clumsy yawn Au, and this reading has other very strong presumptions in its favor, which, not being immediately connected with our subject, we shall pass over.

The addition of one melody to another, both sounding at the same time, which constitutes the harmony said to have been introduced by Guido, is called, in vocal music, *singing in parts*.　This, which compared to the prior state of music, is as great an improvement as the structure of a modern ship is upon the original raft, has been by some simple heads thought to be an infringement upon the decency of divine worship and even a detraction from the solemnity of the music.

There is no accounting for tastes, and this is a pure matter of taste.　Argument would therefore be perfectly misapplied, even were the parties capable of understanding it. It is very possible, yea, it is very true, that conceited and ill informed persons have attempted to execute what they call singing in parts, and have *executed* it with a vengeance.

Certainly it is preferable to hear all singing together in unisons and octaves, than one squeaking out a so called counter tenor at a third below the melody from the beginning to end, not even excepting the close—another aping a tenor at all manner of discordant intervals, and gracing his performance occasionally with half a dozen consecutive fifths to the upper or lower part,—and a third grumbling out what he deems a capital bass, just two octaves from the treble, note for note, excepting where a want of compass compels him to ascend to the upper story of his voice ; all seemingly actuated by a sincere consciousness that they have arrived at the ne plus ultra of the harmonic art, and consequently proceeding with the most vociferous confidence.　Better far, in all places where there is not some one at least of the performers sufficiently well qualified to instruct and correct, when in error, his ignorant brethren, that singing in parts should be altogether discountenanced.

But to return to the responses. As the words are principally the language of the most solemn application, and, as in the instance of the word *Amen*, there is implied an assent and consent to all and every thing contained in the previous prayer, many well meaning persons have objected to their being *sung* at all--having a notion that real prayer can have no alliance with music. It is an absurd notion. There is no feeling of the heart, no emotion of the soul, that can find utterance in words, which may not also have a natural association with harmonious sounds. The powers of music are co-extensive with those of language. They may not all have been yet developed, and of those which have been, many may have been unskilfully employed ; but enough has been done and felt to prove that the mind, in its strongest paroxysms of excitement, finds its most appropriate vent in music. Dr. Blair says " that man is born both a poet and a musician, and that the same impulse which prompts the enthusiastic poetic style, prompts a certain melody or modulation of sound, suited to the emotions of joy or grief, of admiration, love or anger." Well adapted music, therefore, that is, such as correct taste teaches, is the proper channel for the expression of intense feeling. It is the vernacular idiom of nature. Whether the music may not be sometimes employed when the feeling is wanting, or whether that circumstance may not detract from its solemnity, and impair or destroy its effect on the minds of the hearers, are quite different points of inquiry to that which we have been treating, and may hereafter come under our notice.

The ancient ecclesiastical chant, of which mention has already been made, was characterized by the utmost simplicity. The addition of harmony of course rendered it somewhat more complicated ; but still the principal part or melody, was such as might be sung with the greatest ease. With some slight modification, both the name and the thing are still retained.

Chanting has this advantage over all other methods of singing, that by means of it *prose* may be sung without the previous study necessary for the performance of an anthem. Thus the very words of holy writ may be employed, in this delightful part of divine worship, without the mutilation or

redundancy which it must necessarily undergo if turned into metre.

When properly conducted this is the easiest method of
singing, and therefore it is much to be wondered at that it
is not in use among " all sorts and conditions of men ;" but
the same prejudice which has operated to the rejection and
continued exclusion of the organ from an entire division of
the national church has been connected with chanting also.

But the practice of the legitimate style of church music
is reviving. In many parochial churches the hymns following the lessons are regularly chanted, and the congrega-
tions begin to take a part in the performance. This is as
it should be. If, after recovering from the attacks of fan-
aticism and bigotry,it be not choked by the thorns and briars
of empiricism, it will be well ; but there is a danger. The
taste of finery, which seems to pervade, more or less, all the
productions of the present day, has crept even into the
church, and instead of the sober simplicity which actuated
the devotional harmony of our forefathers, modern refine-
ment has introduced difficult passages and chromatic intervals, as though intending to prevent the interference of any
in their execution, excepting those who may have attended
previous rehearsals. It is for this reason that chanting is
so generally and so improperly confined to the choir. It
should not be. The music of a chant is not the proper
place for the display of the agility of some voices to the
discouragement of others, but should be such as that all
might comfortably join in it. All therefore that is required is a simple and natural melody of moderate compass—
for the most part, if not exclusively, written in semibreves
and minims, and accompanied by a well-digested harmony.
These are the characteristics of an othordox chant. All
fine turns, and running passages, and excessive leaps, and
difficult intervals, should be condemned as musical heresies.

The congregation should not seek for *pretty* music, but
for that in which they can most easily join, and which will
least distract their minds from the business which they ought
to be upon. Nor does this hinder that the music be as in-
trinsically good as the ingenuity of man can bring forth, if
that only be good which best fulfils its destined purpose.

Thus much for music. It will be well now to bestow a
few words upon the manner of its performance, in doing
which the writer hopes he shall be excused if he mention a
few particulars which to some persons may appear too well

known to need repetition, but which he believes are not so generally apprehended as is imagined.

The only part of the service commonly chanted, besides the hymns before mentioned, is the portion of Psalms for the day. The whole book of Psalms, which, as Hooker expresses it, contains "the flower of all things profitable in other books," is undoubtedly better adapted to the daily use of the church than any other entire section of the scriptures ; nevertheless no good reason can be assigned why portions selected from other parts of the sacred Writings may not be sung in like manner and thus, in the celebration of divine worship, entirely supercede the use of uninspired metrical compositions, which have within the last three centuries so generally obtained. In that case, it would only be necessary that they should be previously "*pointed*" to be sung in churches.

Perhaps there are thousands who have read this phrase in the title page of their prayer book, and never comprehended its meaning : it may not therefore be altogether useless to explain it.

There will be noticed then in the psalter, as also in some other parts of the prayer-book, a *colon* near the middle of every verse. This colon is not there placed as commonly used in the body, but to guide the singers in the act of chanting, which explanation will be satisfactory to those who have supposed that the passage should be rendered "*appointed* to be sung," &c.

The general rule is as follows. Of the syllables occurring *before* this colon, all excepting *three* are to be repeated [in the manner of reading in an even tone] upon the *first* note ; the three so reserved will be found just enough to conclude the first section or division of the chant : then, of the syllables occurring *after* the colon, all excepting *five* must be pronounced upon the next note [viz. the first of the second section] and the five reserved will carry the singer to the end of the chant, if a single one, and just half way if double : in either case the next verse will be treated precisely in the same manner.

A person desirous of chanting without hesitation, would find it a considerable help to mark or underline these three and five syllables, alternately in his prayer-book ; observing, that if there happen to be too few in any verse, the principal or accented syllable must be longer dwelt upon to fill up the music of the chant, that is, by singing the same word to two or more consecutive notes. A very little practice will soon make the student expert.

It is by no means necessary that the words be gabbled over, as some scandalously abuse them, and thus bring discredit upon the method itself. All the words should be pronounced *distinctly*, with but little more celerity than in ordinary speech, and those which require it *emphatically*. When performed with the organ [which for various reasons is almost indispensably necessary,] as technically speaking, there is *no time* in chanting—notwithstanding some foolishly and ignorantly attempt, whatever the length or shortness of the verses, to bring all to their standard, and Procustes like, mangle or stretch them miserably if they do not happen to fit. The organist is bound to hold out or contract notes, according to the number of syllables, till he hears them orderly pronounced, and then, and not till then, to proceed, somewhat briskly or otherwise, according to the spirit of the language.

In some places, it is usual to hurry out the words as fast as the mouth can utter them, and then go on with the melody quite in the dead march style, making a long pause between each section, this is woeful, and betrays either stupidity or want of authority in the director.

Again you may hear the organ driving on the voices from one section to the other, scarcely allowing time to draw breath; this is indecent, and only manifests the light and careless mind of the organist. The old custom of alternate singing, if revived in our churches, would have an admirable tendency to enliven our dull devotions. How pleasant would it be, thus to witness a large congregation, divided into two bodies, singing alternately the songs of Zion, and how would it interest the soul to hear them all joining in the close with one heart and voice, saying " *Glory be to the Father, and to the Son, and to the Holy Ghost.*" How much like the situation of the Prophet when he saw the Seraphim about the throne, and heard them cry " *one unto the other,*" saying, " *Holy, holy, holy, is the Lord of Hosts, the whole earth is full of his glory.*"

Every age has its fashion. The music now in vogue delights in noise and bustle. Rapidity is more commended than precision, and force more highly valued than feeling.

The genius of harmony, or some other pretending to that title, has converted the piano forte into a velocipede, and reckons her success by the number of miles which she can traverse in an hour, not regarding the awkwardness or ungracefulness of her method of travelling. Other departments of the art have caught the infection ; and now all the rage, even in vocal music, is for velocity of execution ; and the principal singers have, for many years past, with but few exceptions, truckled to this depraved public feeling. This perversion of taste will, it is to be hoped, like the ludicrous machine from which the metaphor has been borrowed, run its little day, and then drop into oblivion.

A hundred years ago nothing was esteemed, in the church or out of it, but the plodding motion of fugue or canon.— The productions of that day were, for the most part, sound and of good body ; and although they sometimes appear to be deficient in animation and vivacity, especially if measured by a modern standard, yet they will generally bear the strictest examination. On the contrary, ours are rather frivolous and superficial, but sparkling as the momentary effervescence of soda water. Thin as this music is, there are many who can relish none other ; they look for it even in the house of God ; and, by their improper influence over the performers, have, it is to be presumed, against their better judgment, succeeded in introducing a style which may be denominated, without speaking passionately, a foul disgrace to the church. However, it must be acknowledged—and it is a circumstance for which all lovers of the art ought to be sincerely thankful—that this spirit of jingle has not as yet made so much inroad upon services as upon some other descriptions of church music.

It is to be lamented that even where there is a good choir, the music is not invariably performed as it should be. It is oftentimes indecently hurried over, as a mere task, in which the vocal organs only are concerned. Suppose yourself deaf, and then present yourself before some choir when in the ordinary execution of their duty, and endeavor to make a probable guess at the nature of their occupation. Who would for a moment imagine that they were singing the praises of their Maker ? Who would but for an instant suppose that they were supplicating for mercy at the foot-stool of the Judge of the quick and the dead ? Who would conjecture that they were petitioning for grace at the hands of the Giver of every good and perfect gift ? Who would not rather sometimes incline to fancy that they were chant-

31

ing the praises of some celebrated toast, or, at best, that
" *Glorious Apollo*" formed the burden of the song ?

Perhaps it is an evil incident to the stated performance
of *any* moral duty, that there will be a tendency to the
preponderance of mere form ; but it is an evil which may
and which ought to be checked. Of the two, open levity is
more hopeful and therefore more desirable (if even the lesser of two great evils can in any sense be desirable) than
hypocritical sanctity.

However, it is not always that devotion is swallowed up
by formality. Sometimes, when the selection of music is
judicious, and appropriate to the circumstances of the meeting as well as to the powers of the performers, those engaged
in it evidently enter into the spirit of the language, and then,
and only then, impart to the words an expression which a
proper feeling of their purport exclusively communicates.
Then may be seen " the rapt soul setting in the eye," as
though, like the first martyr, it were favored with some bea-
tific vision. Then is it that the powers of harmony are applied to their proper use, when they thus carry the soul, on
the wings of the purest devotion, into the celestial regions,
where, purified from the grossness of secular considerations,
it sports itself in an angelic atmosphere, and acquires a fore-
taste of its future occupation.

Whether these words are barely permissive, or whether
they amount to a command, may perhaps be thought dis-
putable. Those who are adverse to the cause of church
music will of course maintain the former ; but perhaps were
something which they approve substituted for that which
they dislike, they might soon learn to construe the sentence
compulsorily. The plain meaning seems to be, that in all
places where the singing of an anthem is at all practicable, it
shall form a regular part of the service. Were there but
half this authority for some other things, we should see how
greedily it would be asserted, and how tenaciously maintained.

THE ANTHEM.

It is much to be regretted, that the anthem is so very rare as it is now become. With a few solitary exceptions on very extraordinary occasions, an anthem in a parochial church is perfectly obsolete ; not, it is to be charitably supposed, from a deficiency of musical talent, but through want of encouragement and opportunity for its exertion and improvement.

Still anthems do maintain their ground in cathedrals ; yet to obtain even permission for their occasional use in a parish church is a matter requiring the exertion of considerable influence. To this circumstance may be distinctly traced many of the extravagancies which have made their appearance in other departments of church music. It has been attempted to convert psalm tunes, from the sober character of congregational melodies, into anthems, by filling them with fugue and imitation points, difficult chromatic passages, and extraneous modulations, fit only for the use of well-trained choirs. This is an absurdity.

An anthem is properly a musical composition on some sacred subject, and generally adapted to words taken from the Holy Scriptures. It admits of the utmost variety, and embraces every possible topic which may be fit to introduce into the church. It follows of course that in the anthem, more than in an any other part of the service, we may look for something appropriate to the peculiar circumstances of the meeting, whether grave or cheerful. It is not adapted to any determinate number of voices—it is not confined to any particular style—it is not restricted to any definite length—it is not embarrassed with any precise laws. Sometimes it very properly occupies but three or four minutes, and at others as many hours ; for an oratorio is but an expanded anthem, in which a unity of subject is observed, and some definite action kept constantly in view. The oratorio and the anthem stand precisely in the same relation one to the other as the epic and lesser poems.

This is the highest walk of church music. In its composition the most exalted genius may find unlimited scope for

the employment of his utmost powers   The Book of Revelation in his hand from which to choose his sacred theme,
the volumes of Nature and Providence spread before him
from which to select his illustrations, and the eternal wel-
fare of his fellow creatures as an object to stimulate his exertions—where can be found a field more extensive, materials more boundless, or a motive more sublime ?   He
may adopt the simplicity of unsophisticated melody, or
he may wander through all the mazes of the most intricate
harmony. He may recal in doleful strains the lamentations
of the weeping prophet, or he may join in the exultation of
the children of Israel when delivered from the hands of
their enemies.   He may enter into the sorrowful cry of the
penitent and disconsolate sinner, or he may unite with the
rapturous hallelujahs of disembodied spirits.

It is with remarkable propriety placed between the prayers, near the end of the service, as a relief which in that
particular place is most sensibly felt.   And truly nothing
can be more delightful ; it is the summit **or** top-stone of our
devotions.   It refreshes and comforts the heart, it revives
and exhilarates the spirits, it lifts the soul above the cares
and disquietudes of mortality, and carries it to the mansions
of the blest.

It is peculiarly appropriate at a funeral. On such occasions
the heart is open and the feelings softened, and the sterner
features of character relaxed, and the mind by the very
circumstances half-severed from the world, so that we become peculiarly susceptible of solemn emotions.

Surely those who would deprive the celebration of Divine
Worship of this its most celestial part, must possess affections dull as the ground on which they tread.   We have
asylums for the blind, hospitals for the sick, infirmaries for
the maimed, receptacles for the insane, penitentiaries for
the unfortunate, and workhouses for the destitute ; but for
this class of beings, as much objects of pity and compassion as either, neither hospital nor workhouse is provided,
but they are suffered to range at large and even to deter
others from the proper exercise and enjoyment of faculties which they themselves do not possess.

Great names may be adduced of individuals, who have
felt no enthusiasm with regard to this most pleasing,
most sacred of the arts, and who may have manifested ev-
en something like an antipathy to it. But what then ?—
This only proves that their minds though large were not

sufficiently capacious to contain more than their own peculiar object of study and regard.

" One science only will one genius fit ;
So vast is art, so narrow human wit."

Those who would shelter their own insensibility by such examples, should be in other respects such as they whose authority they quote ; they might then produce an approximation to an excuse, though even this would not amount to a justification.

Thus, as we have seen, has the Church of England made abundant provision for the solace and comfort for all the sons of harmony. Vocal and instrumental music, separately and conjointly, and in every possible gradation, from the single utterance of words upon one continued sound, to the grandest combinations, and most scientific evolutions of the art, enter alike into the composition of her service. Were but her provisions carried into effect, the most enthusiastic would have nothing to desire. But, alas ! laws however excellent, regulations however salutary, cannot enforce *themselves*. Whatever the constitution in theory, it will be in practice just what the disposition and capacities of the multitude make it ; and therefore we cannot hope for any sensible improvement in church music, without a vast moral change in the great body of the people ; nor will that change take place unaccompanied by the former : they will be simultaneous and mutually indicative.

If any feel inclined to say, what they have repeatedly said already, " all this music is unnecessary," it is at once granted that in a sense it is so. For instance, it is not as necessary as medicine to the sick, as food to the the hungry, or as clothing to the naked. But if not necessary, it cannot be denied that it is useful. Even ornament has a use, when it tends to render that delightful which is too often esteemed irksome, and to allure by its beauty a class of persons who might otherwise be repelled by the severer features of religious observances.

Certainly it is unfortunate that the performance of music occupies such a space of time as it necessarily consumes; as this circumstance makes it obnoxious to a very respectable portion of the clergy, who might not otherwise perhaps be classed among its adversaries and oppugners. Still it behoves them seriously to consider whether, by depriving the outward forms of religion of their pomp and splendor, they do not incur the risk of rendering them less attractive to those who might, by their instrumentality, under the blessing of God, become subjects of its regenerating influence.

There is another objection, which indeed, for its supreme folly, hardly deserves mention. There has been sometimes and somewhere ventured 'the groundless *opinion* that services and anthems, and chanting also, should be utterly disallowed in parochial churches ; and the reason assigned is the most ridiculous that can be imagined, viz. least they become *too common.* If the objection were serious enough to warrant a reply, it might be asked, are not prayers by their very title *common* ? and if one method of performing them be more proper or more edifying than another, ought not that method to be common also ? It is furthermore asserted, that no approximation to the cathedral service should be permitted out of it, and that a psalm tune, drawled out by half a score or half a hundred charity children, is quite good enough for parish purposes—and all this for no other reason than to preserve the superiority of the cathedral manner of worship.

That the cathedrals should be looked up to is undeniably proper. The best way, however, to insure this tribute of respect is, when parish choirs take one step towards good music, for cathedral choirs to take two, and not attempt to thrust their weaker brethren back. If the members of such choirs only improve the advantages which they possess as regularly disciplined forces, they need not fear the rivaly of voulnteer troops ; but if they sleep at their posts, or only bestir themselves to depreciate the skill of others, they may eventually discredit their own.

The lamentable fact is that there are some who have no relish for the pleasures of harmony, and who consequently have no desire for its advancement. There may also be some unworthy members of the profession who feel no zeal for the cause but that which is mercenarily derived. Some go so far as to discover not merely disrelish, but aversion, hatred, abhorrence. Such a character among the labouring poor, though by far the most numerous class of society, is extremely rare. Those persons who *hate* music will be found to be either destitute of the common attributes of humanity, or the powers of whose minds are engrossed by some sublunary object too vast for their grasp, or whose whole affections have been set upon some fancied good, a pursuit of which is incompatible with that state of mind which musical enjoyment pre-supposes. In the first case they are doltish idiots, in the second half-poets or half-philosophers, and in the third generally mammon-moths, alias money-grubs, alias muck-worms, alias misers. It is morally impossible that a man should have an ardent love for music and money at the same time. The demonstration may be sought by the curious ; meantime this fact taken in connexion with the modern difficulty of procuring a subsistence, will account for the pecuniary embarrassments of so many of the harmonic tribe. The love of music, although perhaps it be not, as some are reported to have maintained, " a sign of predestination," is nevertheless an indication that the soul is not torpid and insenible, and consequently that it is at least capable of moral impressions : on the contrary, a hatred of it, as it is clearly inconsistent with the right temperament of the spirit, is a strong symptom of " hardness of heart," which may prove unconquerable. Were all men so constituted, Shakespear's words would soon be realized ; " treasons, stratagems, and spoils" would become common as the sunbeams ; the moral horizon would be dark, cold, comfortless ; and the whole earth re-assume its pristine appearance, " without form and void."

In the composition of a psalm tune, as in that of every thing else, the end proposed should be steadily kept in view. Now the designed use, as has been repeatedly surmised, is the affording to every individual an opportunity of praising his maker. This is so plain that it can bear no contradiction. The ostensible reason why the old music was thrown into the back ground was, that it was so complex that the common people could not join in it ; and the introduction of hymns and such like songs was permitted, " for the comforting of such as delight in music," who before, through the difficult and involved style of Church Music which was then in vogue, unless officially engaged, had neither part nor lot in the matter. It follows then, that a psalm tune should be easy to be comprehended by persons wholly unacquainted with the science, care being always had that it degenerates not into meanness ; or in the words of Queen Elizabeth, that it be " in the best melody and music that may be conveniently devised." Now the best melody for such a purpose, is the most plain and simple, one which may be quickly learned, and not easily forgotten, fit to be the medium of the aspirations of a devout mind, and serve as common carrier from earth to heaven. The species of music best adapted to it is evidently *plain counterpoint*. Of such alas! notwithstanding the number with which our music shops are deluged, how few are to be found.

It should be recollected that a display of skill forms no part of the object of a psalm tune. As it can be neither expected nor imagined that every one should cultivate a talent for music, even if he possess it, that which is provided expressly for the use of all should be free from every avoidable difficulty. The compass of voice required should be small, and all the intervals natural and easy of performance. Let us not be told of the impropriety of men and women, boys and girls, singing all together the same melody. It is an affected objection. No finer musical effect can be conceived than that of a mixed multitude singing at the unisons. Neither do the strictest laws of composition forbid it, nor the example of the greatest masters discountenance it. What is greater than laws or masters, common sense, prescribes it, and both reason and revelation yield it their sanction.*

It is now the fashion to make adaptations from the works of favorite and popular composers, and force them into use as congregational melodies. Considered with reference to its original destination, the music may be most excellent, and yet utterly unfit for the service into which it is thus unmercifully pressed.

It is not sufficient that the tune selected be of the same metre as the psalm or hymn to be sung; the spirit of the music ought to correspond with that of the words; and if an adherence to this principle should even induce a change of tune during the performance of a single psalm, provided it be discreetly done, such a deviation from established usage could not be met by any plausible objection.

There are some tunes which require a repetition of words, sometimes of a whole line, and sometimes of only a few syllables. The employment of these generally leads to the most arrant nonsense; and when the repeats falls upon the middle of a word, it often happens that it becomes converted into a most ridiculous meaning, so as to

---

* The composer should, however, be extremely careful of fourths, which, by the inversion, become fifths.

excite the risibility of persons otherwise serious and devout. Such tunes are on no account desirable, and should never be employed without a previous close and attentive perusal of the psalm.

The next to be noticed is the *giving-out*. If the object of this be, what it is presumed cannot be denied, to apprize the people of the nature of the tune about to be sung, it is plain that it ought to be given out in such a manner as that it may be clearly understood ; instead of which we often witness it so managed as to require the exercise of the utmost ingenuity to discover the melody, buried under turns shakes, and would-be graces of all descriptions. Here the old *Cornet* fashion, though fast dropping into disuse, is to be commended, as it has the decided advantage of giving to melody a distinctness which cannot be misunderstood.

The regulation of the quantum of organ is a matter of great delicacy and no small difficulty ; but it depends upon so many minute circumstances, as for instance the compass of the music, the length of the psalm, the existence or strength of the choir, the number and humor of the people, and even the time of the day, and state of the weather, that to descend to particulars would extend this paper beyond all reasonable bounds.

Most of the old tunes are usually played by far too slow, and this has arisen from a change of fashion with regard to musical notes. They are written in *Minims*, a character to which, two hundred years ago, a much shorter space of time, than is at present, was allotted. Indeed, before the invention of the *crotchet* and its subdivisions, the *minim*, as its name implies, was used to designate the shortest sound. Its old time is preserved in cathedral music, where it is performed almost as fast as the modern *quaver*. This is no doubt the reason why these tunes have fallen into disrepute. They are usually said to be dull, heavy, see-saw, humdrum things ; whereas on their first oming up, the very same tunes were by the then high church party ridiculed as *Geneva jigs*. Strange that what tempted our forefathers to dance should incline their posterity to sleep! These tunes besides being restored to their original time, may be rendered more lively by the addition of short and appropriate interludes, which are as it were a running commentary upon the words sung ; and the whole, so far from being a tiresome and disagreeable exercise, may by proper attention become both pleasing and delightful.

32

There will be then no necessity for the continuance of those barbarous and unholy things which are now so frequently polluting our devotions.

Music has lost the prominent place which it once occupied in divine worship. May not an enthusiastic mind innocently imagine that the violent spirit of the reformation in sweeping away much rubbish, destroyed also much that was "pure and holy and of good report ;" and that in its indiscriminate zeal for the extirpation of tares it plucked up some wheat also ?

The increase of popery, and consequent restoration of of its political ascendency, by some so much and so reasonably deprecated, are principally to be apprehended from its unaccountable connexion with correct taste in the fine arts, especially in music. These have won more victories and made more proselytes than all the swords, and pens which have ever been wielded in its defence. Their influence is all-captivating. How is danger to be obviated? By declaiming against the arts themselves as auxiliaries of the arch-fiend ? No, certainly. As well attempt to arrest the progress of an invading army by prohibiting the use of fire arms. The way is plain. Only let protestantism, instead of, as in some cases, proscribing the arts altogether, in others barely tolerating them, form a firm and indissoluble alliance of the same description as that which is employed with so much effect by the adverse party, and there will be nothing more to fear. Notwithstanding the boasted march of mind, the million cannot reason, but they can feel.